Local Worship, Global Church

Local Worship, Global Church

Popular Religion and the Liturgy

Mark R. Francis, CSV

LITURGICAL PRESS
Collegeville, Minnesota

www.litpress.org

1   2   3   4   5   6   7   8   9

Library of Congress Cataloging-in-Publication Data

Francis, Mark R.
    Local worship, global church : popular religion and the liturgy /
Mark R. Francis, CSV.
        pages   cm
    Includes bibliographical references.
    ISBN 978-0-8146-1879 — ISBN 978-0-8146-3762-3 (ebook)
    1. Liturgics—History.   2. Christianity and culture.   3. Worship.
4. Catholic Church—Liturgy.   I. Title.
    BV176.3.F73   2014
    264.009—dc23   2013041023

*This book is dedicated to the memory of
Dom Anscar Chupungco, OSB
1939–2013
Teacher, mentor, and friend*

CONTENTS

Preface

This book offers a particular perspective on the relationship between liturgy and culture. Long neglected in classical liturgical study has been an attempt to view the worship of the Church from the perspective of the vast majority of the faithful who regularly participate in worship. Rather than first looking at the "official" interpretation of the historical record, these pages attempt to describe how the culture of the common people who identified themselves as Christians down through the ages influenced the official liturgy of the Church. This attempt to look at the liturgy from the "bottom up" rather than the "top down" is admittedly open to critique, since by definition the "common people" do not write history books or theological discourses describing their understanding of what they do at worship. I believe, though, that any attempt at coming to a realistic appraisal of the history of the liturgy must include this perspective that respects the common sense of who we call today "the people in the pew."

This book would not have been possible without the support and encouragement of many people. I would like to first thank my religious community, the Clerics of St. Viator, especially the provincial, Fr. Thomas von Behren, CSV, for encouraging me to take a year's sabbatical after my twelve years in Rome as superior general. Special thanks to Fr. Paul Crowley, SJ, and Sr. Ana Maria Pineda, RSM, for having invited me to investigate the possibility of spending my sabbatical at Santa Clara University and to Fr. Mick McCarthy, SJ, director of the Ignatian Center, for arranging this past year at Santa Clara. I am very grateful to the Jesuit Community of Santa Clara for opening their home to me as a brother and for sharing Eucharist, meals, and conversations. Fr. Michael Zampelli, SJ, rector, and Fr. James Blaettler, SJ, minister, were always gracious, welcoming, and witnesses of real servant leadership in their presence to the local community, including myself. I would be remiss not to thank Dr. Gary Macy, chair of the religious studies department at Santa Clara, and Saralyn Ferrara, secretary at the Graduate Pastoral Ministries, for their companionship and encouragement. I'd also like to thank Diana Macalintal, director of worship for the Diocese of San Jose, who helped to identify some wonderful resources of this culturally rich diocese. Quite simply, I could not have chosen a better place for my sabbatical. Finally, my special thanks to Peter Dwyer and Hans Christoffersen at Liturgical Press for their patience in waiting several years for this book. And last but not least my sincere gratitude to Patrick McGowan, my editor, who patiently read my awkward prose and clarified many of my obscurities.

Abbreviations

AAS	*Acta Apostolica Sedis*
CCC	*Catechism of the Catholic Church*
CSEL	*Corpus Scriptorum Ecclesiasticorum Latinorum*, Edited by the Vienna Academy. Vienna: 1866–present
CCL	*Corpus Christianorum Latinorum*, Turnhout: Brepols, 1953–present
DPPL	*Directory on Popular Piety and the Liturgy* (Congregation for Divine Worship and the Discipline of the Sacraments)
GIRM	General Instruction on the Roman Missal
LA	*Liturgiam Authenticam* (Congregation for Divine Worship and the Discipline of the Sacraments, Instruction on the Use of Vernacular Languages in the Publication of the Books of the Roman Liturgy)
LG	*Lumen Gentium* (Second Vatican Council, Dogmatic Constitution on the Church)
MGH	*Monumenta Germaniae Historica*, Berlin: 1826–present
MD	*Mediator Dei* (Pope Pius XII, Encyclical), AAS 39: 521–595 (1947)
PG	Patrologia Greca (J.-P. Migne) Paris: 1857–1866
PL	Patrologia Latina (J.-P. Migne) Paris: 1878–1890
PRG	Le Pontifical romano-germanique du dixième siècle
SC	*Sacrosanctum Concilium* (Second Vatican Council, Constitution on the Sacred Liturgy)
SCh	*Sources Chrétiennes*
VL	*Varietates Legitimae* (Congregation for Divine Worship and the Discipline of the Sacraments, Instruction on Inculturation and the Roman Liturgy)

CHAPTER ONE

Some Preliminary Considerations

> For the growing good of the world is partly dependent on unhistoric acts; and that things are not so ill with you and me as they might have been, is half owing to the number who lived faithfully a hidden life, and rest in unvisited tombs.
>
> —George Eliot, *Middlemarch: A Study of Provincial Life*

I have always been struck by the appropriateness of a sign in front of a parish in the Hyde Park neighborhood of Chicago that reads: "God's people in extraordinary variety." At this particular parish—like many others around the United States—Catholics from an amazing number of countries and traditions come together to worship every Sunday. Overcoming differences in language is a major challenge, but that is only the tip of the iceberg. While all may be Catholics of the Roman Rite, the principal challenge for the pastor and parish staff in forming a cohesive community is in trying to come to an understanding of the parishioners' often unvoiced attitudes and presuppositions toward faith, worship, and community. These attitudes and presuppositions are often deeply affected by exposure to cultural difference.

In the area of worship, for example, some more traditionally minded Catholics sometimes question why cultural diversity is an issue at all. In the years before Vatican II, most Catholics were taught that the liturgy was the principal and unchanging guarantor of the unity of the universal Church. "One could travel anywhere in the world," it was said, "and the Mass would always be celebrated the same way." This truism, often heard before the Council, was only partially accurate. While the priest's actions at the so-called Tridentine Mass—celebrated in Latin, at an altar in a sanctuary separated by a rail from the nave, with the priest's back to the people—may have been essentially the same, the experience of worship was, in fact, "culturally framed" and often experienced in very different ways. For example, while some of us (especially in Irish or German parishes) remember a very ordered liturgy in which the faithful were largely confined to their pews except for Communion, there was often quite a bit of activity going on in Italian or Hispanic parishes: elaborate processions before, after, or even during Mass; people going to confession or leaving their pew to light candles in front of particular statues; and others moving up the aisles on their knees to fulfill a vow. The music was often very different from parish to parish, from Latin plainchant to hymns in the vernacular composed to parallel the liturgical words and gestures of the priest. Many of these differences were occasioned by culture and by the traditions that could be characterized as "popular religion." It was because of these culturally specific differences—and the fact that homilies were often preached in the language of the old country—that national parishes were such an important part of the Catholic immigrant experience in the United States, giving parishioners a sense of identity and stability in a society that was often experienced as hostile to both their culture and their religion.

Liturgy and Cultural Differences

It was apparent to the bishops in their preparation and discussions on liturgy during the Second Vatican Council that cultural differences needed to be taken into account in the reform of the liturgy. After centuries of enforcing a universal (or at least Latin Rite) liturgical order, the bishops of Vatican II proclaimed in article 37 of *Sacrosanctum Concilium* (the Constitution on the Sacred Liturgy) that "even in the liturgy the church does not wish to impose a rigid uniformity in matters which do not affect the faith or the well-being of the entire community. Rather does it cultivate and foster the qualities and talents of the various races and nations."

It was for this reason that the Constitution announced a new attitude toward the liturgy that allowed for cultural variation in Catholic worship. The conscious awareness of the importance of culture, then, was to be at the heart of the liturgical renewal: "Provided that the substantial unity of the Roman rite is preserved, provision shall be made, when revising the liturgical books, for legitimate variations and adaptations to different groups, regions, and peoples, especially in mission countries" (SC 38).

The Council, while upholding the value of unity in worship, did not insist on uniformity. Rather, the Constitution spoke of the need to safeguard the "substantial unity" of the Roman Rite. While this substantial unity was nowhere defined by the Constitution, it was generally interpreted as that which would be permitted by the introductions (*praenotandae*) and ceremonial directives (*rubrics*) of the official liturgical books (*editiones typicae*).[1] These revised books not only allowed for cultural variation in the Roman Rite but even encouraged this variation in the celebration of the sacraments of baptism and marriage. This newly proposed room for adapting the rites depending on local culture came to be known in the decades after the Council by the word "inculturation."

Popular Piety

One aspect of the cultural and religious diversity that was not discussed in any great depth by the Constitution was arguably one of the principal ways by which many Catholics around the world were led to the liturgy—through their practice of popular piety. Processions, pilgrimages, rosaries, novenas, holy medals, scapulars, and special local customs and rites incorporated in the "standard" celebration of the sacraments all formed a background for the worship of Catholics before Vatican II. The Council made it clear that popular piety and specific devotions were to be commended, provided that "they harmonize with the liturgical seasons, accord with the sacred liturgy, are in some way derived from it, and lead the people to it, since in fact the liturgy by its very nature is far superior to any of them" (SC 13). Apart from this caveat, little else was officially said at the Council about popular piety and its relationship with the worship life of the Church. This issue was taken up by *Varietates Legitimae*, the 1994 instruction of the Congregation for Divine Worship and the Discipline of the Sacraments, that deals specifically with the inculturation of the Roman Rite made possible by Vatican II's Constitution on the Sacred Liturgy. Another official Church body that has been most concerned with this topic has been the Bishops' Conference of Latin America (CELAM), devoting sections of its documents to dealing with the importance of popular

---

[1] This indeed was to be the interpretation of the Congregation of Divine Worship and the Discipline of the Sacraments (CDWDS) in its 1994 document *Varietates Legitimae* (Inculturation and the Roman Liturgy).

religion—or, as it is called in many of their documents, the "people's Catholicism."[2]

The papacy has also discussed the relationship between liturgy and popular piety. In his apostolic letter on worship—written twenty-five years after the promulgation of *Sacrosanctum Concilium*—Pope John Paul II reminded the Church that "this popular devotion should not be ignored or treated with indifference or contempt, since it is rich in values, and per se gives expression to the religious attitude towards God. But it needs to be continually evangelized, so that the faith which it expresses may become an ever more mature and authentic act."[3]

It was not until 2002, however, that the Vatican's Congregation for Divine Worship and the Discipline of the Sacraments would take up the pope's challenge and issue a document that specifically addressed this question. The *Directory of Popular Piety and Liturgy* offers the following definition of popular piety: "The term 'popular piety' designates those diverse cultic expressions of a private or community nature which, in the context of the Christian faith, are inspired predominantly not by the Sacred Liturgy but by forms deriving from a particular nation or people or from their culture" (DPPL 9).

The *Directory* distinguishes "popular piety" from related terms such as "pious exercises" (practices derived from or in harmony with the official liturgy of the Church) and "popular religiosity" (a religious dimension to human life found among all peoples—not limited to Christians—that involves external ritual expression). The *Directory* also uses the term "devotions" to describe "various external practices (e.g., prayers, hymns, observances attached to particular times or places, insignia, medals, habits or customs)" (DPPL 8). All of these practices are described as being in clear contrast to the liturgy, understood as the officially approved prayer of the Church. While it is helpful to make distinctions regarding terminology, we will see that in practice these expressions overlap and are, at times, very hard to distinguish one from the other.[4]

---

[2] Medellin (1968), Puebla (1979), Santo Domingo (1992), Aparecida (2007).

[3] John Paul II, Apostolic Letter *Vicesimus Quintus Annus* (1988), 18.

[4] See James Empereur, "Popular Piety and Liturgy: Principles and Guidelines," in *Directory on Popular Piety and the Liturgy: Principles and Guidelines, A Commentary,* ed. Peter Phan (Collegeville, MN: Liturgical Press, 2005), 10; Peter Fink, "Liturgy and Popular Piety in the Church's Magisterium," ibid., 45–57.

While the *Directory* is an important guide to the liturgical life of the Church, it offers an approach to both inculturation and popular piety that could be called "from the top down." The history presented by official documents such as the *Directory* is often a triumphant march through the centuries, describing a linear and uninterrupted development of the liturgy inexorably leading to our present practices. By ignoring some of the "messiness" that characterizes this same history, the official approach offers an easily understandable exposition of the history of the liturgy but fails to convey the richness of the interaction between liturgy, popular expressions of faith, and the many cultural worlds in which Christianity has moved and developed.[5] In simplifying history, this approach obscures obvious parallels between the experience of the Church in other places and times and what we are experiencing today as a largely Western European institution striving to be, in the famous words of theologian Karl Rahner, "a world Church."

Toward a More Nuanced View of Popular Piety

What would the history of worship look like if we paid more attention to the experience of the "people in the pews"—viewing the liturgy through what we know about their popular piety? This perspective is an undeniable complement to the more official picture presented in the Church's pronouncements on the liturgy.[6] In his book *Through Their Own Eyes: Liturgy as the Byzantines Saw It*, distinguished Jesuit liturgiologist Robert Taft underscored the importance of this approach:

> One can no longer reconstruct the past only from the top down. What we find in liturgical manuscripts was embedded in a socio-cultural ambiance outside of which it cannot be understood as liturgy, something that real people did. Furthermore, such literary monuments are a product of high culture, and hence only half the story. . . . Almost all official Church history has been urban

---

[5] See my "Liturgy and Popular Piety in a Historical Perspective," ibid., 19–44.

[6] A good example of this "official approach" is found in chapter 9 of the *General Instruction on the Roman Missal* (2002) entitled "Adaptations within the Competence of Bishops and Bishops' Conferences," esp. 395–99. See the commentary I offer on these sections with Gary Neville in *A Commentary on the General Instruction of the Roman Missal*, eds. Edward Foley, et al. (Collegeville, MN: Liturgical Press, 2008), 461–67.

history—for it is in the centers of power that history—one view of history at least—is made.[7]

As the demographic center of Christianity (Catholic and Protestant) moves from Europe and North America to Africa and South America, what does the Church have to learn from the history of liturgical inculturation and the way various local churches around the world are receiving the liturgical tradition of the Roman Rite today? How can more sensitivity to the "faith of the people" as expressed in their popular piety aid us in the task of liturgical inculturation? Given the increasingly multicultural nature of our liturgical assemblies, can knowledge of popular religious traditions aid us in preparing liturgies that are sensitive to the often unarticulated but nevertheless deeply held religious sensibilities of the people with whom we minister every Sunday? While many popular religious practices are linked with specific ethnic groups, could popular religious practices unite rather than divide culturally diverse parishes?

Inculturation and Popular Piety

The perspectives of our Catholic forebears, the majority of whom were people of a simple yet profound faith, has often been overlooked or even disdained by those in a position to dominate the historical record. While we hear of the contribution of popes, bishops, kings, and famous theologians, it is rare that liturgical histories speak of the majority of Christians, many of whom were largely uneducated, even illiterate, but who nevertheless passed on to the next generation the traditions and rituals that sustained their lives of faith. In discussing these nameless individuals and their lives of faith shaped by popular religion, lines from the poem "*Los nadies*" (the nobodies) by Uruguayan journalist Eduardo Galeano comes to mind:

. . . the nobodies . . .
Who don't speak languages, just dialects.
Who don't have religions, just superstitions.

---

[7] Robert Taft, *Through Their Own Eyes: Liturgy as the Byzantines Saw It* (Berkeley, CA: InterOrthodox Press, 2006), 7, quoting his *Beyond East and West: Problems in Liturgical Understanding* (Washington, DC: Pastoral Press, 1984), 292–93.

Who don't create art, just handicrafts.
Who don't have culture, just folklore.[8]

It needs to be said that these people, these "nobodies," past and present, have to be taken into account in order to come to grips with the process by which liturgical inculturation has taken place in the history of the Church and continues to take place around the world. This inculturation, at least in part, has been the result of the popular religious imagination that has transformed worship forms received from missionaries into liturgical practices accessible to local cultures. This book is a modest attempt to give some voice to this often overlooked part of the historical liturgical record. It is imperative that we add the perspective of popular piety to our study of worship today since it is one of the primary ways in which the liturgy itself is understood and transformed in the larger process of inculturation. It also offers possibilities for bringing Catholic Christians together in multicultural parishes, respecting their diversity and the particular spiritualties that inform the way they interpret the Roman Rite.

Pope John Paul II has described the process of inculturation as a two-way street. It is not simply a question of the universal Church proclaiming the Gospel in an intelligible way to particular cultures of the world while leaving the rest of the Church unchanged. As he pointed out in his encyclical *Redemptoris Missio*, "Through inculturation the Church makes the Gospel incarnate in different cultures and at the same time introduces peoples, together with their cultures, into her own community."[9] Given this dialogical understanding, how have the cultural contributions of local churches, especially in the form of popular piety, past and present, enriched Catholic worship? Looking at historic and contemporary examples of popular religion and liturgy not often discussed in general historical overviews, this book will attempt to offer an appreciative background for the often unconscious but very real influences of popular piety on Catholic liturgy. The main thesis of this book is that attending to expressions of popular piety and their interplay with the liturgy provides us with a better perspective to work at deepening the "understanding of Christ's message and give it more effective expression in the liturgy and in the many different

---

[8] *El Libro de los Abrazos* (México: Siglo Veintiuno Editores, novena edición, 1994), 59. Translation by the author.

[9] *Redemptoris Missio* 52.

aspects of the life of the community of believers,"[10] which is the whole point of inculturation.

Three Levels on which the Liturgy Communicates

In order to discern how popular piety and liturgy are interrelated, it is helpful to reflect on the different ways in which the liturgy is experienced by the "people in the pews." Liturgy is symbolic activity. As the Constitution on the Sacred Liturgy affirms, "In the liturgy the sanctification of women and men is given expression in symbols perceptible by the senses and is carried out in ways appropriate to each of them. In it, complete and definitive public worship is performed by the mystical body of Jesus Christ, that is, by the Head and his members" (SC 7). As symbolic communication, the liturgy can "mean" many things at the same time since symbols speak simultaneously on various levels. It is for this reason it can be said that the liturgy "speaks" on at least three levels: official, public, and personal.[11]

Official

The official level of meaning is explained and contained in liturgical books and described in ritual introductions (*praenotanda*) such as the *General Instruction of the Roman Missal* (GIRM). Further clarification is offered in the documents issued by the magisterium to explain the objective meaning of the liturgy. Down through the centuries the texts contained in the official liturgical books safeguarded the orthodoxy of the prayers voiced in the name of the assembly. They also protected the faithful from presiders who were amusingly described by the late fourth-century Council of Hippo as *imperiti et loquaces* (inexpert and wordy), mandating that priests use previously approved prayer texts rather than inflict their spontaneous prayers on the assembly.[12]

---

[10] *Varietates Legitimae* 4, quoting *Gaudium et Spes* 58. See also the provocative and insightful article of Anthony J. Gittins, "Beyond Liturgical Inculturation: Transforming the Deep Structures of Faith," *Irish Theological Quarterly* 69 (2004): 47–72.

[11] I am indebted to my colleagues of the North American Academy of Liturgy, especially Professor Margaret Mary Kelleher of the "Ritual-Language-Action" seminar, for this insight.

[12] See Canon 25 of the Council of Hippo (393 CE) in *Concilia Africae a. 345–525*, ed. C. Munier, CCSL 149 (Turnhout: Brépols, 1974).

It is this official level that is especially monitored by the Church in order to ensure that the formulation of the prayers as well as the ritual gestures handed down through the centuries accurately express the Christian faith. It is here that the famous dictum *lex orandi, lex credendi* (how we pray, so we believe) comes into play. Our prayer as Catholic Christians informs what we believe. It is the responsibility of the Church to ensure that the way in which the liturgy is celebrated accurately reflects those beliefs.

In order to explore the three levels, let us take the example of the liturgical gesture of a kiss. This gesture was adopted into the liturgy from the cultural world of the Mediterranean Basin, specifically that of ancient Rome. It was with a kiss that the Romans venerated people and sacred objects. In the current Mass, this gesture is used to venerate the altar at the beginning of the celebration as well as the Book of the Gospels (GIRM 49) after the gospel is proclaimed. In the Tridentine Rite there were many more kisses prescribed: each time the celebrant turned away from the altar to face the people he was to venerate the altar with a kiss. Each time an assisting minister received or gave something to the celebrant in a Pontifical High Mass, his hand was to be kissed. In our current rite, the evangelary or Lectionary is kissed after the proclamation of the gospel. These gestures were inscribed into the normative, official celebration of the Mass to underline the reverence to be shown to the altar (representing Christ himself), the gospel as Christ's word to the people, and the person of the priest who celebrates as an *alter Christus* (another Christ).

Public

The public level of meaning in the liturgy is that which is commonly understood by the people gathered. It may indeed be the same as the official meaning, but it is here that cultural context often intervenes to complicate matters. Let us again take the example of the presider's veneration of the altar with a kiss. In some cultures this gesture poses no problem. In Italy and other Mediterranean cultures people spontaneously kiss sacred objects such as icons, statues, and rosaries. In this context, it seems only fitting that a liturgical gesture of a kiss be used to venerate the altar. In some cultures of the Far East, however, a kiss of any kind in public is considered inappropriate, in bad taste. The "public meaning" of this gesture is different in Japan than it is in Italy. It is for this reason that the GIRM wisely stipulates that the national bishops' conference may establish some other sign of veneration of the altar and gospel book with the consent of the Apostolic See (GIRM 271). Clearly here is a realization that the public meaning of a gesture may need to be taken into consideration, despite the "normative" meaning ascribed to it by the official Roman Rite.

Personal

In addition to having official and public meanings, the liturgy also communicates on a personal level. Each person present at the celebration has a particular history of interaction with the liturgical symbols connected with his or her own particular experience. While the gesture of a kiss expresses veneration in many cultures, it can also have added meaning for someone who associates the gesture with a loved one. A grandmother who taught her grandchildren this particular gesture of venerating objects with a kiss could be linked with this action in the hearts of her grandchildren. This particular connection constitutes a personal meaning that affects how an individual interacts with both the official and public meanings of worship. While the official level of meaning necessarily influences the public and personal, it does not necessarily always dominate. It is here that the popular religious imagination strongly shapes the personal appropriation of the "meaning" of a given image or liturgical gesture, especially since the elders of the family hand down the "meaning" that forms an important part of what anthropologists call the *ideational* and *performance* levels of culture that form cultural identity.

This personal level of meaning serves to explain the emotional resonance and omnipresence of an image such as that of Our Lady of Guadalupe in Mexican culture. While this image portrays the official meaning of "Mary the Mother of God," it also stands for much more. The appearances of Mary to Juan Diego in the sixteenth century (of which the famous image is a "witness"), testify to divine intervention for a people devastated by the Spanish conquest and subsequent collapse of their religious and social world. This image of Mary as *La Morenita* (the little brown one) expresses God's affirmation of the people who are themselves reflected in the image of this maiden that incorporates symbols of the pre-Spanish native worldview. In addition to this "public" meaning, it is an image that accompanies Mexicans from cradle to grave, frequently found on the walls of the humblest of homes and in most Mexican churches. Our Lady of Guadalupe is "one of the family" and remains emotionally linked to the personal experience of Mexicans as she is constantly invoked by parents and grandparents at important moments of life.[13]

Popular Piety and Public/Personal Meaning

In looking at the liturgy from the perspective of popular piety, we will be especially attentive to both the public and personal meanings of worship in different eras and in different cultures. This is not to say that the normative, official meaning ascribed to liturgy by the Church is unimportant. But it is on the level of public meaning, shared by the *plebs sancta Dei*, "the holy, common people of God," that will be of most interest to us, since it points to the interface between faith and culture—the fertile ground that brings forth real inculturation. The myriad personal meanings of liturgy are also important. While it is impossible to exhaustively describe them, they also need to be considered when attempting to get at an adequate understanding of the way people participate in an official liturgical act. This relationship can explain why, in a setting such as Latin America, during the washing of the feet on Holy Thursday, it may be a mistake for the presider *not* to also kiss the feet of those designated for the foot washing, even though this gesture is not prescribed in the official rubrics. The meaning of this gesture in a Latino context on this day, commonly associated with the priesthood, shows the ordained minister's humility and respect for others. It also undoubtedly evokes personal experiences of care and nurture for many of the people present. To omit it may inadvertently send a message on the level of public meaning and personal meaning that the presider is aloof, even conceited. I can personally attest that this interpretation is possible after having presided at my first celebration of Holy Thursday as a priest in Colombia. Being a "new priest," I followed the rubrics faithfully. But since the rubrics say nothing about kissing feet after washing them, I failed to do so. Several people approached me after the service and very publicly scolded me with the accusation that I was "prideful" (*orgulloso*). They pointed out that while this gesture is not in the rubrics, it was done by Pope John Paul, and they pointedly asked me if I thought I was better than the pope!

---

[13] Virgilio P. Elizondo, *Guadalupe, Mother of the New Creation* (Maryknoll, NY: Orbis Books, 1997).

The Challenges of Syncretism and Hybridization

We will also be dealing with the very controversial and complex issue of just how far we can go in allowing our worship to be influenced by popular religious practices. *The Directory on Popular Piety and the Liturgy*, an instruction of the Congregation for Worship, following article 13 of the Constitution on the Sacred Liturgy, states unequivocally that "a superimposing of pious and devotional practices on the Liturgy so as to differentiate their language, rhythm, course, and theological emphasis from those of the corresponding liturgical action, must be avoided, while any form of competition with or opposition to the liturgical actions, where such exists, must also be resolved" (DPPR 13).

This is a reasonable reminder that we need to be aware that there may be popular practices that could convey beliefs that are not consistent with the faith, represent an inappropriate "mixing" of Christian and non-Christian beliefs (syncretism), and distort the meaning of the liturgical rite. The *Directory* is especially concerned about the use of language that does not correspond with what the Church believes. It warns that "great vigilance and a deep sense of discernment are required to ensure that ideas contrary to the Christian faith, or forms of worship vitiated by syncretism, are not insinuated into pious exercises through various forms of language" (DPPL 92).

We will see, though, that this directive is not quite as easy to follow as may at first be supposed. Historically there has often been a tension between various popular practices, some of which were influenced by pre-Christian customs and religious practices and which continued to be practiced by ordinary people even after they embraced Christianity. Although criticism of such syncretism today is often directed at Christians in the "younger churches" of Africa and Asia, it is important to realize that this phenomenon has been present throughout the history of Christianity—in Europe as well as in other areas of the world.

A case in point comes from Rome itself: the veneration of the *Sol invictus*, "the unconquered sun," by many Christians in fifth-century Rome. While Jesus could have been identified as the "Sun of Righteousness," prophesied by Malachi 4:2, it was obvious to Christian leaders that people were continuing an attachment to the cult of the Sun, which had been placed alongside the pantheon of the Roman gods by Emperor Aurelian in the third century (+275) as the divine protector of the empire and the emperor. This veneration was especially practiced at the yearly celebration around the winter solstice on December 25, the *Dies Natalis Solis Invicti* (birthday of the unconquered sun)—a connection that seems to have influenced the date of Christmas in the Roman Church.[14] In one of Pope Leo the Great's (+461) Christmas homilies (*Sermo* 27), he launched an impassioned reproof of the misguided members of his flock who were openly practicing syncretism—not in word, but in gesture. Upon entering St. Peter's Basilica for the dawn Mass on Christmas morning, "when they mounted the steps which lead to the raised platform, they turn around toward the rising sun and bend their necks, bowing in honor of the brilliant orb."[15] In the eyes of Pope Leo, these Christians were "hedging their bets" by continuing to worship the sun—part of God's creation but not God. It would be later in the same century when Pope Gelasius (+496) would preach against the survival of other pagan customs such as a fertility rite known as the *Lupercalia*.[16] Clearly, in reviewing the history of the Roman church, it is important to be aware of Peter Brown's comment that "the historian of the later Roman church is in constant danger of taking the end of paganism for granted."[17] It is clear that traditional, even pagan, practices survived in the lives of many even after they embraced the faith. Many of these modified practices became known as "popular religion."

In a like manner today, in many areas of the world, local, pre-Christian rites and customs continue to be practiced by people who have formally embraced Christianity. It is not unusual, for example, for many Christians in Africa or Asia to celebrate marriage with two rites: a Christian ceremony at which a priest presides and another "traditional" ceremony led by the tribal elders to ensure that the marriage is recognized by the local culture. These two ceremonies are not

---

[14] For an excellent summary of the research on the two hypotheses regarding the origin of the Christmas celebration in Rome see Paul F. Bradshaw and Maxwell E. Johnson, *The Origins of Feasts, Fasts and Seasons in Early Christianity*, (Collegeville, MN: Liturgical Press, 2011), 123–30.

[15] "perveniant, superatis gradibus quibus ad suggestum areae superioris ascenditur, converso corpore ad nascentem se solem reflectant, et curvatis cervicibus, in honorem se splendidi orbis inclinent." Leo Magnus, "Sermo 27 in Nativitate Domini" *Tractatus* Corpus Christianorum Series Latina 138, ed. A. Chavasse (Turnhout: Brépols, 1973), 135.

[16] G. Pomares, *Gélase Ier, Lettre contre les Lupercales et dix-huit messes du sacramentaire léonien*. Introduction, texte critique, traduction et notes. Sources chrétiennes 65 (Paris: Éditions du Cerf, 1959).

[17] Peter R. L. Brown, "St. Augustine's Attitude to Religious Coercion," *Journal of Roman Studies* 54 (1964): 109.

necessarily in opposition, but they reflect an identity that has been called "double religious belonging,"[18] or a "hybridization"[19] of religious identity. This phenomenon is not limited to the non-European parts of the Church but is also found in Europe and North America as a result of the mass migrations and globalization that has taken place in the past several decades. In fact, while some may term these and similar practices "syncretism," the personal and even public synthesis of various religious traditions is becoming more and more commonplace around the world, with or without the oversight of the Church. We will see that this is not a new phenomenon but one the Church needs to take into account if any serious attempt at inculturation of Catholic worship is to take place.

Some Notes on Premodern, Modern, and Postmodern Worldviews

Another way to help us understand the way the liturgy and popular religion "spoke" to our ancestors in faith is to remember that many of these practices developed in a "premodern" world. Most authors use the term "premodern" to describe the historical period in Europe before the secularization brought about by the Enlightenment and the Industrial Revolution in the eighteenth and nineteenth centuries. There are many ways of describing a "premodern" society. Max Weber, one of the first sociologists of religion, contrasted the premodern with the modern by speaking of how modernity "disenchanted," or removed the supernatural from human existence. Before that time, human beings took for granted that the world was indeed "enchanted"—in constant connection with the spiritual realm, which gave legitimacy and order to the universe and which helped all the disparate parts of existence to "hang together," to be "connected." As the old saying goes: "God is in his heaven and all is right with the world."

While the "good old days" should not be romanticized as some kind of ideal past, the "enchanted" vision of the world should not be viewed as a kind of primitive flight from reality either. It was a dif-

---

[18] Michael Amaladoss, "Double Religious Belonging and Liminality: An Anthropo-Theological Reflection," *Vidyajyoti* (January 2002); and Peter Phan, "Multiple Religious Belonging: Opportunities and Challenges for Theology and Church," *Theological Studies* 64 (2003): 495–519.

[19] Robert Schreiter, *The New Catholicity: Theology between the Global and the Local* (Maryknoll, NY: Orbis Books, 1997), 27.

ferent—and reasonable—way of dealing with human reality. Since a premodern worldview would contend that all that exists is dependent on God's will, it is reasonable to assume that one's place and the place of one's family in society is determined at birth. The many choices about marriage, profession, and lifestyle were determined by the tradition of one's religion, family, and tribe. Like Tevye, the poor milkman in the musical *Fiddler on the Roof*, premodern people often simply accepted their lot in life as God's will, even if they sometimes dreamed of being "a rich man."

In a fascinating book describing her experience living with the Amish, Sue Bender, an artist from an average, middle-class American background, commented on the fact that although her choices as a woman became very circumscribed in this premodern cultural setting, there was a certain measure of relief to know that she did not have to make myriad decisions modern Americans need to make every day. She recounted that in going about her daily routine, the sacred and the secular were united. Since all work was considered holy, even the simplest of tasks were imbued with meaning since they corresponded to the will of God.[20] The rhythm of life itself was predetermined by custom that ultimately depended on God. Surprisingly, to those of us living with the freedom of the many choices and options afforded us by our culture, this very limitation is able to create a sense of stability and contentment that modern people often lack. Furthermore, in contrast to our modern (and postmodern) culture that places an overwhelming emphasis on the individual and his or her rights and choices, Jesus and his first followers were born into a sociocentric or "collectivist" society where one's social status was determined by one's relationships of immediate family and tribe lived out in an "enchanted world." Outward identification with one's ancestors, then, is a guiding principle for premodern cultures. Veneration of one's ancestors and loyalty to family and clan often figure in a much more important way in the lives of premodern peoples than in those of typical North Americans.[21]

It could be said that at Vatican II, the Catholic Church finally came to deal constructively with modernity after more than several centuries of trying to shield the faithful from what was regarded as its negative influences. This change was long in coming. The flowering of "secular"

---

[20] Sue Bender, *A Plain and Simple Journal* (New York: HarperCollins, 1991).

[21] Bruce J. Malina and John J. Pilch, *Social-Science Commentary on the Book of Acts* (Minneapolis, MN: Fortress Press, 2008), 187–89.

learning and a newfound interest in the individual sparked by the Renaissance of the fifteenth and sixteenth centuries, coupled with the fracturing of Western Christianity brought about by the Protestant Reformation, marked the beginning of modernity's challenge to the Church. These developments displaced the authority regulating Christian life from the hands of the pope and bishops to personal interpretations of the Bible. This was made possible by the technology of the printing press. The new discoveries of the physical sciences in the seventeenth and eighteenth centuries effectively put into doubt age-old accepted answers regarding the earth as the center of a universe created by God in seven days. The philosophical questioning of the Enlightenment that exalted human reason over revelation forced many to doubt the legitimacy of governmental structures such as monarchy, once thought to be divinely sanctioned. These changes all caused a dramatic evolution in the way Europeans (and North American colonists) thought about God, themselves, and the world.

The Church's negative reaction to modernity is nowhere better summed up than by Pope Pius IX's famous *Syllabus of Errors* appended to his encyclical *Quanta Cura* of 1864. In this document, the pope identifies as erroneous (among other things) democratic government, liberty of conscience, and the separation of Church and state. Pressured by events in Europe that placed the Catholic Church in the crosshairs of hostile régimes that sought to curtail its influence, Pope Pius's response was to insist on the traditional prerogatives of the Church and to reject emerging beliefs in the authority of secular governments and the superiority of scientifically derived learning over revealed truth. Catholics, of course, were not the only believers who reacted with negativity to these cultural currents. The continuing controversy over the teaching of "creationism" rather than evolution in the public schools promoted today by fundamentalist Christians in the United States, for example, is just another example of a rejection of modernity.

It has been said that the Second Vatican Council marked the Church's rapprochement with modernity. Many of the condemnations voiced in the *Syllabus of Errors* are directly contradicted by Council documents such as the Pastoral Constitution of the Church in the Modern World (*Gaudium et Spes*) and the Declaration on Religious Freedom (*Dignitatis Humanae*). The Council recognized that the Church's relationship with the world involved not only proclaiming its faith in the Good News of Jesus Christ to the world but also engaging in a dialogue with human cultures in order for this message to be better understood.

It was ironic, however, that just when the Church seemed to have arrived at a *modus vivendi* with modernity, the world was moving into a period that many cultural critics describe as "postmodernity" (at least in Europe and North America). This development has been noted and discussed by historians, philosophers, sociologists, and theologians.[22] For our purposes it is sufficient that we acknowledge some of its characteristics.

After the disasters of the twentieth century perpetrated by humans, such as the First World War, the Armenian genocide by the Turks, the Nazi attempt at exterminating the Jews of Europe (the Shoah), the numerous Stalinist purges in the Soviet Union, the "killing fields" of Cambodia, and the war in Vietnam, to name just a few, the optimism that reigned in Europe and the United States over the possibility of human progress at the beginning of the century was seen to be illusory. Human reason and technology did not seem to be guaranteeing a better world. Failed political systems such as Communism and the seeming inability of unregulated capitalism to provide a decent life for all have led to a sense of disillusion with any human attempts at establishing a peaceful and just world order. For many in Europe and North America, the world has become "unmoored" and "unreliable." A major characteristic of postmodernity is a lack of confidence in the sureties once used to interpret our history and ourselves. History itself is seen to be untrustworthy and so dependent on interpretation that it cannot be used as a definitive arbiter in deciding between conflicting opinions. All of our institutions, including government and organized Christianity, are in fact seen as largely untrustworthy.

While some sensibilities promoted by postmodernity are based on a rejection of the reliability of the established order, this very rejection has provoked some positive attitudes that could be answered by the Gospel. The quest for a quality of life that goes beyond the utilitarian, fascination with spirituality and contemplation, and awareness of the

---

[22] Among the numerous works available, some of the most helpful books on the topic of modernity (as opposed to postmodernity, which is a different question) are: Louis J. Luzbetak, *The Church and Culture: New Perspectives in Missiological Anthropology* (Maryknoll, NY: Orbis, 1989); Louis Dupré, *Passage to Modernity* (New Haven, CT: Yale University Press, 1993); Michael Paul Gallagher, *Clashing Symbols: An Introduction to Faith and Culture* (London: Dartman, Longman and Todd, Ltd., 1997); and Charles Taylor, *A Secular Age* (Cambridge, MA: Belknap Press, 2007).

heretofore neglected feminine and ecological perspectives on human flourishing are all areas in which the Church has an opportunity to speak to the culture. In effect, postmodernity opens the door to a "re-enchantment" of the world—different from that of premodernity, but one that allows the spiritual side of human life to assume an importance that was downplayed in modernity. Sensitivity to these characteristics of postmodernity, especially when they are expressed in a popular manner, can offer points of convergence with the transformational power of the Gospel.[23]

Finally, because of globalization, it is becoming increasingly difficult to categorize people living "purely" in states of either premodernity, modernity, or postmodernity. As Fernando Calderon has observed, many of us live in *tiempos mixtos* (mixed times) moving continually between these three sensibilities.[24] An example may help to explain this observation.

Several years ago I had the privilege of participating in an ecumenical meeting on the consecrated life in Egypt. Our Coptic Orthodox hosts were very gracious and wanted to share with us the history and traditions of their ancient and long-suffering church. One of the professors at the local university offered a presentation that spoke powerfully of the heroic witness the Copts have given down through the centuries—especially after the Islamic invasion of the eighth century. The beginning of this historical presentation, though, was a biography of Mark the Evangelist, who is considered the founder of the Coptic Church. The presenter spoke with amazing warmth and admiration of St. Mark and went into great detail regarding Mark's parents, the color of his hair, what he liked to eat, the many miracles of healing he accomplished—all of which made this saint come alive. From a scientific, historical-critical point of view, much of what he said was not provable. It was the stuff of folklore and legend, passed down from one generation to the next—in essence, a premodern appreciation of the saint. Later in the same presentation the speaker offered a systematic presentation of the challenges confronting the Coptic Church in an Egypt that even then was chafing under dictatorship and beginning to hear calls for democratic reform. I noticed, though, in the space of this

---

[23] See Gallagher, *Clashing Symbols*, 140–43.

[24] Fernando Calderón, "America Latina: identidad y tiempos mixtos o cómo tratar de pensar la modernidad sin dejar de ser indio," *David y Goliath* 17, no. 52 (September 1987): 4–9.

thirty-minute presentation, the speaker slipped back and forth between sensibilities that were premodern, modern, and even postmodern. In our multicultural and globalized world many people find themselves in the midst of these *tiempos mixtos*, especially in regard to religion. We will return to this observation in the last chapter of this book when we look at a pastoral response to the range of popular religious imagination present in today's parishes.

Overview

In light of popular religious practice, what was the "average person's" way of approaching the liturgy over the course of the centuries? Although much of our discussion will be able to add only peripheral strokes to our picture of the history of liturgy and popular religion, it will help bring us closer to a more accurate understanding of how *los nadies* (the common people) engaged in worship. Through attention to the three levels liturgy communicates through (official, public, and personal) and by an awareness of the constant presence of syncretistic and hybrid engagements with the "official" presentation of the liturgy received by worldviews that are premodern, modern, or postmodern, we will gain a new appreciation of and ability to deal with the challenges of ministering liturgically to our multicultural parishes of the twenty-first century.

The following pages will attempt to take a critical look at the history of the interaction between the popular religious impulse and the official worship of the Western Church. This will be done in order to reflect on current cultural issues confronting Catholicism as it continues this interaction at a level unprecedented in the history of the liturgy. Our focus on these diverse and complicated topics will be not exhaustive but on specific watershed moments in the history of the Western Church. Attention to popular religion and the forms it has taken in Eastern Christianity over the course of the centuries is an important and fascinating area of research but is outside of the scope of this book.

We will begin this history in the second chapter by looking at the interaction of the "Jesus movement" with the culture that gave it birth: the Jewish popular religious impulses of first-century Palestine. The third chapter will look at the definitive entrance of Christianity into the Greco-Roman world, before the legalization and promotion of Christianity by Emperor Constantine in the fourth century. Chapter 4 will discuss how the social and cultural context that gave birth to the Roman Rite in the fourth and fifth centuries began the division between liturgy and popular religious expressions that we know today. In chapter 5, we will take up the radical transformation of Christianity in the West due to the reciprocal cultural and religious influences between the peoples of the Mediterranean world who brought the faith and the Northern Europeans who were evangelized in the seventh and eighth centuries. This interaction led to what many scholars refer to as the "Germanization" of Christianity. The sixth chapter will discuss how popular religion came into play in the extraordinary missionary activity of the Western Church in the "Age of Discovery" in Central and South America. Chapter 7 will look at the papacy's influence on popular piety in the nineteenth century and its relationship to the Counter-Reformation liturgy. Finally, we will look at how the relationship between popular religion and liturgy radically changed after the Second Vatican Council.

The underlying presupposition of this book is aptly summed up by Pope John Paul II in his address to the plenary session of the Congregation of Divine Worship and Discipline of the Sacraments when the *Directory on Popular Religion and the Liturgy* was promulgated:

> Genuine forms of popular piety, expressed in a multitude of different ways, derive from the faith and, therefore, must be valued and promoted. Such authentic expressions of popular piety are not at odds with the centrality of the Sacred Liturgy. Rather, in promoting the faith of the people, who regard popular piety as a natural religious expression, they predispose the people for the celebration of the Sacred Mysteries.

It is my hope that these pages will help those ministering in our multicultural Church to develop a familiarity with and respect for the popular religious sensibility of those with whom we engage in liturgy.

Chapter Two

The Beginnings

Popular Religion and the Worship of the First Christians

The title of this chapter is admittedly anachronistic. "Worship" in the early Church was far from codified, and believers belonging to the first Christian generations did not have a formal authority structure to distinguish an "official" liturgy from "popular" devotion. For this reason it could be argued that there was no real "popular" religion at this early stage of the Church's development. The *Directory on Popular Piety and Liturgy* implies as much by stating that, during the first century, liturgy and popular piety were a blended reality. "In this period Liturgy and popular piety, either conceptually or pastorally, did not oppose each other. Both concurred harmoniously in celebrating the one mystery of Christ, considered as a whole, and in sustaining the supernatural and moral life of the disciples of the Lord" (DPPL 23).

While there might have been a harmony between liturgy and popular religious practices in local Christian communities of the first century, this does not mean elements that *later* generations would judge as "popular" or even "syncretistic" and "superstitious" were not part of the way these first Christians worshiped. Often these elements are downplayed or even overlooked by general presentations of the history. In part, authors engage in this simplification in order to avoid overcomplicating the narrative. Some historians, however, seem reluctant to describe practices that no longer correspond to the way that Christians later worshiped—or to practices that were abandoned by the larger church but maintained by groups of Christians that were later judged to be heterodox.

Due to the diversity of practice within the early Church, it is very dangerous to generalize about exactly how the first Christians worshiped. The way in which the first Christian communities gathered—whether a full meal was shared or just elements of bread and wine (or water, or cheese) were blessed, who presided at these gatherings—has been the object of much recent research.[1] If this is true for what were to become the principal forms of worship (Eucharist, baptism), it is even more so for those practices that could be deemed "popular" (such as charismatic prayer). Much depended on the cultural and religious background of the group under discussion. In order to better appreciate this "messiness," we will look at the cultural diversity of Roman Palestine and how it influenced the first Christian believers. Then, in order to get a more realistic picture of the liturgical life of the early Church, we will look at the contributions made by recent research on religious experience and altered states of consciousness. Finally, we will comment on a cultural reality that was to have lasting consequences for the spread of Christianity outside of the Roman Empire yet largely unknown by Christians in the West: the Semitic Church. How can acquaintance with a Christianity that has not been directly influenced by Hellenism aid us in understanding the religious experience and liturgical concerns of Christians in Africa and Asia?

Cultural Diversity among the First Generation of Believers

An easy way of appreciating the cultural and religious world of first-century Palestine is to look briefly at the languages spoken in the region. The first Christians were Jews. But the Jewish culture of this time was not monolithic, and the Jews were not the only cultural group living in this part of the Roman Empire. Palestine at this time was culturally complex and far from linguistically uniform. The people of Northern Palestine (Galilee), descendants of the Jews who had returned from the Babylonian Exile, spoke Aramaic—a Semitic language related to Hebrew that had become the trade language of the Near East under the neo-Assyrian and Persian Empires and had "gradually supplanted

---

[1] On the amazing variety of eucharistic celebrations, see Andrew McGowan, *Ascetic Eucharists: Food and Drink in Early Christian Ritual Meals* (Oxford, UK: Oxford University Press, 1999).

Hebrew in most of Palestine as a common tongue."[2] It seems likely, though, that Jesus and his followers were also acquainted with Hebrew, though there are scholarly disagreements as to how proficient they were in this language that was used more commonly in the south (the area of Judea). While Hebrew was used in worship and closely associated with the longing for national independence, especially during the Maccabean revolt against Antiochus Epiphanes II in the middle of the second century BCE, Aramaic was more commonly spoken, especially in Galilee. As scholars have pointed out, there is no doubt that Aramaic overwhelmed Hebrew after the second century CE and that Hebrew gradually became restricted to liturgy and writing.[3]

If the non-Jewish part of the population is considered, the language that was the most widely spoken in Palestine was *koine* (common) Greek, although many Jews also spoke Greek as a first or second language. Greek had begun to displace Aramaic as the *lingua franca* of the region after Alexander the Great's conquest of the old Persian Empire at the end of the third century BCE. This conquest resulted in the Hellenization of the region. Greek was the primary language of commerce and government, spoken in the towns established along the trade routes or those that supplanted previous settlements within the borders of Israel: Ptolemais (Acco), Sebaste (Samaria), Scythopolis (Beth Shean), the Dekapolis, and Tiberias. Greek was also the principal language of the Roman administrators, bureaucrats, and even soldiers who maintained the language of government and public order that had been established under the successors of Alexander, the Ptolemids in Egypt and Seleucids in the Near East.[4] Even though Rome held political and military sway in Palestine, very little Latin was spoken there. Apart from its use by Roman authorities in official documents and some inscriptions, as was the case generally throughout the Eastern empire, Greek remained the language of choice of the Gentile political and merchant classes and with those Jews who regularly interacted with Gentiles.[5]

---

[2] Joseph E. Fitzmyer, "The Languages of Palestine in the First Century CE," *Catholic Biblical Quarterly* 32 (1970): 502.

[3] Steven E. Fassberg, "Which Semitic Language Did Jesus and Other Contemporary Jews Speak?," *Catholic Biblical Quarterly* 74 (2012): 263–80.

[4] Martin Hengel, *The 'Hellenization' of Judaea in the First Century after Christ*, trans. John Bowden (London: SCM Press, 1989), 14–16.

[5] Fitzmyer, "The Languages of Palestine," 507.

Being aware of this linguistic and cultural diversity is important for any adequate interpretation of the life of the early Church in Palestine. Apart from the idyllic description of the Christian community in Jerusalem found in the Acts of the Apostles (Acts 2:42-47), tensions soon arose, occasioned by cultural differences among Jesus' first followers. These tensions are described in Acts 6:1-7 as discrimination against the Greek-speaking widows. Two separate groups of Jewish Christians are named: the Hebrews and the Hellenists. It is important to note that, at this point, we are still speaking of a religious movement within Judaism. The Pentecost event in Acts 2:1-6 describes *Jews* who have come from the diaspora to Jerusalem for the Jewish pilgrimage feasts of Shavuot (Weeks). While many use this first account of Pentecost to speak of the universalism of the "Jesus movement" ("Christians" as a name will not be used until later, in Antioch), the real outreach to the Gentile world is not described until Acts 10, when the Holy Spirit comes upon the Roman centurion Cornelius and his household, thus clearly indicating to Peter that they ought to be baptized into the new community.

Raymond Brown has helpfully reminded us that the early diversity of the Church was not only due to the Gentiles entering the Church but also because of the diversity among the Jews who had embraced Christ as the Messiah. Brown describes the presence of four different Jewish-Christian responses to the Gentile mission of the first Christians before the destruction of the temple in Jerusalem by the Romans in CE 70.[6] Since the first generation of Christians were all Jews, the way they saw their relationship to the Gentiles who wished to embrace the new religion was key in forming the various factions in the early Church. Each of these four groups had a different theological and practical approach, and it seems the basis for these approaches was often just as linguistic and cultural as it was theological. The first group were "Jewish Christians and their Gentile converts who practiced full observance of the Mosaic Law, including circumcision, as necessary for receiving the fullness of the salvation brought by Jesus Christ."[7] In fact, this group simply continued the Jewish discipline surrounding the admission of proselytes into the people of Israel. They still saw the temple sacrifices

---

[6] Raymond E. Brown, "Not Jewish Christianity and Gentile Christianity but Types of Jewish/Gentile Christianity," *Catholic Biblical Quarterly* 45 (1983): 74–79.

[7] Ibid., 77.

as having permanent value and insisted that even Gentiles embrace a Jewish life, now simply reinterpreted with Christ as the central focus.

The second group, championed by James and at times Peter, was composed of "Jewish Christians and their Gentile converts who did not insist on circumcision as salvific for Gentile Christians but did require them to keep some Jewish purity laws."[8] This was a modified position, but this group too continued to go to the temple and maintained a separation between Jews and Gentiles at meals. This group was also in favor of maintaining the practice of pilgrimage to Jerusalem for the three major feasts of the year, the so-called *shalosh regalim*: Pesach (Passover), Shavuot (Pentecost), and Sukkoth (Tabernacles).

The third group was composed of "Jewish Christians and their Gentile converts who did not insist on circumcision as salvific for Gentile Christians and did not require their observing Jewish purity laws in regard to food."[9] They would not, however, have automatically discarded the following of certain parts of the law by those Christians who were Jews. Brown describes the apostle Paul, who sought to be "all things to all people" as one of the leaders of this group.[10]

Finally, the fourth group is made up of "Jewish Christians and their Gentile converts who did not insist on circumcision or on following the Jewish food laws. They saw no abiding significance in the cult of the Jerusalem Temple. (Only this type is properly Hellenist in contrast to the three preceding varieties of 'Hebrew Christianity;' indeed, only this type may be considered fully non-law-observant.)"[11] These would be people like Stephen, Philip, and also those represented by the Fourth Gospel and the Letter to the Hebrews. This predominantly Greek-speaking part of the early Church represents a more radical break with the traditions of Judaism. For this group, the sacrifices of the temple have been abolished by the Christ event and since following the Law of Moses is part of the old covenant, it has nothing to do with salvation in Christ.[12]

---

[8] Ibid., 77.

[9] Ibid., 78.

[10] Ibid.

[11] Ibid.

[12] For further elaboration of this pluralistic reality of the first-century "Jesus Movement," see James G. D. Dunn, *Unity and Diversity in the New Testament: An Inquiry into the Character of Earliest Christianity* (London: SCM Press, 1977); and F. F. Bruce, *Peter, Stephen, James and John: Studies in Early Non-Pauline Christianity* (Grand Rapids, MI: Eerdmans, 1979).

After the destruction of the temple in CE 70, the issue of linking religious identity to the temple in Jerusalem became a moot point—for both the more strictly observant Jews and the Jewish Christians of the first three groups described above who had seen the need for continuing observance of the Law in whole or in part. It was from these initial groups that Christianity as a predominantly Gentile religion later emerged, but it is important to note that despite evidence of Christian hostility toward Jews present in the New Testament corpus, this hostility was not necessarily universal or uniform among all Christians all the time. In some cases, both Christians and Jews continued to identify with each other. While this identification takes different forms in different places, the "double identification," or at least sympathy, between Jews and Christians during the first several centuries is attested to by scholars. To illustrate this sympathy (at least in some circumstances), Daniel Boyarin cites the consumption of kosher meat by the Christian martyrs of Lyon in 177, the observance of both Saturday and Sunday as holy days by fourth-century Egyptian monastics, and the dependence of some Christians in Asia Minor on rabbis to determine the date of Easter because of its relationship to Passover.[13] The most important witness to sympathy between Jews and Christians was in the case of martyrdom. Both groups were persecuted and at times put to death over refusing to burn incense to an effigy of the emperor, and there are instances of rabbis praising Christians for suffering death rather than engaging in idolatry.[14]

Popular Religious Practices in First-Century Palestine

But what of the popular religious practices among the culturally diverse Jews of Palestine? Would the Jewish Christians have inherited any of these practices? The topic of Jewish popular religion is one that has only relatively recently attracted the attention of scholars of the Old Testament.[15] Since popular religion was more oral than written, much of the information that we have has come to us from archaeology: epigraphic (inscriptions on tombs, monuments) and surviving mate-

---

[13] See Daniel Boyarin, "Martyrdom and the Making of Christianity and Judaism," *Journal of Early Christian Studies* 6, no. 4 (1998): 582–84.

[14] Ibid., 626–27.

[15] For an overview on research in the area, see Jules Gomes, "Popular Religion in Old Testament Research: Past Present & Future," *Tyndale Bulletin* 54, no. 1 (2003): 31–50.

rial objects (mosaics, statuary). In his work on early Israelite religion, William Dever offers a helpful definition of popular religion that could also be applied to first-century Palestine. He defines popular religion as

> an alternate, nonorthodox, nonconformist mode of religious expression. It is noninstitutional, lying outside priestly control or state sponsorship. Because it is nonauthoritarian, popular religion is inclusive rather than exclusive; it appeals especially to minorities and to the disenfranchised (in the case of ancient Israel, most women); in both belief and practice it tends to be eclectic and syncretistic. Popular religion focuses more on individual piety and informal practice than on elaborate public ritual, more on cult than on intellectual formulations (i.e., theology). By definition, popular religion is less literate (not by that token any less complex or sophisticated) and thus may be inclined to leave behind more traces in the archaeological record than in the literary record, more ostraca and graffiti than classical texts, more cult and other symbolic paraphernalia than scripture. Nevertheless, despite these apparent dichotomies, popular religion overlaps significantly with official religion, if only by sheer force of numbers of practitioners; it often sees itself as equally legitimate; and it attempts to secure the same benefits as all religion, namely, the individual's sense of integration with nature and society, of health and prosperity, of ultimate well-being.[16]

Dever may be overemphasizing the individual and private nature of popular religion, but what he says is helpful to orient our study. While the temple priesthood could no longer serve as a source for determining "official" Judaism, the relocation of the Sanhedrin to Jamnia (a small town in Palestine) after the destruction of the temple in CE 70 opened a way for the survival of an authority structure in Judaism that would eventually determine "official" teaching in what was to become Rabbinic Judaism. It is commonly believed that it was the debates among the religious authorities at Jamnia that set in motion the eventual exclusion of those Jews who believed that Jesus was the awaited Messiah.[17]

---

[16] William G. Dever, "The Silence of the Text: An Archaeological Commentary on 2 Kings 23: The Contribution of Archaeology to the Study of Canaanite and Early Israelite Religion," in *Scripture and Other Artifacts: Essays on the Bible and Archaeology in Honor of Philip J. King*, eds. M. D. Coogan, C. J. Exum, and L. E. Stager (Louisville, KY: Westminster John Knox, 1994), 160.

[17] On the restructuring of Judaism just before and after the destruction of the temple, see J. W. Doeve, "Official and Popular Religion in Judaism," in *Official and*

If we are to take the pages of the New Testament at face value, though, many of the members of the Jesus movement were drawn to belief in Jesus not only through the preaching of the Master's first disciples but also because of the signs and wonders worked publicly that substantiated their claims that Jesus was of God. Among these signs and wonders were exorcisms and healings that are present in the gospels and also figure in the pages of the Acts of the Apostles. While the importance of exorcism should not be exaggerated,[18] it is useful to recall that the religious worldview of most people of first-century Palestine presupposed the existence of demons who had power to do evil and who could even possess human beings. In this premodern age, before the advances in medical science, God was directly invoked in healing diseases and disabilities. People imbued with God's spirit and power were commonly thought to have the ability to heal and to restore the afflicted to wholeness. Jesus and his followers, then, in announcing God's reign, were necessarily involved in healing and exorcisms—signs of the advent of God's power on earth. Healing itself "was a central ministry of the Christian community, whether such healing appears in the guise of miracles performed by apostles (Acts) or other charismatic healers (I Cor. 12:8-10, 28-30), or whether it is a task assigned to elders (James 5:13-18). Above all, however, the Gospels highlight healing, for at the core of their narratives of Jesus' public ministry lies his activity as healer."[19]

The New Testament accounts of exorcisms and healings attest to this public and private belief in the involvement of the spirit world in human life. This belief was undoubtedly expressed in both the formal and informal gatherings of the first Christians. These gatherings probably would have at times resembled healing services that one could find today throughout two-thirds of the world (Africa, Asia, Latin America) in Pentecostal gatherings and in healing services among charismatic movements within the Roman Catholic Church.

Popular Religion: Analysis of a Theme for Religious Studies, eds. Pieter Henrik Vrihof and Jacques Waardenburg (The Hague: Mouton Publishers, 1979), 325–39.

[18] An important part of Jesus' ministry in the Synoptic Gospels is exorcism, but it features not at all in the Gospel of John. On the place of exorcism in the New Testament and the early Church see Graham H. Twelftree, "In the Name of Jesus: A Conversation with Critics," *Journal of Pentecostal Theology* 17 (2008): 157–69.

[19] John T. Carroll, "Sickness and Healing in the New Testament Gospels," *Interpretation* 49, no. 2 (April 1995): 131.

The role of marginal people in the new Jesus movement should also not be overlooked. There is evidence to suggest that women enjoyed a much more prominent place in the early Christian community than they did in subsequent generations. In a Jewish context, their involvement in positions of leadership (Church leadership, leading prayers, ministry) would have been considered rather "popular" by more traditional patriarchal Jewish standards.[20] There is evidence to suggest that by the end of the first century this revolutionary aspect of the Jesus movement would be discouraged by the imposition of Church orders that emphasized the unique leadership of men.[21]

Popular Religion in the New Testament and Altered States of Consciousness

Those with a premodern worldview tend to believe strongly that their societal customs and beliefs—as they relate to the divine—are directly inspired by God. Consequently, only a powerful experience of the divine—a vision or a divine revelation—would be capable of changing their fundamental religious convictions. Evidence of these kinds of experiences is found in practically all major religious traditions and figures prominently in the Bible.

Building on insights from cognitive neuroscientists and anthropologists, biblical scholar John Pilch, in his commentary on the Acts of the Apostles, identifies numerous instances where the text describes an encounter with God, the risen Christ, or angels that indicate a level of awareness different from normal waking consciousness.[22] Among

---

[20] See, for example, Barbara E. Reid, *Taking up the Cross: New Testament Interpretations through Latina and Feminist Eyes* (Minneapolis: Fortress Press, 2007); Dorothy Jean Weaver, "'Wherever This Good News Is Proclaimed': Women and God in the Gospel of Matthew," *Interpretation* 64, no. 4 (October 2010), 390–400.

[21] On the ongoing role of women in ministerial roles in the early Church, see *On the Cutting Edge: The Study of Women in Biblical Worlds: Essays in Honor of Elisabeth Schüssler Fiorenza*, ed. Jane Schaberg, Alice Bach, and Esther Fuchs (New York: Continuum, 2004).

[22] The list of these incidents is impressive: Acts 1:1-11 (ascension of Jesus); 2:1-4 (descent of the spirit); 2:5-13 (glossolalia); 6:1–8:3 (Stephen [7:55-56]); 8:4-40 (Philip); 9:1-9 (Paul); 9:10-19 (Ananias); 9:43–10:8 (Cornelius); 10:9-16 (Peter); 10:17-23 (interpretation of Peter's vision); 10:23-48 (soldier's house in Caesarea; Cornelius repeats; Peter explains; glossolalia; trance experience); 11:1-18 (Peter explains in Jerusalem); 12:5-19 (Peter escapes arrest); 12:12-17 (maid's reaction); 13:1-3 (commissions in Antioch); 4:12 (Paul and the curse); 14:1-20 (healing);

others, he identifies the accounts of Jesus' ascension into heaven, the coming of the Spirit at Pentecost, and the appearance of the risen Christ to Paul on the road to Damascus as references to "altered states of consciousness" (ASC). Studies have found that this phenomenon of altered states is widespread and that "at all times and in all places people have been capable of and actually entered into a variety of altered states of consciousness. Indeed the potential to shift, voluntarily or involuntarily between different states of consciousness is a function of the universal human nervous system."[23]

The interpretation of these altered states of consciousness is very much influenced by one's culture (its basic religious attitude and whether it is premodern, modern, or postmodern) and helps to explain how

> Mediterranean believers are more likely to interpret an altered state of consciousness experience as an encounter with someone from the realm of God, while a scientifically sophisticated Western believer may be inclined to interpret such an experience as a "hallucination," that is, something pathological, or perhaps an "alien from outer space" or an "unidentified flying object (UFO)." The society, country, or culture of origin influences the way in which the visionary interprets an experience. In their ecstatic trance experience of Jesus' Transfiguration (Luke 9:28-36), the disciples identified the two men talking with him as Moses and Elijah, not Zeus and Apollo.[24]

Altered states of consciousness are an aspect of religious experience that needs to be taken into account when trying to gain a total picture of the worship life of the early Church. Pilch points out that these experiences can be divided into two categories, spontaneous or induced, and that intentionally induced trances ordinarily occur in the

---

16:6-10 (ASC experience of the Spirit); 22:6-21 (Paul's vision); 23:10-11 (the Lord speaks to Paul); 26:9-18 (Paul's vision again); 27:23-26 (angel tells Paul his destiny). Bruce J. Malina and John J. Pilch, *Social-Science Commentary on the Book of Acts* (Minneapolis: Fortress Press, 2008), 186.

[23] Jean Clottes and David Lewis Williams, *The Shamans of Prehistory: Trance and Magic in the Painted Caves*, trans. Sophie Hawkes (New York: Harry N. Abrams, Inc., 1996), 12.

[24] John J. Pilch, *Visions and Healings in the Acts of the Apostles: How the Early Believers Experienced God* (Collegeville, MN: Liturgical Press, 2004), 3.

Scriptures in the context of a rite. He further specifies that "ceremonial rite" such as fixed prayer can be the occasion for just such altered states of consciousness.[25] We know from Paul's discussion of the *charismata* or "spiritual gifts" enumerated in 1 Corinthians 12 that these rites were exercised by members of the Christian community during their gatherings. *Glossolalia* (speaking in tongues) and their interpretation are but one example of a kind of communal experience of ASC that continued in the worship by Christians during the apostolic period and beyond. In a real way, glossolalia and acts of healing could be considered "popular religious practices" in the worship life of the early Church. As Wayne Meeks points out regarding glossolalia in assemblies in the Christian house churches:

> We are led to a conclusion that at first may seem paradoxical: that such exotic and presumably spontaneous behavior as speaking in tongues was also ritual. It occurred within the framework of the assembly, performed by persons expected to do it. It happened at predictable times, accompanied by distinctive bodily move-ments, perhaps introduced and followed by characteristic phrases in natural language.[26]

Lest we relegate this phenomenon to an early "immature" period of the Church, it is important to remember that these manifestations of the presence of the Spirit never completely die out. They reemerge in other ways over the course of Christian history: in the mystical tradition during the Middle Ages, in the eruption of Pentecostalism in early twentieth-century United States, and in the charismatic renewal movement in Roman Catholicism after Vatican II.

The Importance of Christianity's Often Overlooked Semitic Heritage

While the usual history of Christian worship—based on the ac-count found in the Acts of the Apostles—often moves without much delay from the first followers of Jesus in Roman Palestine who were of Jewish background to the definitive entry of the Church into the Greco-Roman world, recent scholarship has taken another look at this history and turned its attention to the ongoing existence of a Semitic

---

[25] Ibid., 9.

[26] Wayne Meeks, *The First Urban Christians: The Social World of the Apostle Paul*, 2nd ed. (New Haven, CT: Yale University Press, 2003), 149.

Christianity largely unaffected by the Hellenistic culture of the Roman Empire.[27] As Peter Phan has commented,

> Historical studies of early Christian missions have also shown the fallacy of the conventional reading of Acts, with its version of the Christian expansion toward Rome and the West. In fact, in the first four centuries, the most successful fields of mission were not Europe but West Asia and Africa, with Syria as the center of gravity of Christianity before 500. The most vibrant and influential Christian centers were found in Asian and African cities such as Damascus and Alexandria, Axum and Antioch (where, incidentally, the followers of Jesus first became known as "Christians"); and in countries such as Armenia (the first Christian nation), India, and somewhat later, in China. Of the five ancient patriarchates, only Rome was located in the West, and of the remaining four, three were located in Asia (Jerusalem, Antioch, and Constantinople) and one in Africa (Alexandria).[28]

In many ways, the traditional Jewish approach to the Scriptures was more faithfully maintained in those regions that were not influenced by the Greek *paideia,* or education, especially the Aramaic-speaking Church of Syria. Jewish influence seems to continue longer in this part of the world and gradually gives rise to a theological approach influenced by a Semitic culture that is just as venerable as the form it will take in the West.[29] In commenting on the theological tradition of the Syrian Church that is just as "traditional" as the Greco-Roman version that developed within the Hellenized Roman Empire, Joseph Amar writes about Ephrem, the great Syriac father of the Church (+373). His theology—his very manner of presenting the truths of the faith—is quite distinct from that of the Latin and Greek fathers such as Augustine or Athanasius.

---

[27] Philip Jenkins, *The Lost History of Christianity: The Thousand-Year Golden Age of the Church in the Middle East, Africa, and Asia—and How It Died* (San Francisco: HarperOne, 2008); Lamin Sanneh, *Disciples of All Nations: Pillars of World Christianity* (Oxford, UK: Oxford University Press, 2008); Andrew F. Walls, *The Cross-Cultural Process in Christian History* (Maryknoll, NY: Orbis Books, 2002).

[28] Peter Phan, "Speaking in Many Tongues: Why the Church Must Be More Catholic," *Commonweal* 134, no. 1 (January 12, 2007).

[29] Sten Hidal, "Evidence for Jewish Believers in the Syriac Fathers," in *Jewish Believers in Jesus: The Early Centuries,* ed. Oskar Skarsaune and Reidar Hvalvik (Peabody, MA: Hendrickson Publishers, 2007), 568–80.

Though few would contest his inclusion among these luminaries [the fathers of the church], little that pertains to this mostly Greco-Roman company prepares us for him [Ephrem]. Grounded in the classical curriculum, the fathers wrote in Greek and Latin, and used the abstract language of philosophy to shape the central beliefs of the faith. Ephrem, on the other hand was a Semite who wrote exclusively in Syriac; and while he shares some of the theological concerns of his contemporaries who wrote in Greek and Latin, there is a crucial difference that goes beyond language. What sets him emphatically apart from the mainstream Christian authors of his day is his utter abhorrence of rationalism—"the poison of the Greeks," as he called it. For Ephrem, abstract philosophical language and cleverly constructed epistemologies had no place in theology. Divine truth, like life itself, required a subtler, more comprehensive language. Only poetry was sufficiently allusive to intimate the truths of God.[30]

Ephrem and other Syriac fathers such as Aphraat (the Persian Sage) promoted a Middle Eastern Christianity that was eventually eclipsed by the advent of Islam in the seventh and eighth centuries. But this attitude toward rationalism as "the poison of the Greeks" may offer new possibilities for evangelization that we in the West have heretofore neglected. The recovery of this part of the Christian story is timely in light of the new situation in which the Church finds itself. The peoples of Asia and Africa, many of whom still have a premodern worldview unaffected by the rationality of the Enlightenment (or the Greek philosophical categories that were so decisive in the West) have interpreted the Bible and the sacramental system of the Church in ways consonant with a Semitic worldview.[31] Through their eyes, we can more easily imagine how the early Jewish Christians first accepted the Good News of Christ. The Gambian theologian Lamin Sanneh remarks that "the West can encounter in the world Christian movement the gospel as it is being embraced by societies that had not been shaped by the Enlightenment, and so gain an insight into the culture that shaped the origin of the NT church. That might bring about a greater appreciation

---

[30] Joseph Amar, "The Loss of Syria: New Violence Threatens Christianity's Ancient Roots," *Commonweal* 139, no. 17 (October 12, 2012): 14.

[31] The relatively recent approval of the ancient anaphora (eucharistic prayer) of Addai and Mari by the Congregation for the Doctrine of the Faith illustrates this new awareness on an official level. See Robert F. Taft, "Mass without the Consecration?," *America* 188, no. 16 (May 12, 2003): 7–11.

for the NT background of Christianity. It might also shed light on the issues the early church faced as it moved between the Jewish and Gentile worlds."[32]

The New Testament and early Christian writings that narrate the miraculous are more understandable and can be seen in a more positive way by Western Christians who are conscious of this newly refocused history and have difficulty—even embarrassment—in trying to explain many of the elements of the New Testament that do not jibe with a postmodern worldview. Rather than writing off the numerous examples of trances, exorcisms, and miraculous healings ascribed to Jesus and his first followers as simply a premodern way of dealing with mental disorders and hallucinations, seeing this world through other cultural lenses offers an interpretation that takes our ancestors in the faith more seriously. The author of the Letter to the Ephesians, along with many modern Christians in the developing world, is convinced that "our struggle is not with flesh and blood but with the principalities, with the powers, with the world rulers of this present darkness, with the evil spirits in the heavens" (Eph 6:12). Our challenge is not to dismiss this view out of hand but to reinterpret it for our globalized world of the twenty-first century.

Christians of the North are also challenged over their particular monopoly of the theological mainstream that in many cases is just as culturally contingent as that of the emerging churches of the South. Philip Jenkins describes well the questions of the two sides:

> Why, for instance, do these churches [of the South] so emphasize healing, visions, and prophesy? Perhaps, one might suggest, they are rather too much in contact with their pre-Christian roots, with traditional worlds of healing or magic or shamanism. For Northern liberals, contemplating a belief in demons and exorcisms based on a fundamentalist reading of scripture, this seems to be the realm of cults, not Christianity. . . . Yet many Africans and Asians respond that their views are grounded in the abundant evidence of scripture; they ask how any reasonable reader could exclude healings and miracles from the Christian message. Have liberal Americans and Germans never read the gospels or the book of Acts, in which miracles and exorcism so proliferate? If Southern Christians have

---

[32] Lamin Sanneh, *Whose Religion Is Christianity? The Gospel beyond the West* (Grand Rapids, MI: Eerdmans, 2003), 26.

compromised with animism, have not Northerners sold out to scientism, materialism, and determinism?[33]

Being aware of the sensibilities occasioned by these worldviews and drawing on a wider range of Christian cultural experiences than only those of the West will be useful skills for pastoral agents who seek to serve in a globalized pastoral context where members of some cultural groups may indeed have a premodern worldview.

Converts not Proselytes

One major element eventually distinguished the Jesus movement from the mainstream Judaism of the first century: the way non-Jewish believers were received into the community of believers. With the fall of Jerusalem and the dispersal of its Jewish-Christian community after the destruction of the temple in CE 70 and the subsequent Bar-Kokhba revolt in CE 135, the Romans no longer permitted Jews to enter their ancient capitol. In this difficult time of displacement and transformation of Jewish identity, the "hard line" Jewish-Christians who demanded that Gentile converts effectively become Jews before becoming Christians lost influence. Had their point of view prevailed, the history of Christianity would have been very different indeed. As Andrew Walls points out:

> Had the Jesus Community retained the proselyte model, Christians would almost inevitably have been taken out of the intellectual mainstream and shut up in their own sacred books. But as converts, believers in Jesus were required to turn their processes of thought toward Christ, to think Christ into the intellectual framework of their time and place. The eventual result was Christian theology as we know it.[34]

Apart from Jewish-Christian groups that did not recognize Jesus as divine and became identified with heterodox groups such as the Ebionites,[35] the decision of the so-called First Council of Jerusalem

---

[33] Philip Jenkins, *The New Faces of Christianity: Believing the Bible in the Global South* (Oxford, UK: Oxford University Press, 2006), 16.

[34] Andrew F. Walls, "Converts or Proselytes? The Crisis over Conversion in the Early Church," *International Bulletin of Missionary Research* 28, no. 1 (January 2004), 6.

[35] For an exhaustive study of this fascinating group see Oscar Skarsaune, "The Ebionites," in Skarsaune and Hvalvik, *Jewish Believers in Jesus*, 419–62.

recorded in Acts 15:28-29 that Gentile converts abstain from meat offered to idols, from consuming blood, from eating the meat of strangled animals, and from fornication opened the Jesus movement to the surrounding non-Jewish cultural influences. Other than these restrictions, even during this early period, Gentiles were able to enter the Christian community retaining their culture—including their worldviews expressed in cultural practices—as long as these practices were not directly related to paganism.

The first Christian communities were largely an urban phenomenon since the Church expanded in cities located along the trade routes of the Roman Empire. The influence of the urban, multicultural backdrop of the Roman Empire will be an important element in the development of the early Jesus movement—at least in the Mediterranean world.[36] In fact, it is to this cultural mix that we owe many of the particular characteristics of what will become Western Christianity. It would be a mistake, though, to think that the cultural influence of Greco-Roman civilization was incorporated into the practices and rites of the early Church in an orderly fashion. Since the sacred and the secular in this premodern context were largely fused, it would take real discernment and negotiation for the Church to accept some cultural practices and reject others that were regarded as too wedded to pagan beliefs. Not unlike the process that is at work today in the "new churches" of Africa and Asia, the early Church was forced to determine what part of the surrounding culture was compatible with the Gospel and what popular practices had to be rejected. As Lamin Sanneh points out, the new religious movement that became known as Christianity entered into a real dialogue with local cultures. Despite the best efforts of Christian authorities, this dialogue never defined completely and absolutely the cultural forms that the nonnegotiable content of the faith would take.[37]

Conclusion

It is particularly difficult for us to bridge the historical and cultural chasm that would allow us to more accurately imagine the life of the first Christians. These first followers of Jesus had very different cultural

---

[36] Abraham Malherbe, *Social Aspects of Early Christianity* (Philadelphia: Fortress Press, 1983), 63.

[37] Lamin Sanneh, *Disciples of All Nations: Pillars of World Christianity* (New York: Oxford University Press, 2008), 31.

and religious presuppositions than most Christians who live in twenty-first-century North America. This chapter has attempted to point to some of these differences in order to see early Christianity with a new perspective that may help us to better appreciate Christianity's roots in Judaism. The worship of these first Christians was undoubtedly more spontaneous and informal than it would be at later stages. It was also more influenced by popular religious practices and beliefs. This heritage is especially relevant when appreciating the attraction of Christianity in today's global South—an area of the world that is not a direct cultural heir to Greco-Roman civilization. It is to this new cultural chapter in the history of Christianity that we now turn.

Chapter Three

The Greco-Roman Religious World and Christian Popular Piety

As the Church moved more fully into the Greco-Roman world, it attracted Gentile adherents who brought to their belief in Christ a religious background naturally influenced by their culture. How did this pagan context influence the religious imagination of the people who embraced belief in Christ? More to the point, did their previous religious grounding affect the way they understood and participated in the worship life of the Christian community? Did a "popular" set of beliefs and practices exist alongside the "official" portrait of Christianity that we find in the New Testament corpus and the early Christian writers? This is a complex question that cannot easily be answered, especially because like Christianity itself, the religious backdrop of the Greco-Roman world was both varied and complex.

The General Religious Situation of Greece and Rome

Perhaps the best place to start to answer such a question is to try to avoid falling into anachronistic assumptions about the religious worldview of the people of the Roman Empire of the first centuries. There has been a tendency among some modern Christian writers to view Greco-Roman paganism as an exhausted and discredited religious system that was ripe to be transformed by the preaching of the Gospel. It is true that the religious world of these centuries, especially the official pantheon of the gods of Greece and Rome, had suffered a crisis of confidence as early as the fifth century BCE due to advances in astronomy and the birth of philosophical schools (Epicureanism and Sophism) that gave rise to a new cosmology that questioned the traditional role of the gods.[1] It is important to note, however, that while this lack of confidence took hold in the more elite strata of society, it was by no means universal.

Much recent scholarly work has been done to better clarify the contours of this religious world that was sometimes presented in an oversimplified way by earlier historians. From the seventeenth century onward, many of those who studied the influence of Greco-Roman religion on Christianity fell into a one-dimensional pattern, naming the pagan "mystery religions" as the only dominant outside influence on early Christianity. These religions, such as the Eleusian Mysteries, celebrated death and rebirth and initiated adepts through ceremonies whose details were kept secret from the uninitiated. For some Protestant authors, this influence was regarded as the beginning of the corruption of a Catholic Church that had by their time strayed from simple biblical faith. This pure faith would be recaptured only when the nonbiblical aspects were removed from the practice of the faith by the reformers.[2] In a less polemical way, Catholics too looked to the mystery religions of the first centuries as an influence on the early Church, tracing their influence on the way in which the sacraments came to be celebrated.

The most famous exponent of proposing the mystery religions as an influence on the development of the Christian sacraments was the Roman Catholic liturgical pioneer Dom Odo Casel, a Benedictine of the Monastery of Maria Laach. His 1928 book, *Mysteriengegenwart* (mystery presence), was controversial and met with opposition from more traditional theologians who regarded his theory as a threat to the integrity of Catholic worship. Many theologians later contended that Pius XII's encyclical on the liturgy, *Mediator Dei*, contained a condemnation of Casel's theory—although Casel himself saw it rather as a vindication.[3]

---

[1] Antonia Tripolitis, *Religions of the Hellenistic-Roman Age* (Grand Rapids, MI: Eerdmans, 2002), 14–16.

[2] See, for example, Alexander Hislop, *The Two Babylons: or, The Papal Worship Proved to Be the Worship of Nimrod and His Wife* (Edinburgh: James Wood, 1858). This polemical work is available on Amazon.com.

[3] See Pope Pius XII, *Mediator Dei*, AAS 39 (1947), 521–95, in which some have seen his criticism of certain "recent theories" which overemphasize the objective nature of the rites at the expense of "subjective" or "personal piety." See also Hugo Rahner's critical review of the literature that attributes a direct relationship

Recent scholarship has offered a much more nuanced appraisal of the influence of Greco-Roman religion on the early Church—one that does not center on just the mystery religions but considers the whole of the pre-Christian religious experience of the people on its own terms, rather than simply a deficient approach to the divine that was finally corrected by Christianity. One of the most helpful approaches is that proposed by Luke Timothy Johnson. In his book *Among the Gentiles: Greco-Roman Religion and Christianity*, Johnson provides an important new perspective on this influence.[4] He starts his reflections by offering a preliminary profile of Greco-Roman religion that also helps describe the religious context in which the early Christians lived and attracted new believers. Using five alliterative adjectives, he describes religion in the Roman Empire of the first centuries as pervasive, public, political, pious, and pragmatic.

Greco-Roman polytheism was a pervasive phenomenon in the ancient Mediterranean basin. Unlike the North American tendency to relegate religion to select moments and areas of people's lives, religion was omnipresent in the Greco-Roman world. Shrines to the gods were on every street corner, their temples built on the acropolises of practically every major city. Every aspect of life—every profession and state of life (e.g., agriculture, fertility, motherhood, war, etc.)—was placed under the purview of certain gods. As Johnson points out, "Religion for Greeks and Romans was not something done only with a part of one's time, space, attention. It demanded attention in virtually every time and space, because every time and space was potentially an opening to a divine presence and power."[5]

Because it was so pervasive, pagan religion also had a decidedly *public* character. It is easy for many of us raised in Europe or North America to be unaware of the gregarious nature of other cultures. We tend to value the private and the individual and feel that demands of the larger society infringe on our rights. The premodern, ancient world (and also many current non-Western cultures) regarded an individual's

---

between the mystery religions and early Christianity in *Greek Myths and Christian Mystery* (New York: Biblio & Tannen, 1971), 3–46, as well as Edward Kilmartin's appraisal of Casel's influence on *Mediator Dei* in his *The Eucharist in the West: History and Theology* (Collegeville, MN: Liturgical Press, 1998), 295–300.

[4] Luke Timothy Johnson, *Among the Gentiles: Greco-Roman Religion and Christianity* (New Haven, CT: Yale University Press, 2009), 32–49.

[5] Ibid., 33.

isolation and separation from family and community as an evil that religious practice was meant to overcome. Religion was seen as a way of helping individuals express their belonging to a given society and therefore needed to be expressed publicly. Both calendars (time) and urban planning (space) were all religiously determined. The Romans accommodated many of the actions of their lives according to days designated as *fasti* (available for commerce and public activity) and *nefasti* (assigned to the worship of a god and therefore unlucky for other business). Cities and towns were also consecrated to certain deities and put under their protection. These gods, then, needed to be continually "cultivated" by worship and sacrifice in order to guarantee continued good luck and prosperity.

Because of the pervasive and public nature of religion, it was also political. It was in the emperor's interest to ensure that proper devotion was offered the gods since the well-being of the state depended on it. Good harvests, victory in war, and commercial prosperity were a concern for all the members of the state, and these depended on the right worship of the gods, undertaken by people specially chosen to carry out this worship in the "correct" way. Following the traditional ceremonial directives concerning gesture and dress in offering a sacrifice and speaking the established accompanying prayers without error were regarded as essential if the gods were to continue their protection of the state. In ancient Rome a precise set of conditions and cultic formulae were found in a compendium called the *ius divinum* (the divine law). In order to ensure the favor of the god in offering a sacrifice, the accompanying prayer had to be proclaimed perfectly by the priest. The perfect recitation of the prayer was so important that a *promptor* near the priest suggested the exact word of the prayer to help him avoid mistakes since, if a mistake were made, the whole prayer needed to be recited from the beginning.

Given the demanding nature of the cultic law and its connection to the favor of the gods, the choice of religious functionaries was of crucial importance. Part of the *cursus honorum* (the series of political and administrative posts for an aspiring Roman politician) included seeking appointment as an *augur* (a reader of omens) or a *pontifex* (priest of the state religion). With these appointments came much prestige and power. Indeed, though not a formal part of the *cursus honorum*, serving as a Vestal Virgin (priestess of the goddess Vesta, keeper of the sacred flame in her temple in the Forum) conferred on a woman a social preeminence and influence just below that of the emperor himself.

The regulation of religion, then, was considered very important for the safety of the state. Rome, however, was usually very open to the importation of foreign gods, provided that they did not threaten social stability. Syncretism was long practiced in Rome from the very foundation of the city through its exchanges with the neighboring Etruscans and other local Italic tribes. The erection of temples to the Egyptian goddess Isis and her consort Osiris, the worship of the fertility goddess Cybele from Asia Minor, and the widespread presence of centers of devotion to the Persian god Mithras throughout the empire all attest to the capaciousness of the Roman attitude toward the various manifestations of the divine. The Romans had no problem adding the worship of these deities to the traditional pantheon of Greco-Roman gods and goddesses such as Zeus/Jupiter, Hera/Juno, Poseidon/Neptune, and Artemis/Diana.

This religious tolerance, however, did not extend to people following a philosophy that denied that the gods were involved in everyday affairs or that they were concerned about the safety of the state. Followers of Epicurus and members of other philosophical schools that openly questioned the need to sacrifice to the gods were condemned by Roman writers like Plutarch, who charged them with threatening the stability of the empire. In the same way, Jews and Christians, in their refusal to sacrifice to the gods (and specifically to the emperor) were charged with "atheism" and thus were guilty of *amixia* (failure to mingle or participate) that "was tantamount to *misanthropia* (hatred of humanity)."[6]

Finally, the polytheism practiced in Rome and throughout the empire was both *pious* and *pragmatic*. It was pious in the sense that it was inextricably linked to the family—the ancestors whose veneration took place in every Roman home in the form of the *lares*, or ancestral spirits, whose effigies were honored at specified times of the year. The *penates* were household deities related to Vesta and were believed to look after the well-being of a family. By extension, the Roman state itself had public *lares* and *penates* whose role in maintaining the well-being of the state was regularly acknowledged. Roman religion was pragmatic in that it did not provoke much theological speculation. The rites, if duly conducted, guaranteed the security of the state and the family. If conditions for offering a sacrifice were not just right, the sacrifice was postponed. The important thing was to fulfill the *ius divinum*, which was necessary to obtain the gods' favorable response.

[6] Ibid., 34.

It would be a mistake, though, to judge religious practices such as offering sacrifice to the gods or reading the omens as empty formalism. Undoubtedly the level of belief and "piety" varied from person to person. Some people were more fervent than others, and charges of superstition and credulity were voiced by otherwise pious believers toward those who were easily taken in by charlatans making use of religion for their own gain. Also, while certain official sacrifices were done by an elite group of priests at the expense of the state, this religious activity was paralleled by religious practices done in the home by the head of the family (*paterfamilias*). In this sense, Greco-Roman religion had a very strong base among the people and could itself be considered "popular." Meat obtained from sacrifices and sold at the market was also a normal part of the diet of most city dwellers, facilitating a sharing at the gods' table within the home (much to St. Paul's disapproval[7]). The strongly domestic component of Roman religion, as well as its pragmatic characteristics, will have a real influence on the way Christianity will be later interpreted by Gentile converts.

Having described some of the general characteristics of Greco-Roman religious sensibility, we can now turn to some of its specific expressions in order to round out the cultural and religious context in which the early Church proclaimed the Gospel. The mystery religions, prophesy, healing, and pilgrimage all serve as points of reference for what Gentile converts would experience as members of the Christian Church.

Mystery Religions

The early Church was seen as a religious movement not completely dissimilar to that of the so-called "mystery religions" that were popular throughout the empire. Several characteristics of these religions underscore their difference from Christianity. However, it needs to be noted that these were not separate "religions" but were, in fact, part of pagan religious practice for centuries. They were dubbed "mystery religions" only in the sense that the tenets and especially the acts of worship were reserved to initiates who learned the deeper significance

---

[7] Recall St. Paul's disapproval of this practice and his characterization of the pagan gods as demons. "You cannot drink the cup of the Lord and also the cup of demons. You cannot partake of the table of the Lord and of the table of demons" (1 Cor 10:21).

of certain objects and gestures used in the course of their initiation that would in turn bring about a saving relationship with the god or goddess being worshiped.

These religions seem to have developed from nature rites focused on issues of fertility and life. Using natural symbols of water, fire, and wind, they held initiatory rituals that introduced adepts into the central "mystery" of the particular cult. The most common examples are the Eleusinian rites that celebrated Demeter and Persephone, the Greek goddess of vegetation and fertility and her daughter. Another popular mystery was that of the Egyptian god Osiris and his sister Isis that celebrated death and rebirth and featured lustrations using the water of the Nile. Mithras, whose worship was popular among Roman legionnaires, featured the god's slaying of a mythic bull, ritual meals of communion, and a calendar regulated by the solstices.[8]

Part of the attraction of these religions was the emphasis they placed on the initiatory rituals themselves. These rituals were thought to transform the initiand through the power of the god or goddess and place him or her under special divine protection. It was through experiencing the ritual, rather than learning any didactic content, that led to a greater understanding by which the individual was believed to attain a new level of intimacy with the god. Aristotle himself summed up the point of entering the mysteries by juxtaposing two words: *mathein* (to learn) and *pathein* (to experience). He said, "The purpose of the mysteries is not to learn (mathein) but rather to experience (pathein) and gain a disposition."[9] It was this religious experience that transformed and united the initiand to other members of the cult rather than any formal adherence to a set of doctrines. We will compare and contrast this attitude to the Christians' approach to initiation.

Prophecy

Much of pagan religion was concerned with knowing the will of the gods. This will was revealed in a variety of ways—in inspecting the entrails of sacrificed animals or in consulting the priests and priestesses at the temple of certain gods known for their ability to predict the fu-

---

[8] Edward Yarnold, *The Awe Inspiring Rites of Initiation: Baptismal Homilies of the Fourth Century* (Middlegreen Slough, UK: St. Paul Publications, 1971), 55–62.

[9] τοὺς τελουμένους οὐ **μαθεῖν** τι δεῖν, ἀλλὰ **παθεῖν** καὶ διατεθῆναι (Aristotle, frag. 45, 1483a19).

ture. The famous oracle at Delphi in Greece where the god Apollo was worshiped and which was considered the center of the world (*omphalos tou kosmou*) was perhaps the best-known place to learn the god's will. This was the place where the ancients consulted a priestess of Apollo who sat on a tripod over a vent in the earth that emitted vapors. After exposure to these vapors, she went into a trance and uttered enigmatic words that were in turn interpreted by the *prophetai* of the shrine. The various Sibyls (female prophets also associated with Apollo, the most famous of whom spoke at a cave north of Naples at a place called Cumae) were long held to be important intermediaries of the will of the gods and the well-being of Rome. The belief that somehow the gods could possess a human being and use that person to pronounce words that conveyed the divine will and announced future events was commonly held in the Greco-Roman world.

Widespread belief in astrology also permeated all walks of Greco-Roman society. Foretelling the future by the movement of the stars and extraordinary celestial portents was a commonplace in underlining the importance of the famous people celebrated in the ancient world. Many people consulted astrologers before embarking on a new venture since these experts were capable of telling the suppliant which god or goddess would be particularly involved, thus guaranteeing good fortune.

Pilgrimage

Each god was known to be concerned about certain specific issues. If a person was concerned about a particular issue, he or she would likely pray to a specific god. While one might pray to the gods anywhere, to make a formal request—usually by offering the god special worship in the form of sacrifice—an individual had to travel to temples especially associated with them. Thus, to obtain an oracle from Apollo, one had to make the difficult journey to Delphi. In order to dedicate oneself as a soldier and to ask for protection in battle, one needed to go physically to the Temple of Mars the Avenger in Rome. It was in the physical place associated with the god or goddess that their power was the strongest and where the suppliant had the best chance of obtaining the sought-for favor.

Healing

A special reason for pilgrimage was to seek healing. Those in search of a cure frequented shrines of the physician god Asclepius that were spread throughout the ancient world in places such as Epidaurus in

Greece, Pergamum in Asia Minor, and Rome. By spending the night within the temple precincts—a practice called incubation—many sought a physical cure for their disease. It was considered to be especially fortunate if the sacred snakes associated with the god crawled over the sick person while asleep. This association with snakes and healing seems strange to us, but we have a remnant of this association depicted in the modern symbol for medicine itself, the rod of Asclepius that consists of a snake coiled around a stake.

Special individuals were believed to be endowed by the gods with the gift of healing as well. The Emperor Vespasian had such a reputation, as did the neo-Pythagorean philosopher Appolonius of Tyana—both were considered *theioi andres* (divine men) by their contemporaries, able to bring about healings and exorcisms by channeling the power of the gods.[10]

Magic

Greco-Roman religion was very concerned with obtaining the power of the gods—whether over fertility, sickness, enemies, commercial ventures, or other human activity. The line between seeking the help of the deity and trying to manipulate divine power to obtain it is sometimes difficult to discern. According to Johnson, "There is some validity to the classic distinction between being acted on by divine powers and seeking to control divine powers (the difference between prayer and a spell). The more closely we examine all the forms of Greco-Roman religion, however, with its constant concern for access to power that benefits humans here and now, the hazier that distinction becomes."[11]

The use of spells to obtain health or good fortune (or to curse enemies) and the widespread use of physical objects such as amulets to ward off evil underscore a basic religiosity that was involved in the everyday of human life. The use of spells and amulets was often the only recourse ordinary people had to cope with life's challenges and sufferings.

Breaking with Paganism and Becoming a Christian

It is only after having sketched in broad strokes the religious climate in which Christianity lived and moved in the Greco-Roman world—one that emphasized the search for divine power to obtain benefits and

---

[10] Johnson, *Among the Gentiles*, 40.
[11] Ibid., 43.

ensure the safety and prosperity of society—that we can understand how popular pagan beliefs and practices may have influenced the lives of the new converts to Christianity. In looking at the history of the early Church, it is obvious that the attitude of Christians toward many pagan practices changed after the Emperor Constantine declared the faith a *religio licita* (legal religion) in 313. As we have seen, during the centuries of periodic persecution, Christianity was regarded by the wider pagan society as both secretive and suspect. The refusal of Christians to participate in what was considered the simplest of public actions (offering sacrifice to the deified emperor or to other gods) was damning proof to the pagan world that they were out to undermine the public order. Because of this refusal both Jews and Christians were branded "atheists" by their pagan neighbors and were the object of distrust and the focus of sensational accusations. They became the object of sporadic violent persecutions since their lack of *pietas* was thought to result in the disfavor of the gods, which in turn exposed the empire to disaster.[12]

Christians, through apologists like Justin Martyr (+165), Irenaeus (+202), Tertullian (+220), and Origen (+253) tried to assure the Roman authorities that their religious beliefs and practices, while different from the mainstream, were not seditious. It is important to note, though, that adherence to Christianity was a decision that would have radically separated the new convert from pagan society. The Church itself made clear that a decisive break with pagan customs and values had to take place before a person could even enter the first stage of the catechumenate. A third-century list of prohibited professions included in the *Apostolic Tradition* traditionally ascribed to Hippolytus[13] clearly spells out which professions were unacceptable. Not surprisingly, brothel keepers, idols makers, pagan priests, gladiators or gladiator trainers, makers of charms, astrologers, dream interpreters, and magicians are all barred from beginning the catechumenate. Even more countercultural was the prohibition against soldiers (since they could be ordered to kill),

---

[12] See Minucius Felix's second- or third-century account of calumny against Christians in *Octavius* 9: CSEL 2, 13–14. English translation: Minucius Felix, "Octavius," in *The Ante-Nicene Fathers*, trans. R. E. Wallis, vol. 4 (Buffalo, NY: The Christian Literature Publishing Co., 1887), 177–78.

[13] On the complex issues of dating and provenance of the *Apostolic Tradition*, see John Baldovin's useful summary in "Hippolytus and the *Apostolic Tradition*: Recent Research and Commentary," *Theological Studies* 64, no. 3 (September 2003): 520–42.

charioteers (whose teams were placed under the protection of various gods), and actors (known for their "loose" lifestyle and portrayal of pagan gods on stage). Teachers of young children are encouraged to give up their profession since a required part of the curriculum was teaching the pagan myths and observing pagan festivals. The most telling prohibited profession, though, is that of rulers.

> The prohibition against admitting rulers into the catechumenate is paralleled in Tertullian by an attack on Christians assuming an office that required involvement in pagan sacrifices, temples, festivities, and such like, or even wearing the dress and insignia of office without performing any of the functions, since such things carried the implication of idolatry.[14]

It is obvious that during the Church's first several centuries, Christians could not appear to be like "everyone else," since their customs directly challenged much of the existing public order.

Even though Christians distinguished themselves from pagans, is there any evidence to suggest that popular practices found in the dominant Greco-Roman culture influenced Christian worship before the Peace of the Church in 313? And if so, did these influences affect how new converts from paganism understood their initiation as a follower of Christ? To use our categories, did the "public meaning" of the process of initiation correspond to the official meaning found in the writing of the authoritative teachers like bishops and other "orthodox" writers?

Popular Religious Elements in Baptism

As we have already learned, the most obvious influence on Christian practice in the first centuries noted by scholars was that of the pagan mystery religions. There is current debate about just who influenced whom, with more recent scholarship contending that some pagan mysteries borrowed practices from the Christians. While Christianity was not a religion that necessarily hid its practices, it came to resemble the mystery religions in withholding detailed information about its rites and beliefs from those who were not instructed. In his response to the criticism of Celsus, a second-century pagan philosopher and polemical adversary of Christianity who accused Christians of being just another

---

[14] Paul F. Bradshaw, Maxwell E. Johnson, and L. Edward Phillips, *The Apostolic Tradition: A Commentary* (Minneapolis, MN: Fortress Press, 2002), 94.

exotic mystery cult, Origen of Alexandria maintained that Christianity's beliefs were for the most part openly shared, but he conceded that there were some aspects of the faith that could not be revealed to outsiders.[15]

In a way, Celsus could have been forgiven for mistaking Christianity for just another mystery religion—at least superficially. Justin Martyr, for example, in his description of baptism in chapter 61 of his *First Apology* (written around the year 150 CE), speaks of prayers for purification (scrutinies) celebrated with the initiands. In addition, he names the effect of baptism that comes with the washing with water *photismos*, or enlightenment. All of these elements were common in the practice of the mystery religions. According to Edward Yarnold, who has closely studied the evolution of the rites of initiation,

> apart from common terminology, there are other striking points of resemblance between the Christian and pagan ceremonies themselves: scrutinies, catechesis, the learning of sacred formulas, fasting, stripping, anointing, immersion, the putting on of a white robe, consignation (even with a permanently visible sign in the form of a tattoo or brand), a meal of initiation (a honeyed drink forms a part of both the Eleusinian rites and the neophytes first communion) all feature in both Christian and pagan rites.[16]

The adoption of the cup of milk and honey to be given to the newly baptized at the eucharistic celebration is a particularly interesting development. Found in several of the manuscript traditions of the *Apostolic Tradition*[17] and also mentioned by Tertullian at the end of the second century, the origins of this custom can be interpreted on various levels. The *Apostolic Tradition* admonishes the bishop to explain that this drink symbolizes "the fulfillment of God's promise to our ancestors that he would lead them to a land flowing with milk and honey." This

---

[15] "Then since he often calls our doctrine *secret*, in this point also I must refute him. For almost the whole world has come to know the preaching of Christians better than the opinions of philosophers. . . . The existence of certain doctrines, which are beyond those which are exoteric and do not reach the multitude, is not a peculiarity of Christian doctrine only, but is shared by the philosophers." Origen, *Contra Celsum*, trans. Henry Chadwick (Cambridge, UK: Cambridge University Press, 1980), 10.

[16] Edward Yarnold, "Baptism and the Pagan Mysteries in the Fourth Century," *The Heythrop Journal* 13, no. 3 (1972): 248.

[17] Bradshaw, Johnson, Phillips, *The Apostolic Tradition*, 28.

biblical reference fits the ritual context. After crossing the waters of the Jordan (baptism) God leads the neophyte into the promised land (the Christian community). There is reason to believe, however, that while a biblical explanation is plausible, it is highly possible that the custom itself may have originated in a practice that would have been well known in Rome: that of the *susceptio* or the *munus susceptionis.*[18] A parallel remark on this practice from Tertullian in the late second century may give a clue. Following baptism and after being welcomed or received (*suscepti*) by the bishop, Tertullian states that "we taste the cup of milk and honey that signifies concord."[19] A Roman family rite was practiced at the birth of a child. A cup of milk and honey was given to a newborn after the head of the household, the *Paterfamilias*, stooped to pick up the infant that had been placed at his feet. This gesture showed the father's legal acknowledgement of the child and his right to be nurtured by the family from that moment on. It was also believed to protect the young child from evil spirits. The use of this symbol for Christian *neophytes* (literally, newborns) would have had a great deal of cultural resonance.

It is also possible, however, that this practice of milk and honey came from the Eleusinian mystery religion that also used milk and honey in their mysteries of initiation. It is impossible to say with certainty whence the influence came, other than the general cultural context of the third century.

The Development of Holy Week and Popular Religion

One of the most instructive places to view the dramatic evolution of Christian liturgical practice—specifically, fourth-century developments in the Holy Week liturgy—is Jerusalem. A center of pilgrimage for the Christian world because of its association with Jesus' last days on earth, Jerusalem has been amply documented as a center of liturgical practice through two sources. First, there are the writings of Cyril of Jerusalem. Cyril became bishop of Jerusalem in the year 349 and left a series of catechetical lectures to the newly baptized that

---

[18] Anscar Chupungco, "Cultural Setting of Baptismal Liturgy," in *Worship: Progress and Tradition* (Washington, DC: The Pastoral Press, 1994),12.

[19] "Inde suscepti, lactis et mellis concordiam praegustamus." Q. Septimi Florentis Tertulliani, *De Corona*, ed. Jacques Fontaine (Paris: Presses Universitaires de France, 1966), 3.

describe the rites of Holy Week.[20] Second, there is the travel journal of a woman pilgrim (possibly a nun) from Spain by the name of Egeria. Egeria traveled to Jerusalem in the years 381–384 and recounted her impressions of worship in the churches of the Holy City during Holy Week. Her work gives us detailed information about the liturgy as it was celebrated at the end of the fourth century.[21]

In order to appreciate what we learn from these sources regarding the liturgies of Holy Week, it is important to keep in mind that this information marks a sea change in Christian attitudes toward the liturgical year. During previous centuries, Christians seem not to have had a need to celebrate an annual commemoration of the death and resurrection of Christ since every Sunday was a celebration of the resurrection.[22] After the initial yearly commemoration that centered on Christ's death rather than his resurrection was separated from its direct link with the Jewish calculation of Passover,[23] and the focus of the Sunday celebration shifted to the Lord's resurrection (leaving the prior Thursday, Friday, and Saturday free to focus on the events leading up to Easter), the evolution of a full presentation of the particular events became possible. This "historicization" of the events of Holy Week was also abetted by the construction of churches over the very sites where these events took place: the Mount of Olives (the *Eleona*), Golgotha (the *Martyrion*), and Christ's tomb and place of resurrection (the *Anastasis*).

Given the prestige that Jerusalem enjoyed in the Christian world, the various celebrations that developed there were influential in the local development of the liturgical year elsewhere. This is how the Palm Sunday procession with branches was imported to the Western Church, as well as the particular focus of the rites that would become the most important part of the week: the three days or the Triduum.

---

[20] See *The Works of Saint Cyril of Jerusalem*, trans. Leo P. McCauley and Anthony A. Stephenson (Washington, DC: Catholic University of America Press, 1969).

[21] John Wilkinson, *Egeria's Travels* (Warminster, UK: Aris and Phillips, 1999).

[22] See this discussion in Paul F. Bradshaw and Maxwell E. Johnson, *The Origins of Feasts and Seasons in Early Christianity* (London: SPCK, 2011), 39–67.

[23] The *Quartodecimans* or "fourteeners" insisted that a yearly commemoration of the passion take place on the same date as the Jewish celebration of Passover, i.e., the fourteenth day of Nisan. With the ascendency of those who favored a Sunday celebration after the first full moon after the vernal equinox, Easter or the Pasch became focused on the Resurrection.

This initial development of Holy Week, though, was also influenced by what could be called a "spontaneous" popular piety.

Liturgist Kenneth Stevenson, in his book *Jerusalem Revisited: The Liturgical Meaning of Holy Week*,[24] offers a helpful analysis of the Holy Week liturgy that explains how the rites that originated in Jerusalem in the fourth century can be read on various levels. Using the term "pieties," by which he means "religious attitudes," he identifies different levels or kinds of rites informed by three distinct pieties: "unitive," "rememorative," and "representational."

The "unitive" piety is both the oldest and the one that would reflect the attitude of the most experienced and educated. It could also be termed the most "liturgical" in that it seeks to hold together the entire paschal mystery of Jesus Christ in each celebration. When we celebrate any one aspect of the life of Christ, we do not do so as if we are ignorant of the saving details of his entire life. So, for example, although we focus on Christ's death on Good Friday, we do so fully aware of the resurrection that will follow. The same is true for the Eucharist celebrated on Holy Thursday evening. This harkens back to a time when there was a single celebration for Triduum, at which the entire paschal mystery was the focus of the worship. The current entrance antiphon in the Roman Rite for Holy Thursday does not speak of the institution of the Eucharist. Rather, it is drawn from St. Paul's Letter to the Galatians 6:14. "We should glory in the cross of our Lord Jesus Christ, for he is our salvation, our life and our resurrection; through him we are saved and made free." When we celebrate the liturgy as Christians, even to recall a key event of our salvation like the Last Supper, the liturgy constantly tries to keep all the saving events before our eyes since they are intrinsically related: Christ's suffering, death, and resurrection.

The second "piety" that influenced the rites of Holy Week Stevenson calls the "rememorative." Because it is often difficult to remember and keep in tension all the aspects of Christ's life, the "rememorative" separates the principal events of our salvation in order to help us meditate on them one at a time. This is the piety that encouraged the splitting-up of the original annual Christian celebration of Christ's suffering, death, and resurrection into three distinct days that recall chronologically the major steps of the passion and resurrection. It is for this reason, on

[24] Kenneth Stevenson, *Jerusalem Revisited: The Liturgical Meaning of Holy Week* (Washington, DC: The Pastoral Press, 1988).

Palm Sunday, we remember Christ's triumphant entry into Jerusalem by carrying palm or olive branches in procession. On Holy Thursday we focus on the institution of the Eucharist at the Last Supper. The immediate events that led to the crucifixion are recalled on Good Friday. At the Easter Vigil on Holy Saturday, the celebration reaches its climax with the proclamation of the resurrection.

The third piety—the representational—is different from the "rememorative" in a very important way. It is dramatic. It goes beyond a remembering to a reenactment. Although Palm Sunday has been described as being formed by a "rememorative" piety, once there are people costumed as Jesus and the disciples and a donkey for Jesus to ride, we have entered into popular, representational, or "dramatic" piety. What happened during the first Holy Week is not simply recalled through word and gesture—it is reenacted. The same would be true of the washing of the feet—the *mandatum*—that takes place on Holy Thursday. It is not a simple remembrance. We do not hear about feet being washed—we wash feet. This aspect of the dramatic will constantly reoccur as the Holy Week liturgy evolves. Stephenson cites the example of the Medieval *quem queritis* ("whom do you seek") drama based on John 20:15 and often staged in the middle of the Paschal Vigil. Various ministers would suddenly act out the parts of the women at the tomb and one would take on the part of Christ. This drama was done primarily to strengthen the faith of unlearned common people or those just baptized.[25] We will see that in the late Middle Ages there was a flowering of the "representational" piety that influenced the liturgy for centuries and brought to the New World by the Spanish and Portuguese during the first wave of evangelization in the sixteenth century.

These pieties, which had their beginnings in the context of Jerusalem of the late fourth century, reflect a new need. Unlike the majority of Christians during the age of persecution who sought for and largely received a more intense formation, the late fourth-century pilgrims that attended Holy Week celebrations in Jerusalem were not only divided by language but also divided by differing levels of understanding of the faith and familiarity with the liturgy. The liturgy, as it developed, instinctively sought to reach out and communicate to these different levels at the same time. Stevenson sums up:

---

[25] Ibid., 10.

In Holy Week the three pieties coexist. Unitive piety is austere, primitive, and, if you are liturgically patient, it likes the kind of liturgical celebration which is theologically the least demanding in *detail*. Rememorative is [*sic*], as we have seen, midway, still employs subtle symbolism and requires elaboration, preparation, and (most important of all) a vibrant community in order to provide continuity and concentration. Representational, on the other hand, is the culmination of the pictorial mind, the result of popular piety. [26]

An interesting parallel to these different levels is found in the plays of Shakespeare. His writings are filled not only with profound philosophical discourse and erudite allusion to classical myths, but he often fills the mouths of his more "common folk" characters with ribald humor in order to "play to the groundlings" (entertain the uneducated poor who had to stand on the ground of the theater rather than sit in the expensive seats). One of the reasons for the continued popularity of Shakespeare's writing is that he was able to alternate between various levels in order to communicate with the audience: sophisticated and learned for the educated, popular and earthy for the common people. In a way the late fourth-century liturgy, at least for Holy Week, seems to have operated in the same way.

Conclusion

The *Directory of Popular Piety and Liturgy* speaks of the first few centuries as a time of "spontaneous convergence" between the cultural and religious symbols of the Greco-Roman world and the Christian liturgy. It notes, though, that beginning in the fourth century, due to the Church's stronger position vis-à-vis the surrounding culture, a conscious reflection starts to take place regarding the relationship between liturgy and popular piety. It goes on to say that:

The local Churches, guided by clear pastoral and evangelizing principles, did not hesitate to absorb into the Liturgy certain purified solemn and festive cultic elements deriving from the pagan world. These were regarded as capable of moving the minds and imaginations of the people who felt drawn towards them. Such forms, now placed at the service of the mystery of worship, were seen as neither contrary to the Gospel nor to the purity of true

---

[26] Ibid., 11.

Christian worship. Rather, there was a realization that only in the worship of Christ, true God and true Saviour, could many cultic expressions, previously attributed to false gods and false saviours, become true cultic expressions, even though these had derived from man's deepest religious sense. (DPPL 24)

While things might not have been this clear "on the ground," it is undeniable that the Church was more open to pre-Christian cultic elements and forms once it came into the ascendency, at least politically. But even during the centuries of persecution, Christians meeting in house churches in relatively small numbers (fifty to one hundred people) understandably brought with them the assumptions of their surrounding religious worldview, reinterpreted in light of their commitment to Christ. For example, the presence of visionaries and prophets in the worship of these small Christian gatherings is well attested, and these roles clearly have parallels in pagan religion.[27] Belief in the power of "demons" now identified with the pagan gods seems to have been widespread. Allusions to their activity and the way in which the power of Christ is capable of overcoming their power are also well attested—both in the writings of the New Testament and in early patristic literature. Since Christianity in the first centuries was experienced in house churches, it is entirely understandable that pagan domestic traditions would influence Christian organization and worship. A house church conceived as the "family of God" would naturally take on some of the elements of an extended Greco-Roman household.

The marked change in the Church's position vis-à-vis the larger culture in the fourth century gave birth to more formal liturgical practices. Christians now celebrated in large, lavishly appointed basilicas with hundreds if not thousands of people in attendance. The development of more public and dramatic elements in Christian worship was both logical and inevitable. Processions, use of lights, incense (at least in the East), special liturgical dress, and insignia of office—all elements that earlier Christian writers had criticized in paganism as "empty show"—now become a normal part of formal Christian worship in the larger cities of the empire. It is at this time that the dramatic is introduced into the liturgy due to its capacity to attract and catechize

---

[27] See Robin Lane Fox's description of these parallels in *Pagans and Christians* (New York: Knopf, 1987), 375–418.

an ever-growing number of new Christians whose formation was less intense than during the period of persecution.[28]

We will now turn to a specific example of the absorption and re-interpretation of pagan cultic elements into the liturgy by looking at the formation of the "classic" Roman Rite. We will also explain how this evolution was the harbinger of the centuries-old division between liturgy and popular religion with which we live today.

[28] Theodor Klauser, *A Short History of the Western Liturgy: An Account and Some Reflections*, trans. John Halliburton, 2nd ed. (Oxford, UK: Oxford University Press, 1979), 31–37.

Chapter Four

The Birth of the Classic Roman Rite and Popular Religion

We will now turn our attention to one of the most notable examples of liturgical inculturation in the history of Christian worship: the formation of the "classic" Roman Rite. The birth of a particularly Roman way of Christian worship evolved over a period of around three hundred years (from the fourth to the sixth centuries). The decisions made regarding *how* to inculturate Christian worship in Rome during this time will have long-ranging repercussions, not only on the Church in Western Europe, but on many places around the globe evangelized centuries later by Europeans who will take this tradition of worship along with the Gospel. The beginning of the Roman Rite will also mark the start of a break between the official liturgy and popular religious practices.

At the outset it is useful to note that the emergence of the Roman Rite parallels the development of other liturgical rites that gradually coalesced around the four traditional patriarchates of the East. Alexandria in Egypt, Antioch in Syria, Constantinople (Byzantium) in modern-day Turkey, and Jerusalem witnessed development of distinct ways of celebrating the mystery of Christ in their worship that were strongly influenced by their particular languages and cultures. From the liturgical traditions of Rome, Seleucia-Ctesiphon (in the old Persian Empire), and Armenia come the origins of the six rites and twenty-one autonomous churches that make up today's Catholic Church.[1] The way the liturgy developed in Rome was no exception to the others.

---

[1] The twenty autonomous (*sui juris*) Catholic Churches following liturgical traditions other than the Latin are: The Alexandrian Rite: Coptic and Ethiopian; the

We will begin this chapter by looking at the initial, formative period of the liturgy in Rome just before and during the pontificate of Pope Damasus (+384). It was during the reign of Damasus that the language of the liturgy changed from Greek to Latin and a distinctive style of worship developed that was influenced by the values of traditional Roman culture.[2] In many ways, this shift of language serves as a convenient way of identifying the cultural characteristics that were adopted into the Roman way of worship. All of this took place at a moment of profound transformation in the relationship between the Church and its surrounding social, political, and cultural context.

The Church's Changed Position vis-à-vis the Empire

With Constantine's embrace of Christianity and the promulgation of the edict of toleration of 313, the Christian Church not only became a legal entity alongside its pagan rivals but attained a quasi-official status in Roman society. Even before Christianity was made the official religion of the empire under Emperor Theodosius in 391 (it was still a minority religion in the time of Constantine), it became advantageous for pagans to convert to the religion of the emperor. Especially for the lower and middle classes, conversion to Christianity brought about undeniable political and social advantages.

The Church, however, paid a price for its newfound status in Roman society. Its very self-understanding as a community of believers changed, as did the image of Christ that dominated the hearts and minds of the first generations of believers. Christians during the age of persecution, provided they persevered, were regarded as "saints." In the second and third centuries the Church was constituted by tiny

---

Antiochene (West Syrian) Rite: Syrian, Maronite, Syro-Malankar, and Armenian; the Chaldean (East Syrian) Rite: Chaldean and Syro-Malabar; and the Byzantine Rite: Byelorussian, Bulgarian, Greek, Hungarian, Italo-Albanian, Melkite, Romanian, Ruthenian, Slovak, Ukranian, Albanian, and Russian. *Annuario Pontificio* (Città del Vaticano: Libreria Editrice Vaticana, 1999), 1158.

[2] For a more detailed examination of this important stage in the development of the liturgy, see Theodor Klauser, *A Short History of the Western Liturgy: An Account and Some Reflections*, trans. John Halliburton, 2nd ed. (Oxford, UK: Oxford University Press, 1979); Marcel Metzger, *History of the Liturgy: The Major Stages*, trans. Madeleine Beaumont (Collegeville, MN: Liturgical Press, 1997); Enrico Cattaneo, *Il culto cristiano in Occidente: Note storiche*, B.E.L. Subsidia 13 (Rome: Edizione Liturgiche, 2003).

groups of committed individuals who had received an intense preparation for baptism and the Christian life. These first Christians always
recognized that their commitment could end in persecution and even
death. They counted on their faithfulness to Christ in this life to bring
them salvation in the next. The images of Christ that dominated the
walls of the catacombs were those of good shepherd, healer, teacher,
and philosopher. By the late fourth century, however, because of the
greater number of converts who sought baptism (at times out of mixed
motives), the intense formation in the Christian life that was the rule
during the age of persecution became much less rigorous. As Peter
Brown has pointed out "it was far less certain that the masses who had
passed through a perfunctory baptism in this world would be saved in
the next. Men's anxieties, therefore, shifted to a more distant event: to
the drastic settling of accounts at the Last Judgment. The earlier imagery of the afterlife, which showed a quiet group of initiates enjoying
their sheltered idyll in another world—resting in the cool glow of the
stars or in the shade of an arbour—gave place to the awesome thought
of Christ as Emperor and Judge."[3]

This change in mentality was occasioned by the Church's gradual
assumption of the role of moral arbiter of the social order and guardian of the empire. Like the old paganism whose public sacrifices and
feast days marked and ordered the life of the cities of the Roman
world, Christianity, through its organization of bishops and local
urban communities, little by little supplanted the old religious and
civil order. At the same time, though, the Church also adopted some
of the characteristics of Roman civic and religious culture. We saw
in the last chapter that Greco-Roman religion was pervasive, public,
political, pious, and pragmatic. The same can be said for Christianity as it gradually assumed the privileged position of state religion.
Christian worship under the Christian emperors gradually became
the *cultus publicus* directed by a new class of officials who assumed
many of the prerogatives of the both the former pagan *pontifices* and
the civil magistrates of the empire.

---

[3] Peter Brown, *The World of Late Antiquity: AD 150–750* (London: Harcourt
Brace Jovanovich, 1971), 107. To see an illustration of this shift, one need only
compare the frescoes of the catacombs to the apsidal mosaics in churches built in
the fourth and fifth centuries: from images of Christ as the good shepherd or philosopher in the catacombs to the depiction of Christ as a beardless young emperor
astride the globe of the world in the apse of the church of St. Vitale in Ravenna.

Recent scholarship has helped us gain a better perspective on the position of this quickly evolving Church and its fourth-century leaders. While the Church had gained the patronage of the emperor—except for the short reign of Julian the Apostate (361–363)—Christianity, especially in the western part of the empire, was not the religion of the majority or of the traditional "old families" of Rome whose identity and prestige were linked to the worship of the old gods. These "old families" were consequently highly distrustful of this upstart religion from the backwater of Judea. Constantine, however, had radically changed the religious landscape by putting himself and the empire under the protection of the Christian God. The liturgy of the Church now became a means of gaining and keeping God's favor. Christian worship soon began to replace the sacrifices of the pagan civil religion. Brown states that "in return for this protection, Constantine rewards the Christian clergy with appropriate privileges. For it was they (and not the average Christian) who were the ritual experts. They knew best how to conduct the worship of the Most High God."[4]

In order to understand the development of the Roman Rite in the fourth century, then, it is important to keep in mind the rather unsure social and political position in which the bishops had been placed by Emperor Constantine. As Peter Brown has remarked, "The first Christian emperor thrust the bishops and clergy of the Christian church forward as a privileged body. But at the same time, he denied them any purchase on the upper reaches of west Roman society."[5] The Christian clergy were rarely drawn from the aristocratic class. Because of this, the traditional Roman families looked down on them as social inferiors and *arrivistes*. Nevertheless, they were charged by the emperor with the task that had been traditionally exercised by the aristocratic classes who made up the priesthoods and colleges of augurs of the old religion: that of offering official prayer for the protection of the emperor and the safety of Rome. It was this group who were the architects of what was to become the Roman Rite.

It is important to keep in mind that while privileged, bishops did not enjoy the unquestioned obedience of their flock that they were to enjoy in later centuries. Other persons of reference for the Christian

---

[4] Peter Brown, *Through the Eye of a Needle: Wealth, the Fall of Rome, and the Making of Christianity in the West, 350–550 AD* (Princeton, NJ: Princeton University Press, 2012), 32.

[5] Ibid., 31.

community had both influence and real power. As Kim Bowes points out, we need to avoid an anachronistic assumption that the bishops functioned according to the well-defined role they would have in subsequent centuries.

> The average late antique bishop was a rather anemic creature with an uncertain job description and more authority than actual power. . . . Other figures, particularly holy men and women and powerful laypersons, often rivaled or trumped bishops' still-nascent authority. And while in some instances, holy man, aristocrat, and bishop merged into a single person, in the first century of public Christendom those well-publicized cases were probably more exceptional than typical.[6]

The Roman Rite, then, was born in a social and political context that was in the process of transformation and where the leaders of the Church were searching for legitimacy vis-à-vis the Roman aristocracy. Around this same time, the Roman Church was increasingly called upon to promote both stability and tradition in a Rome that had been "demoted" by the naming of other cities as political and administrative centers of the empire in the West (Milan, Trier, Ravenna) and the designation of Constantinople as the "New Rome" and Eastern capital in 330. The people of Rome, both pagan and Christian, felt their identity being threatened and were very aware of the need for stability and tradition during this contentious period.

The Liturgical Shift from Greek to Latin

The religious context of Rome, then, was quickly evolving. But it would be a mistake to assume that this evolution happened easily or all at once. The seventy-eight years that fell between the edict of Milan legalizing Christianity (313) and the law establishing the new religion as the official and exclusive religion of the Roman Empire (391) saw the establishment of the criteria that guided the inculturation of the liturgy in the city of Rome. These criteria, influenced by Christianity's newfound status as a "public" religion, were especially reflected in the change of the liturgical language of the Church of Rome from Greek to Latin.

---

[6] Kim Bowes, *Private Worship, Public Values, and Religious Change in Late Antiquity* (Cambridge, UK: Cambridge University Press, 2008), 4.

It should come as no surprise that Greek was the liturgical language of the first Roman Christians. Up until the fourth century, the language most used by Christians in Rome was Greek because the majority of the members of the early Roman Church were immigrants or children of immigrants from the eastern part of the empire who had taken up residence in the city. Interestingly, the first Latin Christian writers active during the second and third centuries hailed not from Rome but North Africa. Since the bulk of theological writings were done in Greek in these early centuries (both in the eastern and western parts of the empire) much of the work of these first Christian Latin writers was in translating and explaining a faith that had been originally expressed in Greek.[7]

The shift to Latin in the Roman liturgy took place during the long pontificate of Damasus (366–384). This change was occasioned by several factors. Surprisingly, one of the least important reasons seems to have been concern to make the words of worship more accessible to the Christian community of Rome who had by then become mostly Latin speaking. It was more important to bishops like Damasus that Christianity be "upgraded" from a religion that was regarded by the Roman cultural elite as foreign, unsophisticated, and lacking in a respectable literary style. There was also a desire on the part of Church leaders to take advantage of this linguistic change to use a Latin liturgical language as close as possible to the kind of language used in the old pagan cultus so that Christianity could replace paganism and assume its status as the true *cultus publicus* of Rome and of the empire.[8]

---

[7] It is to North African writers such as Tertullian (+225) that we owe the first Latin writings in theology. It was Tertullian, for example, who coined the word "sacrament" to translate the Greek "mysterion."

[8] See Joseph Jungmann, *The Mass of the Roman Rite: Its Origins and Development (Missarum Sollemnia)*, trans. Francis A. Brunner, vol. 1 (New York: Benziger Brothers, 1951–55), 50–58; Christine Mohrmann, "Les origines de la latinité chrétienne à Rome," *Vigiliae Christianae* 3, no. 3 (July 1949): 70; Christine Mohrmann, "Quelques observations sur l'évolution stylistique du canon de la messe romaine," *Vigiliae Christianae* 4, no. 4 (October 1950): 1–19; Christine Mohrmann, *Liturgical Latin: Its Origins and Character* (Washington, DC: Catholic University of America Press, 1957); Charles Pietri, "Liturgy, Culture and Society: The Example of Rome at the End of the Ancient World (Fourth-Fifth Centuries)," *Concilium: Liturgy, A Creative Tradition* 162 (Edinburgh: T&T Clark, 1983): 38–46; Maura K. Laferty, "Translating Faith from Greek to Latin: Romanitas and Christianitas in Late Fourth-Century Rome and Milan," *Journal of Early Christian Studies* 11, no. 1 (Spring 2003): 21–62.

The choice of this *style* of Latin liturgical prayer will have long-lasting consequences for the history of the liturgy in the West and in the development of popular religious practices. What were some of its characteristics? First, it was very different from both the Latin of the Bible and the spoken language of the people. For several centuries Latin translations of the Bible had been available and were read in church. But they were an embarrassment to educated Roman Christians.[9] The Latin of these Scripture translations was full of loan words from Hebrew, Aramaic, and Greek. It employed grammatical constructions and turns of phrase that were merely literal renderings of the Greek text. For this reason much of the Scriptures appeared to be the product of poorly educated people who had no feeling for good Latin prose or poetry.[10]

In contrast with the poorly crafted Scripture translations, the style of Latin adopted by the bishops for the liturgy—especially the Roman Canon—was hieratic and technical. It was modeled after the archaic and legalistic Latin prescribed by the old *ius divinum* in which the pagan sacrificial prayers had been composed. Even for educated Romans, these texts were difficult to understand. But understanding or accessibility was not the point. The use of this traditional language—however archaic—was meant to promote "mystery," a sense of religious awe. With a concern for the rhythm of the words, a very typical characteristic of the sacral language of Rome was to pile up synonymous adjectives of a sacral or juridical nature. Scholars have noted that this betrays a certain scrupulosity with regard to higher powers that is reflected in the composition of the old Roman prayers.[11]

An example from the Roman Canon (Eucharistic Prayer I in today's missal) may help illustrate this dependence of the new Christian liturgical Latin on its pagan antecedents. In one of his mystagogical catecheses given at the end of the fourth century, St. Ambrose cites a fragment of the earliest version of the Roman Canon that prays for the acceptance of the offerings. Its style is remarkably like the old pagan Roman prayers. For example, the prayer for the acceptance of the bread and wine is: "*Fac nobis hanc oblationem scriptam, rationabilem,*

---

[9] See Mohrmann, *Liturgical Latin*, 39. This noted authority makes the distinction between colloquial language (*sondersrpach*)—how the words of Scripture were translated from koine Greek—and the formal, cultivated language prized by the upper classes (*kunstsprach*).

[10] See Cattaneo, *Il culto cristiano*, 87–91.

[11] Mohrmann, *Liturgical Latin*, 68.

acceptabilem . . ."[12] (literally: "Make this oblation legally recognized, spiritual, acceptable"). This kind of listing of synonymous adjectives is a common characteristic of pagan Roman prayer. This petition will become even more pronounced in the sixth-century text of the Roman Canon that serves as the basis for our present text in English: *Quam oblationem tu, Deus, in omnibus, quaesumus benedictam, adscriptam, ratam, rationabilem, acceptabilemque facere digneris* (the recent English Missal translation: **"Be pleased, O God, we pray, to bless, acknowledge, and approve this offering in every respect; make it spiritual and acceptable"**). It is not difficult to see why an expert in liturgical Latin, Christine Mohrmann, compares this phrase to pagan Roman prayer and describes its style as one of "monumental verbosity" and "juridical precision." It also illustrates the great challenge of putting these texts into anything resembling good English style.[13]

The choice of this mode of prayer by the Church of the fourth century underscores its need to offer a culturally resonant, sophisticated style of prayer in keeping with Roman pagan tradition. Again, the primary goal is not one of intelligibility but of establishing a relationship of religious awe with elegance of expression. It is, after all, liturgical prayer that, as Mohrmann points out, needs to be different from everyday speech. As she puts it, "In all religious or hieratic languages, communication more or less always takes a back seat to expression."[14] The important issue, though, is the way that this style of prayer differs from colloquial speech. Greek Christian prayer, the language of the Divine Liturgy of John Chrysostom, for example, and the style of language of the Syrian churches, are both much more dependent on direct quotations from the Bible (centonization) and are much more open to poetry and imagery. Roman prayer, however, rarely quotes the Scriptures directly. Even when the Bible was the source or inspiration for a liturgical text in the Canon of the Mass, it was restyled by the redactors of the Latin text to reflect this hieratic balanced mode of expression.[15] Klauser, noted liturgical historian, mentioned that although

---

[12] Ambrose of Milan, *Des Sacrements Des Mystères: Explication du Symbole*, trans. Bernard Botté (Paris: Sources Chrétiennes, 2007), 114.

[13] Mohrmann, *Liturgical Latin*, 68.

[14] ". . . dans toutes les langues religieuses ou hiératique, la communication est refoulée, d'une manière plus ou moins complète, au profit de l'expression." Bernard Botte and Christine Mohrmann, *Ordinaire de la Messe: Texte critique, traduction et etudes* (Paris: Les Éditions du Cerf, 1953), 33.

[15] Ibid., 38.

patristic writing is full of quotations from the Bible and allusions to Sacred Scripture, this is not the case with Roman liturgical prayer. "I hope I shall not be misunderstood if I say that, fundamentally, the Roman liturgy is far removed from the Bible."[16]

Because of this tradition of juridical scrupulosity, another characteristic of the Roman prayer tradition (euchology) is its tendency to be terse and abstract. Consequently, classic Roman prayer is not open to human feeling in the same way as are Byzantine or Coptic styles of prayer. As Klauser remarks: "The consequence of constructing prayers according to the laws of Roman rhetoric and using the ancient sacred language of Rome has been that not only is the way in which these prayers are written far above our everyday language (to a certain extent this is necessary in every liturgy), but indeed is so far above it that it is certain that the average Roman Christian of the fourth, fifth, and sixth centuries was not always able to follow the prayer."[17] Robert Taft, with his usual directness, underscores the point that we cannot use our modern criteria for judging the lack of intelligibility of the prayers and sung texts of the liturgy of late antiquity.

> Did the people understand what they heard? Here we must dispense with another cliché. We in the English-speaking world have the good fortune to live in a culture where universal education is a long-standing acquisition and linguistic unity centuries old, where the language everyone speaks is basically the same, and where the gap between the spoken and the written language is narrow to minimal. Do not think things were that way in Late Antiquity, when even if the people did hear the homily and liturgical prayers, that does not mean they understood them. Before the modern era most of the Christian faithful were illiterate and unschooled, spoke and understood a dialectical form of their native language, and had a very limited vocabulary. The language used in the liturgy, even if a literary form of their mother tongue, was of a quite different level from the vernacular they spoke, and employed a vocabulary at least partly beyond their grasp.[18]

The gulf between the language of liturgy and the capacity of average people to understand the words goes a long way to explain why

---

[16] Klauser, *A Short History of the Western Liturgy*, 42.

[17] Ibid., 41.

[18] Robert F. Taft, *Through Their Own Eyes: Liturgy as the Byzantines Saw It* (Berkeley, CA: InterOrthodox Press, 2006), 84–85.

many Christians sought "supplementary" and "extra-liturgical" ways to express their faith, developing what came to be known as popular religious practices. But words are not the only "language" used by the liturgy to communicate and engage. Movement, gesture, song, environment, and vesture are also important ways in which people are invited to enter into the liturgical event. Like the words themselves, these non-verbal languages were influenced by late Roman culture and came to constitute what scholars have called "the Genius of the Roman Rite."

"The Roman Genius"

Edmund Bishop, the great English historian of the liturgy, described in what is now a classic presentation on the Roman Rite a key characteristic of what he termed the "Roman Genius"—the typical way the liturgy of the city of Rome evolved in the fourth to sixth centuries. By genius, Bishop means "a characteristic and distinguishing spirit that manifests itself in all that a people says and does, in its history and its literature; determining the character of both, and affecting the general character even of its thought."[19] Basically Bishop is talking about what we would call "cultural patterns" that distinguish Roman culture of the late empire from other cultures. We have already discussed some of the characteristics of Roman cultic language that influenced the public prayer of the Church. It is important, though, to keep in mind that other Roman cultural values helped formed what we know today as the Roman Rite. According to Bishop,

> [T]he genius of the native Roman Rite is marked by simplicity, practicality, a great sobriety and self-control, gravity and dignity. . . . We must not separate in idea the Roman pre-Christian days and the Roman under the Christian dispensation; at bottom in his instincts, in his powers, in his limitations, he is the same.[20]

Despite the tendency to "monumental verbosity" inspired by a preoccupation with fulfilling the "legal requirements" traditionally demanded for official prayer, and the influence of the ceremonial of the imperial court, the classic Roman Rite tends toward the simple and the practical. Romans were not theoreticians. The Romans of the

[19] Edmund Bishop, "The Genius of the Roman Rite," *Liturgica Historica: Papers on the Liturgy and Religious Life of the Western Church* (Oxford, UK: The Clarendon Press, 1918), 2.

[20] Ibid., 12.

earlier ages were sober, no-nonsense people who were not given to much speculation and emotion about the gods. In contrast to Greek, the Latin language "always retained something of the concrete rigidity that had always characterized it as the language of a rural population."[21] The main concern in regard to worship was that it be performed in the "correct" manner so that it would be pleasing to the gods.

These characteristics are observable in both the ancient Roman ritual of the Church as well as in the prayer texts themselves. In contrast with the Canon, which because it was a sacrificial formula was the most influenced by Roman cultic legal language, the other presidential prayers of the Mass were simpler. For centuries, the president of the assembly offered those prayers that later became known as the collect, the prayer over the gifts (offerings), and the prayer after Communion spontaneously but following a set structure. They began with an invocation, usually a very austere "Deus" (God), followed by a relative clause, a statement about what God has done, a petition, and then a doxology. Attention was paid to rhythm, to rhetorical forms of late antiquity such as antithesis, and to the use of what Mohrmann has called "traditional prayer terms" such as *quaesumus* (we pray, we beseech) and *dignari* (to deign). A fine example is a collect ascribed to Pope Leo the Great (+461) for Christmas morning in the current Roman Missal:

> *Deus qui humanae substantiae dignitatem*
> *et mirabiliter condidisti*
> *et mirabilius reformasti,*
> *da quaesumus nobis*
> *eius divinitatis esse consortes*
> *qui humanitatis nostrae fieri dignatus est particeps.*

> O God, who wonderfully created the dignity of human nature
> and still more wonderfully restored it,
> grant, we pray,
> that we may share in the divinity of Christ
> who humbled himself to share our humanity.

While this prayer represents a profound contemplation of the mystery of the incarnation, it is composed with simplicity and sobriety. Although a certain rhetorical flourish is evident, there is no extraneous emotion discernable in the composition. All of these elements are also characteristics of prayer compositions of the Roman Rite.

---

[21] Mohrmann, *Liturgical Latin*, 44.

But what of the other ways in which liturgy speaks? The Roman Rite of the Eucharist, as celebrated in the fifth century, was quite simple. Though often celebrated in large basilicas, the practice of Rome was to emphasize the essential. As Bishop himself points out, what we take for normal parts of Sunday eucharistic worship today, the *Kyrie* (Lord have mercy), the *Gloria* (Glory to God), the Creed, and the Lamb of God were all imported elements and not part of the original Roman Rite.[22] Nothing could be simpler. No incense was called for unless a bishop or the pope was present. No instruments were heard in church because of their association with pagan worship. The singing of Latin hymns based on nonbiblical texts, though very popular outside of the city of Rome—in Milan and parts of Gaul, for example—was met with resistance by the Roman authorities for centuries. The natural conservatism of Rome would exclude hymns from the Mass and limit singing to biblical chants that eventually became Gregorian chant or plainchant. A procession in and out of the church, movement for the reception of Communion, facing east at certain times in the celebration were the basic movements associated with the liturgy.

One factor that did complicate the liturgy of the Roman Rite was the presence of the pope or another bishop. Because Constantine had bestowed upon the upper clergy the prerogatives of civil magistrates, in formal liturgical settings they were attired as if at the imperial court. Like other notables of the empire, they received insignias such as the pallium/lorum (a distinctive stole), the mappula (a ceremonial napkin), the *compagi* (special shoes), the *camalaucum* (a distinctive head covering), as well as a golden ring. As imperial level dignitaries, they were to be accompanied by lights and incense and greeted with a kiss on the hand. The person of the pope was accorded even higher honors, since he was considered to have a dignity similar to that of the emperor himself. He was to be served by attendants with covered hands and seated on a throne during the liturgy. People who approached him would genuflect and kiss his foot. All of this ceremonial was technically not liturgical. But it came into liturgical usage through the imperial privileges granted the bishops by Constantine and his successors.[23] These practices were

---

[22] See Bishop, "The Genius of the Roman Rite," 7. See also Jungmann, *The Mass of the Roman Rite*.

[23] See Klauser, *A Short History*, 34. See also Anscar Chupungco, "The Early Cultural Settings of Ordination Rites," *Worship: Progress and Tradition* (Washington, DC: The Pastoral Press, 1994). See also the earliest extant detailed description

very influential for the later development of the Roman Rite outside of the city since Rome, as the sole Patriarchate of the West, had immense prestige. Pilgrims from many places in Western Europe would bring back from Rome ceremonial customs they had observed. It was in this way that the imperial court ceremonial, as well as the style of Roman prayer, would be gradually adopted throughout the Latin West.

The development of the distinctive characteristics of the liturgy of the Roman Rite as a direct consequence of the need for the Church and its leaders to establish a place in a sophisticated Roman society that had long disdained Christianity as a religion of rustics and illiterates needs to be understood in order to evaluate the Roman inculturation of Christian worship.

> In late antiquity, bishops were more concerned with incorporating the Roman elite and elite culture into Christianity and with establishing their own position at the top of the hierarchy of the church and as arbiters of spiritual and ecclesiastical matters, to be consulted and deferred to even by emperors, than with widespread accessibility. For Damasus, the adoption of a Latin liturgy allowed him to identify the Roman church more closely with traditional Roman culture, to appropriate the values and prestige of that culture for Christians, and to claim a share in the aristocratic life of the city for the rulers of the Roman church.[24]

The consequences of embracing what was at the time the culturally elite strata of Roman society, linked with the ever-growing number of people at worship, also meant that the common people, who in previous centuries found worship more accessible, would inevitably be displaced by a growing class of "professionals." This clerical class, following a path of career advancement in a Christian version of the old Roman *cursus honorum* and connected to the governance of the Church by the pope and his court, gradually transformed what was a largely domestic ritual, done by relatively small groups of people, to a more complicated service of worship influenced by the ceremonial of the imperial court.[25] It is this move that sowed the seeds of a later

---

we have of a papal eucharistic liturgy in Rome, Alan Griffiths, *Ordo Romanus Primus: Latin Text and Translation with Introduction and Notes*, Alcuin Club 73 (Norwich, UK: Canterbury Press, 2012).

[24] Laferty, "Translating Faith," 62.

[25] On this development see Chupungco, "Early Cultural Setting of Ordination Rites," 43–65.

clericalism that would effectively discourage lay participation in the official worship of the Church and encourage the growth of popular religious customs outside the direct control of the religious authorities.

The simplification and reordering of the Roman liturgy that took place under Pope Gregory the Great (+604) could be seen as an attempt to attenuate this growing division between clergy and lay people. The *Directory on Popular Piety and the Liturgy* identifies the pontificate of Gregory as "an exemplary reference point for any fruitful relationship between Liturgy and popular piety." His ordering of the Rogation Days in April, for example, officially transformed the ancient pagan Roman observance of *robigalia* (a rite to pray for the fertility of the fields and the protection of crops against disease) into three days of fasting and ceremonies that included the litany of the saints and public processions to bless the fields. The *Directory* states:

> Through the organization of processions, stations and rogations, Gregory the Great undertook a major liturgical reform which sought to offer the Roman people structures which resonated with popular sensibilities while, at the same time, remaining securely based on the celebration of the divine mysteries. He gave wise directives to ensure that the conversion of new nations did not happen without regard for their own cultural traditions. Indeed, the Liturgy itself could be enriched by new legitimate cultic expressions and the noble expressions of artistic genius harmonized with more humble popular sensibilities. He established a sense of unity in Christian worship by anchoring it firmly in the celebration of Easter, even if other elements of the one mystery of Salvation (Christmas, Epiphany, and Ascension) were also celebrated and the memorials of the Saints expanded. (DPPL 27)

Unfortunately, a complete record of Gregory's reform of worship of the Roman Church has not come down to us intact. We do know many of the details of his reform, however, from secondary sources and from ancient sacramentaries that bear his name but were compiled at a later date.[26] Undoubtedly this simplification of the liturgy helped to bridge a growing gap between the liturgy and the common Christian. Gregory's renewed emphasis on regular papal eucharistic celebrations at parish churches within the city of Rome (stational liturgies) and oc-

---

[26] For an enumeration of Gregory's simplifications of the Roman liturgy, see Cattaneo, *Il culto cristiano*, 109–13.

casions for public religious processions in and around the city did much to bring the expressions of the faith as well as the ministry of the pope to the people. However, although the *Directory* seems to present the pontificate of Pope Gregory as a "golden age" of the complementary existence of popular piety alongside the official liturgy, there is evidence to suggest that this relationship was not quite so harmonious.

Popular Religion in Late Antiquity

The source of the tension between the "official" liturgy and popular religious practices came from two different social directions: the common people and the elite of Roman society. As we noted earlier, the aristocrats in the city of Rome tended to resist conversion to Christianity as a religion that was foreign and unsophisticated. The inculturation of the Roman Rite in the fourth century, following cultural patterns already present in the Roman religion and reflecting values of the upper class, did much to bridge this gap. Once converted, though, the Roman aristocrat came with a religious mentality inherited from generations of Romans who saw directing and promoting religion as part of their role in society and as an activity that was at least partially a "family affair." This often worked in favor of bishops who were in need of allies to advance the reach of the Church in the broader society. Bishops like Pope Damasus sought the aid of wealthy Romans—especially widows—to help finance a range of Church projects. For this reason his enemies called him an *auriscalpius matronarum* (ear-tickler of noble ladies).[27] The interest of the nobility in religion, however, was not without its headaches for the bishops. Because of their independence and higher social standing, many aristocrats were just as influential in the practical affairs of religion as the hierarchy. Historian Kim Bowes, in *Private Worship, Public Values, and Religious Change in Late Antiquity,* offers an intriguing picture of the influence that nobles exercised on public and domestic rituals as well as their part in the growth of the cult of the martyrs through their construction of mausoleums and churches to accommodate their desire to maintain ancestral rites, now re-interpreted though a Christian lens. As Bowes points out:

[27] J. Fontaine, "Un sobriquet perfide de Damase: Matronarum auriscalpius," in *Hommages à Henri le Bonnec: Res sacrae,* ed. D. Porte and J.-P Néraudau, Collection Latomus 201 (Brussels: Latomus, 1988), 180–81.

> For these new Roman converts, the blurriness between public and
> private religiosity, personal rituals and civic status, and household
> and the broader "public," was one of the facts of life, part of being
> an elite. It was this persistence of a social habit that would turn out
> to be so troubling to bishops, and so difficult to alter. That is, for
> Christian bishops, the challenge of the pagan past was not limited
> to animal sacrifice or a fondness for Plato, but extended into the
> deeper realms of social structure, structure that was embedded
> in the mentalité of the most fervent and wealthy new converts.[28]

The Church in the persons of bishops was also challenged by lower
echelons of Roman society in a way not totally dissimilar from the
challenge posed by the aristocrats. They, too, had come to the faith
with certain cultural presuppositions that needed to be attended to,
regardless of what the leaders of the Church might say. Nowhere is
this better illustrated than in the persistence of Greco-Roman funerary
customs among the new Christians. Despite strong condemnations by
many bishops, people continued age-old practices regarding burials and
commemorations of the dead that differed very little from the customs
of their pagan ancestors.

In order to appreciate popular customs surrounding death during
this period, it is important to keep in mind the very different ideas
about the afterlife held by Christians from the fourth to the seventh
centuries. At this stage in the life of the Church there were no "official"
funeral rites. Much of what was done by the survivors at the death
of a loved-one was guided by traditions inherited from Greco-Roman
practices and modified to correspond to Christian beliefs. Unlike the
very recent North American assumption that the soul of a loved one
immediately goes to heaven after death, Christians at this time were
more circumspect about the immediate fate of the soul once someone
had expired. Liturgical historian Cyrille Vogel, explains that

> the eschatology that prevailed before the beginning of the sev-
> enth century, the "soul" of the deceased, or more accurately, his
> "double," his likeness, dwelt after death in a place of waiting and
> in a shadowy state in which he looked forward to the one final
> judgment that would take place at the end of time. The *refrigerium
> interim* ("interim refreshment"), in the broad sense of a provi-
> sional, intermediate state included two "places": the *refrigerium*
> in the proper sense, which was a place of relative liberation and

---

[28] Bowes, *Private Worship, Public Values*, 222.

rest, and the *tormentum,* where the most unfortunate and sinners found themselves in complete deprivation.[29]

Neither the *tormentum* nor the *refrigerium* were permanent locales for the soul. The ultimate fate of the individual depended on the final judgment at the end of time, when Christ will come to definitively judge all people. Martyrs, however, those who had suffered because of the faith, those whose lives most resembled that of the Savior, were believed to bypass the *refrigerium* and were immediately admitted into the presence of Christ. For this reason martyrs could be counted on to intercede for the living. On the other hand, the living needed to offer comfort and solace to their dear departed through regular remembrance. It was the Greco-Roman custom to celebrate a meal at the gravesite, also called the *refrigerium,* where the name of the deceased would be mentioned and prayers and libations would be offered for the rest of their spirit. This meal usually occurred on the day of internment or on the third day after the burial and on anniversaries of the death. The pagan Roman commemorative days of *Parentalia* in February—culminating in the celebration of *Cara cognatio* on February 22—involved eating and drinking to remember the ancestors. This practice may have had an influence on the choice of a feast dedicated to St. Peter on February 22.

What did these meals look like? *Refrigeria* were also termed *laetitia* (joyful celebrations) among the pagans. Ramsay MacMullen describes them:

> Such loving times in the recall of the dead went on for as long as the celebrants' mood and their wine might last, even as an "all-nighter," a *vigilia.* The dead themselves participated. They needed such remembrances for their tranquil existence in the Beyond. They were to be offered whatever food was at hand and, most especially, a toast in wine to be tipped onto their sarcophagus or into a pipe leading down to the head-end where they rested, athirst and happy. A party mood was essential. Participants, if they were challenged to defend the bad behavior that might attend too much eating and drinking, answered indignantly that loving thoughts, respect, and the recollection of fleshly pleasures offered to ancestors whose

---

[29] Cyrille Vogel, "The Cultic Environment of the Deceased in the Early Christian Period," *Temple of the Holy Spirit: Sickness and Death of the Christian in the Liturgy,* ed. Achille M. Triacca, trans. Matthew J. O'Connell (New York: Pueblo Publishing Co., 1983), 260.

> favor was certainly of more effect than any mere human's—all
> this was not just picknicking. This was religion.[30]

This custom was widely practiced in the Roman world and offers an important cultural backdrop in answering the question: how did the large number of new converts participate in the life of the Church during the fourth century? Given that the liturgy of the grand basilicas in Rome was being inculturated in a way that would correspond to the cultural expectations of the more elite echelons of society, there is evidence to suggest that the vast majority of new Christians engaged in Christian worship that was, in effect, a baptized version of pagan celebrations at the graveside of their beloved departed. These celebrations, though, were transformed into specifically Christian affairs when *refrigeria* were celebrated at the tombs of the martyrs following the old pattern of ancestor veneration already established in the Roman world. These celebrations were the occasion to ask for favors through eating and drinking at the tomb of the martyr who had been transported to the presence of God and thus able to act as an intercessor. It also became the custom to want to bury one's loved ones as close as possible to these tombs, since on the Day of Judgment at the resurrection from the dead the martyr in question would be close on hand to intercede for those who had been buried nearby.

The conflation of Roman burial customs such as the *refrigerium* with the cult of the martyrs is attested to archaeologically in the Roman world. In fact, scholars such as Ramsay MacMullen believe the archaeological evidence suggests that the building of Christian places for worship outside the walls of Rome that took place in the fourth century was not uniquely or even primarily for eucharistic gatherings but to accommodate the *refrigeria* offered at the tombs of saints by common people. Some (but not all) of these meals were preceded by the Eucharist. Drawing on the archaeological work of several scholars, the cemetery areas upon which great basilicas called "martyria" would be built, such as San Sebastiano, San Lorenzo, St. Paul Outside the Walls, and even St. Peter itself, were places where Christians celebrated *refrigeria* in honor of the martyrs and of their own dead. Later, these spaces became roofed-over cemeteries and dining halls where the "mensa" or table used at times to both celebrate the Eucharist and to

---

[30] Ramsay MacMullen, "Christian Ancestor Worship in Rome," *Journal of Biblical Literature* 129, no. 3 (Fall 2010): 603.

eat the *refrigerium* was the top of the tomb itself. In other cases, portable altars were brought in on the feast day to celebrate a Eucharist. But the more common celebration—much to the chagrin of many of the bishops—was the *refrigerium*. MacMullen described this popular activity as evidence for a "second Church"—a popular Church whose principal ways of participating in Christianity evolved independently of episcopal control during the late patristic period.

While the assertion that a "second Church" existed at this point in the history of Christianity has been criticized as an exaggeration, it does seem likely that the Christians in the late antique period did not simply abandon their traditional ideas about the dead and filial piety due their ancestors when they converted.[31] As MacMullen explains, these Christians

> had joined the church from a traditional background, or their parents had done so. They had thus been raised in beliefs that lay beyond the boundaries of any church and were close to the heart. They believed the dead needed a helping hand, as we must suppose from the common leaving of coins in their sarcophagi, or a variety of little gifts, it might be only in fragments; or again for children, toys and diversions stuck in to the plaster that closed a *loculus*. The unseen interim-world has its needs, so everyone believed; it had a reality and life known also in the forms of its guardian spirits, the Manes, who *were* the deceased, and to whom epitaphs were routinely addressed. The formula was, in abbreviation, "to the gods and Manes," *D(is) M(anibus)* on hundreds of Christian tombstones. In so many ways, Christians and non-Christians were thus at one.[32]

As Peter Brown points out, though, it is the cult of the martyrs—popular religion—that eventually brings together both the elite and popular elements of the Christian Church in the late antique period, providing a point of reference that could be used by the local bishops around which to rally disparate members of the urban community. Christians, in counter distinction to pagans, were concerned about bringing together not just the elites and the lower classes (the plebeians)

---

[31] See the exchange between Robert Louis Wilken and Ramsay MacMullen on MacMullen's book in *Conversation in Religion and Theology* 8, no. 2 (November 2010): 120–25.

[32] Ramsay MacMullen, *The Second Church: Popular Christianity A.D. 200–400* (Atlanta, GA: Society of Biblical Literature, 2009), 76.

but also "two unaccustomed and potentially disruptive categories, the women and the poor."[33] The promotion of the cult of the martyrs was part of a policy put forward by bishops like Ambrose, Augustine, and Paulinus of Nola to unite all the members of the city into common acts of worship. In fact, it seems that this form of worship, while different in some ways from the previous pagan practices of ancestor veneration upon which it was based, engaged the newly converting pagan population to a much greater extent than the formal liturgies in the urban basilicas of the Western empire.[34]

Finally, in speaking of these grand basilican *martyria* located outside the wall of Rome and other Roman cities of the Western empire, we need to remember that they also functioned as the locale for some of the more dramatic aspects of Christianity in late antiquity: healings and exorcisms. The reputation enjoyed by these shrines as places where God's power was made manifest through the intercession of the saints played an important part in the "liturgical life" of Christians at the end of the Roman Empire and into the Middle Ages. As Peter Brown points out, especially in considering exorcism, the vanquishing of the demons (often identified with the old gods) dramatized and supported the Christian worldview: the victory of God and the restoration of creation to God's original intentions. Now divine power was not to be found tied to nature and the passage of the seasons as it was in paganism but to historic holy individuals whose feast days were determined outside of the cycle of nature. It was in cultivating an interpersonal relationship between the suppliant and the saint, along the Roman model of patronage, that healing and liberation were obtained by the power of God made manifest at the shrine.[35]

Bishops and Supervision

In the face of this seemingly irresistible perdurance of popular customs surrounding reverence for the dead (which in turn influenced the celebration of the cult of the martyrs), bishops in late antiquity embarked on a gradual reform. For many, the need for reform was obvi-

---

[33] Peter Brown, *The Cult of the Saints: Its Rise and Function in Latin Christianity* (Chicago: University of Chicago Press, 1981), 41.

[34] See Robin Darling Young, "Martyrdom as Exaltation," in *Late Ancient Christianity*, ed. Virginia Burrus (Minneapolis, MN: Fortress, 2005), 74–75.

[35] Peter Brown, *Cult of the* Saints, 106–26.

ous. Their biggest objection was that the *refrigeria*—with its celebratory mood that included sharing wine and dancing at the graveside—led to excess and even debauchery. St. Augustine famously critiqued the *refrigeria* by explaining their origin. "When peace came to the church, a mass of pagans who wished to come to Christianity were held back because their feast days with their idols used to be spent in an abundance of eating and drinking."[36] His mentor, St. Ambrose, was even more critical and forbade the practice in Milan. We have an interesting explanation of this situation from St. Augustine himself. Augustine describes an incident in which his mother, Monica, was admonished to change her long-held practice of veneration of the saints.

> It had been my mother's custom in Africa to take meal-cakes and bread and wine to the shrines of the saints on their memorial days, but the doorkeeper would not allow her to do this in Milan. When she learned that the bishop had forbidden it, she accepted his ruling with such pious submission that I was surprised to see how willingly she condemned her own practice rather than dispute his command. . . . She used to bring her basket full of the customary offerings of food, intending to taste a little and give the rest away. For herself she never poured more than a small cupful of wine, watered to suit her sober palate, and she drank only as much of it as was needed to do honor to the dead . . . for her purpose was to do an act of piety, not to seek pleasure for herself. But she willingly ceased this custom when she found that this great preacher, this holy bishop, had forbidden such ceremonies even to those who performed them with sobriety, both for fear that to some they might be occasions for drunkenness and also because they bore so close a resemblance to the superstitious rites which the pagans held in honor of their dead.[37]

Unlike Ambrose, however, Augustine, as bishop of Hippo, did not totally forbid the practice of the *refrigeria*—whether because he saw its absolute prohibition to be impossible or because he regarded a modified version of these customs a way of effectively countering the cult of pagan deities, thus making the practice of the *refrigeria* a tool for evangelization.

---

[36] Augustine, *Ep.* 29.9.
[37] Augustine, *Confessions* 6.2, trans. R. S. Pine-Coffin (Hammondsworth, UK: Penguin Classics, 1961), 112–13.

The Persistence of Pagan Worship Practices

In addition to the *refrigeria*/cult of the saints, other popular pagan religious practices continued into late antiquity. These practices provide an important example of how pagan Greco-Roman popular worship continued in a modified form among Christian communities of late antiquity in a way that clearly underscores their new Christian orientation. The procession of cult statues through the villages and cities of the late antique world continued as Christianity slowly but surely became the majority religion. These public processions—often including the relics of the martyrs—became a feature of medieval Christian life. They were often employed to avert catastrophe and served to publicly bring the power of God into the everyday lives of the people in their own squares and streets. This is an example of a more accessible form of worship—usually accompanied by a litany that was easy to join and offering a more participatory worship experience than a formal eucharistic liturgy in a basilica. It also serves to make religious belief public and to bring together the members of the town. As William Christian points out, "As images of social wholeness, the processions have an added significance. The villagers for once in the year see the village as a social unit, abstracted from the buildings and location that made it a geographical unit." [38]

Other practices such as the use of amulets to ward off evil and the frequenting of astrologers to find out about the future (despite frequent condemnations by religious authorities) indicate the old beliefs, though reinterpreted, died very hard. "By the sixth century, astrology too has established itself again with many Christians, despite the strong opposition of Christian teaching. Its art was the study of God's 'signs,' not his 'causes,' a view which pagan practitioners had also accepted. The arts of the horoscope and the old 'book of fates' thus passed usefully into the Middle Ages."[39]

Conclusion

As Roman Catholics we still live today with the decisions made in the fourth century to inculturate the worship of the Church into late an-

---

[38] William Christian, *Person and God in a Spanish Valley* (New York: Seminar Press, 1972), 70.

[39] Robin Lane Fox, *Pagans and Christians: Religion and the Religious Life from the Second to the Fourth Century A.D.* (New York: HarperCollins, 1988), 678.

tique Roman culture. While the Roman Rite will also be influenced by other cultures, the choice of "continuity" with the pagan hieratic style of prayer still has consequences for our own style of prayer today—especially when we consider the recent, more literal translation of the Roman Missal. This style is theologically orthodox yet usually devoid of direct citations from the Bible. It is juridically precise and abstract. It cannot, however, lay a claim to be automatically "universal" just because it originated in Rome. We will see that as the Church moved into the Franco-Germanic world. While respecting Roman tradition, the people of northern Europe will adapt the Roman style of prayer to their own tastes. The same is true for the austere, simple, and sober ritual style that characterized the classic Roman liturgy. The prestige of the papacy and Rome as a pilgrimage center for Western Europe will help propagate a Roman style of worship that, while simple, is also influenced by the etiquette and dress of the old imperial court.

The effect of these choices on the "common people"—both within the lands of the Roman Empire and beyond its borders—will be to encourage two ways of entering into common worship. On the one hand, being present for the great celebrations performed by the clergy in a language scarcely understood will induce awe and reverence. On the other hand, awe and reverence, while important, are not sufficient to express a person's relationship with the transcendent. Popular religion in the form of processions, drama, blessings of the people, and objects of daily life will become important ways for common people to enter into communion with one another and express their faith in the mystery of Christ.

We will now examine the ways in which the classic Roman Rite was received into another cultural context: that of northern Europe. While the Roman Empire itself was in its death throes, an amazing missionary effort took place to Christianize the barbarian tribes that had overrun the borders of what was then considered the civilized world. How these peoples received the Roman Rite and in turn transformed and supplemented it with their own popular expressions of faith will be the focus of our next chapter.

CHAPTER FIVE

THE GERMANIZATION of CHRISTIANITY

LITURGY AND POPULAR RELIGION

The missionary expansion of the Church into northern Europe transformed the cultures of the barbarian tribes that had taken control of vast areas of the former Roman Empire. But in its missionary encounter with peoples whose worldview differed markedly from that held by Romanized Christians, the Church itself was changed. Speaking about this period of Church history, noted liturgical historian Joseph Jungmann makes the astonishing claim that "we may safely assert that in all the two thousand years of the Church's history, no period has ever seen a greater revolution in religious thought and institutions than that which took place in the first five centuries between the close of the patristic age and the dawn of scholasticism [600–1100]."[1] This mutual cultural transformation between the Franco-Germanic peoples and the late antique culture of the Roman Church gave birth to a distinctive form of Catholic Christianity that differed markedly from that of the Eastern Church and contributed to the eventual break between West and East. We will now look at the basic cultural characteristics of this revolution and how this change brought about a popular religiosity that both influenced and developed apart from the liturgy.[2]

---

[1] Joseph Jungmann, "The Defeat of Teutonic Arianism and the Revolution in Religious Culture in the Early Middle Ages," in *Pastoral Liturgy* (New York: Herder and Herder, 1962), 1.

[2] The *Directory on Popular Piety and Liturgy* notes that this period marked the separation between liturgy and popular religion. "Between the seventh and

The Germanic Religious Worldview and Christianity

In order to understand the magnitude of the religious revolution that took place in Western Christianity during these centuries, it is helpful to use a distinction developed by specialists in comparative religion. They make the distinction between "folk" and "universal" religions. James Russell, in his fascinating book *The Germanization of Early Medieval Christianity,* uses these labels to contrast the fundamental structural differences between the religious outlooks of the Indo-European Germanic tribes that gradually adopted Christianity at the beginning of the Middle Ages to the faith of the missionaries sent from the Irish monasteries and from the Mediterranean South. The pre-Christian religious worldview of the Germanic peoples would be best described as "folk," "ethnic," or "natural." In the context of such a worldview there is not a great deal of concern for the afterlife, but with the "here and now" and how religious devotion can help obtain the good things in life: children, the fertility of the fields and flocks, health, victory in war, etc. In this sense it is a "world-affirming" religion that often offers ways of obtaining the good things of life through not only prayers but also by means of magic. Christianity, by contrast, is described as a "universal," "revealed," "prophetic," or "historical" religion.[3] This kind of religion is structured to regard the world as a place of spiritual struggle from which human beings need to be rescued. In Christianity, though, this rescue is not focused on the present world but will ultimately take place at the end of time and in the next life. For this reason, Christianity (along with Judaism and Islam) could be described as a "world-denying" religion.

Furthermore, Germanic religion was nondogmatic. Its "sacral locus" focused on the folk community itself. "The sacrality of the community is expressed in ritual ceremonies that celebrate its relationship with its own exclusive gods and that promote a strong sense of in-group identification and loyalty."[4] In contrast, a universal, historical

---

the fifteenth century, a decisive differentiation between Liturgy and popular piety began to emerge which gradually became more pronounced, ending eventually in a dualism of celebration. Parallel with the Liturgy, celebrated in Latin, a communitarian popular piety celebrated in the vernacular emerged" (DPPL 29).

[3] James C. Russell, *The Germanization of Early Medieval Christianity: A Sociohistorical Approach to Religious Transformation* (Oxford, UK: Oxford University Press, 1994), 46.

[4] Ibid., 48.

religion like early Christianity focuses on the salvation of the individual believer through initiation into a community of belief and adherence to a universal ethical code.[5] Each religion system, then, was very different in outlook and was geared to answer different questions and concerns about the human condition.

As we have seen, Christianity adopted elements of the world-affirming, status quo supporting functions of a natural religion when it became the official religion of the Roman Empire. Nevertheless, even though the second coming of Christ became less imminent in the minds of Christians, Christianity maintained an eschatological orientation by offering salvation in the next life through the community of those who accepted the truth of this revelation and ordered their lives according to Christ's teachings. It also continued to address a sense of rootlessness, of *anomie* and disillusionment in the Roman Empire that had primarily affected the lower classes of society. Christianity held up a message to the marginalized and disaffected that countered a loss of confidence and promoted a hope for the future. The early Christian Church, by challenging the old religion and civic religious structures that had lost credibility, offered a new, more hopeful vision of the world through its extensive charitable networks and the proclamation of the brotherhood of all believers. Christianity gave marginalized people a sense of order and purpose. As Mircea Eliade explains:

> For all the rootless multitudes of the Empire, for the many who suffered from loneliness, for the victims of cultural and social alienation, the Church was the only hope of obtaining an identity, of finding, or recovering, a meaning for life. Since there were no barriers, either social, racial, or intellectual, anyone could become a member of this optimistic and paradoxical society in which a powerful citizen, the emperor's chamberlain, bowed before a bishop who had been his slave.[6]

It was this aspect of Christianity that was modified in the eighth and ninth centuries when it underwent what Russell called "a process of Germanization." The culture of the Germanic tribes did not suffer from *anomie* or the lack of group cohesion. On the contrary, they had a very clear sense of cultural identity and were largely unconcerned with

---

[5] Ibid., 49.

[6] Mircea Eliade, *A History of Religious Ideas*, vol. 2, trans. Willard R. Trask (Chicago: University of Chicago Press, 1982), 413.

issues about the fate of individuals after death. For that reason, Christianity's offer of a savior and redeemer was the answer to a question they were not asking. As Russell points out, "Neither the cohesive social structure nor the Indo-European ideological heritage of the Germanic peoples predisposed them to desire salvation." Furthermore, "whereas early Christianity was generally world-rejecting and universalist, the important universal ethical and doctrinal components, [Germanic] religiosity was generally world-accepting and folk-centered, without formal ethical and doctrinal elements, and usually possessing heroic, religiopolitical, and magicoreligious characteristics."[7] Many of the missionaries sent to evangelize the Northern tribes instinctively knew that in order to make the Gospel both appealing and comprehensible to the Germanic peoples, the Gospel would have to be presented in a new way.

Different Missionary Approaches

Since Christianity offered answers to questions about life and faith that the Germanic peoples were not asking, it is hardly surprising that missionaries often had a difficult time in convincing many of the tribes of the relevance of this new religion. But Christianity, as presented by the missionaries to the Germanic peoples in the seventh and eighth centuries, had the advantage of representing a civilization that impressed these less sophisticated peoples. As Aylward Shorter notes, "The new, pagan rulers of Europe were eager to appropriate the remnants of Roman civilization and to make use of its bureaucracy and Latin literacy." [8] In many of the areas where the missionaries worked, they relied on the permission of the rulers to preach and convert. In some cases they were supported by the military power of the pagan or Christian monarchs who supported the missionaries for political if not for religious reasons.

The evangelization of the Anglo-Saxons was a case in point. The pagan ruler of Kent, Ethelbert, welcomed Augustine and his fellow monks who had been sent to England by Pope Gregory the Great in CE 597 and gave them a place to stay and permission to preach in his domains. In a famous letter to Mellitus, a companion of Augustine who was to join him in England, Pope Gregory spells out what

---

[7] Russell, *Germanization of Early Medieval Christianity*, 102.

[8] Aylward Shorter, *Toward a Theology of Inculturation* (Maryknoll, NY: Orbis, 1988), 141.

could be called a "gradualist" or "accommodationist" approach to evangelization:

> We wish you to inform him that we have given careful thought to the affairs of the English, and have come to the conclusion that the temples of the idols in that country should on no account be destroyed. He is to destroy the idols, but the temples themselves are to be aspersed with holy water, altars set up, and relics enclosed in them. For if these temples are well built, they are to be purified from devil worship, and dedicated to the service of the true God. And since they have a custom of sacrificing many oxen to devils, let some other solemnity be substituted in its place, such as a day of Dedication or the Festivals of the holy martyrs whose relics are enshrined there. On such occasions they might well construct shelters of boughs for themselves around the churches that were once temples, and celebrate the solemnity with devout feasting. They are no longer to sacrifice beasts to the Devil, but they may kill them for food to the praise of God, and give thanks to the Giver of all gifts for his bounty. If the people are allowed some worldly pleasures in this way, they will more readily come to desire the joys of the spirit. For it is certainly impossible to eradicate all errors from obstinate minds at one stroke, and whoever wishes to climb to a mountain top climbs gradually step by step and not in one leap. It was in this way that God revealed himself to the Israelite people in Egypt, permitting the sacrifices formerly offered to the Devil to be offered thenceforward to Himself instead. So he bade them sacrifice beasts to Him, so that, once enlightened, they might abandon a wrong conception of sacrifice, and adopt the right. For, while they were to continue to offer beasts as before, they were to offer them to God instead of to idols, thus transforming the idea of sacrifice. Of your kindness, you are to inform our brother Augustine of this policy, so that he may consider how he may best implement it on the spot. God keep you safe my very dear son.[9]

It is important to note that the letter presupposes that the Christian missionaries had the support of the king who had been baptized in 597. This made it much easier for the pope to advise a more gradual process of evangelization. Yet it also should be noted that while the pope speaks of appropriating the old centers of pagan worship and

[9] Bede, *A History of the English Church and People*, trans. L. Sherley-Price (Harmondsworth, UK: Penguin, 1955), 30. Original Latin text found in *Monumenta Germaniae Historica: Epistolae 1*, ed. Ernst Dummler, vol. 2, p. 331.

substituting Christian meaning for pagan religious practices, there is no real encouragement to evangelize from "within" the culture. The pope, while trying to be sensitive to religious traditions, takes it for granted that the missionaries have the superior culture and religion and that this faith must now be imposed on the people with the help of the king. The policy of making this kind of accommodation of Christianity to pagan ritual practices and sacred places was to change in the Anglo-Saxon mission to evangelize their continental relatives due to the wedding of the Christian message to the Frankish sword.

However difficult it was to convert pagan peoples, the Roman missionaries to England seemed to find tougher opposition to their particular version of Christianity from the remnant of the Celtic Christians displaced by the Anglo-Saxon invaders. These "Celtic Britons" survived the presence of the Anglo-Saxons and held customs that varied from the Roman "standard" that was being preached by the missionaries. They differed from the Roman missionaries in having an organizational structure centered on monasteries rather than urban centers with bishops, as well as on the date they celebrated Easter. It would not be until the Council of Whitby in 664 that the Roman version of Christianity, rather than the Celtic, would prevail.[10] At any rate, the missionaries sent from Rome seem to have been aware that some accommodation with the local culture had to be made in order for their evangelization efforts to bear fruit.

The seventh and eighth centuries witnessed an amazing international missionary effort on the continent of Europe that came not directly from Rome but from the monasteries of Ireland and England. The Irish monastic practice of *peregrinatio* encouraged monks to see missionary work as part of monastic life. The foundation of monasteries in today's France (Gaul), Switzerland, Austria, and Germany attest to the zeal of these Irish monks. St. Columba, who began monastic establishments in Gaul (Vosges, Annegray, and Luxueil) and in Lombard, Italy (Bobbio), was the most famous of these intrepid founders. He also inspired the founding of Frankish monastic communities, wedding the Rule of St. Benedict to certain Celtic practices.[11]

The missionary wave of Irish monks was followed by monks from England who maintained a more uncompromising attitude toward the

---

[10] See Roger Collins, *Early Medieval Europe 300–1000* (New York: St. Martin's Press, 1999), 183–86.

[11] Ibid., 245–48.

local pagan cultures. The most famous example of these Anglo-Saxon monks who labored in the Frankish Empire was Boniface, who became known as the apostle of Germany. As G. Ronald Murphy notes, Boniface represents a different missionary approach.

> In 719 Boniface secured a papal commission to convert the pagan Germans and, significantly, was instructed to use the Roman baptismal formula rather than the Celtic form of the ritual, which he and others must have been using from the monasteries in the British Isles. We know that when he returned to the German territory he was much more ruthless both toward the German pagans and toward the Irish missionary clergy there, whom he regarded as too paganized. Can it be that he objected to the earlier missionaries' attempts to "accommodate" ritual and formulation to the native Germanic culture and insisted instead on the Romanization of the pagans in the preaching of the Gospel?[12]

The most memorable confrontation between Boniface and the pagan Germans was the felling of the sacred oak of Thor at Geismar. The tree was cut down "while a great number of pagans present . . . kept on cursing this enemy of their gods under their breath with the greatest fervor."[13] Of course, the reason why Boniface was able to destroy this powerful pagan symbol was due to the nearby Frankish army of Charles Martel that supported his action. As Murphy notes, "Boniface converted by confrontation and direct threat of violence . . . and his method appeared to be so successful that there seems at the time to have been little need to worry about German hearts and minds."[14]

The Gospel as Saxon "Good News"

The Carolingian policy of forced conversion continued the method practiced by Boniface and the Merovingian authorities at the beginning of the eighth century. The region of northern Germany known as Saxony became a target of Charlemagne's policy of converting all the peoples of his realm to Christianity in order to consolidate his

---

[12] G. Ronald Murphy, *The Saxon Savior: The Transformation of the Gospel in the Ninth-Century Heliand* (Oxford, UK: Oxford University Press, 1989), 13.

[13] ". . . magna quippe aderat copia paganorum, qui inimicum deorum suorum intra se diligentissime devotabant." *Bonifatii Epistolae: Willibaldi Vita Bonifat*, 2nd ed. Reinhold Rau (Darmstadt: Wissenschaftliche Buchhandlung, 1968), 494.

[14] Murphy, *The Saxon Savior*, 14.

rule. Unlike the more gradual conversion of Merovingian Gaul and Anglo-Saxon England—where pagans and Christians had coexisted for several generations, often within the same family—"the conversion of Saxony . . . was a sudden operation, carried out under Charlemagne's military banner. There had been earlier missionary efforts in Saxony, mostly by Anglo-Saxons such as St. Boniface, but they had not met with much success. Saxony did not become even nominally Christian until Charlemagne's time."[15] "Conversion" often took place at spear point, with the people of the village being marched into the nearest body of water while priests on the nearby banks screamed out the baptismal formula. Like Boniface's destruction of the sacred oak, Charlemagne utterly destroyed the Irminsul, a pillar or tree trunk located near the headwaters of the River Lippe "which was probably a representation of Yggdrasil, the cosmic tree, the tree of life, support of the universe, and the center of Saxon worship."[16]

Not surprisingly, many questioned the genuineness of the conversion of the Saxons. Alcuin, Charlemagne's ecclesiastical adviser, wrote to him that "one should consider very carefully that the office of preaching and the sacrament of baptism be done properly, lest the washing of the body in baptism be to no avail if the knowledge for the Catholic faith in the soul does not precede it."[17] The policy of forced conversion seemed to work more effectively with the upper-class Saxons who were impressed by the more Romanized Frankish culture. They also stood to gain socially and politically by acquiescing to Frankish power. Ruth Karras points out:

> Many noble Saxons readily embraced Christianity in order to be assimilated into the Frankish upper classes and to gain the favor of the king. Christianity to the nobility was a symbol of a higher, more civilized culture. Many noble families founded proprietary monasteries with their own patron saints, and the monasteries to which the peasants paid tithes were full of sons of nobles who sought to imitate the Franks. During the ninth century 177 young Saxon nobles became monks at one monastery, Corvey, alone.[18]

[15] Ruth Karras, "Pagan Survivals and Syncretism in the Conversion of Saxony," *The Catholic Historical Review* 72, no. 4 (October 1986): 554.

[16] Murphy, *The Saxon Savior*, 15.

[17] Alcuin to Charlemagne, CE 796, *MGH Epist.* 4, ed. Ernst Dummler, sec. 110, p. 158.

[18] Karras, "Pagan Survivals," 556.

But the majority of the Saxons—especially those of the lower classes—were less inclined to embrace both Christianity and Frankish rule. The imposition of tithing and the suppression of Saxon religious and political activity led to numerous rebellions in the late eighth and ninth centuries. The hold that Christianity had on the majority of Saxon minds and hearts was evidently not very profound.

It was in this troubled context that around the year 840 a Saxon Christian poet was commissioned by Charlemagne's successor, Louis the Pious, to write a version of the gospels that would be more readily understood and embraced by the Saxons. Modeled after Tatian's *Diatessaron*, this conflation of the four canonical gospels written as a German epic poem, has come to be known as the *Heliand* (the Savior).[19] The *Heliand* represents a Saxon interpretation of Christianity that transformed the Christian message in a way understandable to the Saxon people. Jesus is described as a *drohtin,* or chieftain, living on the shore of the North Sea who gathers around him a group of thanes (warrior retainers). Presented as a more powerful version of the god Woden, the Holy Spirit in the form of a dove is described as sitting on Jesus' shoulder, like the usual image of Woden who was depicted with the Nordic mythical bird of consciousness and memory resting on his shoulder.[20] The author subtly parallels the political and military oppression of the Romans with that of the Franks under Charlemagne, obliquely criticizing the Frankish policy of forced conversion and the total destruction of the old ways.

One of the most fascinating elements of this Germanic interpretation of the Gospel is the way it treats the presence and communication of the holy through "magic." We saw that a characteristic of folk or natural religion is a belief that "magic"—the use of spells and incantations—can procure desired results. This use of special, secret words has been described as "performative speech" that in Germanic religion takes the form of spells or "runes"—words that possess the power to

---

[19] On the dating, provenance, and authorship of the *Heliand* see Murphy, *The Saxon Savior,* 3–9.

[20] The *Heliand* describes the aftermath of Jesus' baptism as a distinctively German theophany: "As [Christ] stepped out onto the land, the doors of heaven opened up and the Holy Spirit came down from the All Ruler above to Christ—it was like a powerful bird, a magnificent dove—and It sat upon our Chieftain's shoulder, remaining over the Ruler's Child." G. Roland Murphy, *The Heliand: The Saxon Gospel* (New York: Oxford University Press, 1992), 35.

carry out what they say. G. Ronald Murphy, one of the acknowledged experts on the *Heliand*, suggests:

> The *Heliand* does, I believe, reveal various distinct traces of Germanic magic. In several incidents . . . it is my thesis that [the Saxon author] forces the reader to surmise the presence of magic by surrounding the event with dramatic secrecy and/or refers to "powers" in the description of the event or object. This magic reinterpretation of a scene occurs in his expanded description of the "powers" possessed by the consecrated bread and wine in the Last Supper scene, in the curious secrecy that is made to surround Christ's transformation of the water into wine at Cana, in the introduction of the "Pater Noster" as a secret runic mystery, and in the depiction of the creation of the world—and the writing of the gospel—as instances of word magic ordained by God.[21]

Murphy even goes so far as to title a whole chapter of his commentary on the *Heliand* by referring to Jesus as the "Lord of the Runes."[22] At crucial moments in his interpretation of the gospels, the author of *Heliand* describes Christ, by means of the runes, conferring holy power on certain objects. At the Last Supper Christ describes the theological meanings of the eucharistic bread and wine to his twelve thanes (apostles) "as if he were revealing the secret magic powers possessed by the eucharistic power-objects, and urging them to use them."[23]

> "Believe me clearly," he said, "that this is my body and also my blood. I here give both of them to you to eat and to drink. . . . This is a thing which possesses power; by doing it you will be giving honor to your Chieftain. This is a holy image: keep it to remember me, so that the sons of men will do it after you and will preserve it in this world, and thus everyone all over this middle world will know what I am doing out of love to give honor to the Lord."[24]

The Eucharist is described as "a thing which possesses power." Murphy points out that in the original old Saxon, the lines read: "thit it mahtig thing." This could be reasonably translated as "this is a *magic* thing." In effect, the bread and wine are described in the very Germanic

[21] G. Ronald Murphy, "Magic in the *Heliand*," *Monatshefte* 83, no. 4 (1991): 386.
[22] Murphy, *The Saxon Savior*, 75–94.
[23] Murphy, "Magic in the *Heliand*," 388.
[24] Ibid., 389.

way of having performative power—capable itself of bringing about the effect promised. Murphy observes:

> In cross-culturally interpreting the Eucharist in this manner, the *Heliand* poet in the early ninth century may be one of the first to have participated in the shift of sacramental emphasis from the earlier semitic and biblical focus on God himself (as the personal prime cause of the performative effect of any sacrament or miracle) to the instrumental, or secondary causes beloved of Northern Europeans: the water used in baptism, the oil used in ordination and confirmation and anointing the sick, and, of course, the bread and wine, together with their accompanying formulae and gestures (now perceived and presented as performative spells). [25]

Murphy supplies many other examples of this Germanic fascination with instrumental or secondary causes in the author of the *Heliand*'s description of the miracle of the multiplication of the loaves and fishes, the transformation of water into wine at the Marriage at Cana, and the power-filled words (runes) of the Lord's Prayer given to the disciples. The *Heliand*, then, interprets the Christian message to a Saxon audience to allow them to grasp the importance of the "good news" in a concrete, tangible way that corresponded to their religious worldview.

The "Germanization" of the Eucharist and Eucharistic Devotion

While we can easily see the author's transformation of the Gospel in the *Heliand* in order to more effectively present the Christian message to hard-to-convert Saxons, can we find evidence that this Germanization also affected the rest of the non-German Western Church? Significantly, a contemporary document, commonly accepted as the first extended catechetical treatise on the Eucharist, *De Corpore et Sanguine Domini*,[26] written by the Frankish monk Paschasius Radbertus around the year 831, demonstrates just such an influence. Mary Collins, drawing on the scholarship of Dom Idelfons Herwegen as well as that of G. Ronald Murphy and James Russell, offers an important description of "how this particular eucharistic catechesis so engaged our Germanic ancestors in the faith that it effectively shaped the western church's

---

[25] Ibid.
[26] Paschasius Radbertus, *De Corpore et Sanguine Domini*, ed. Bede Paul, Corpus Christianorum: Continuatio Mediaevalis 16 (Turnhout: Brépols, 1969).

approach to eucharistic belief throughout the entire second Christian millennium."[27]

Abbot Herwegen, a German scholar active between the two world wars of the twentieth century, wrote of the early medieval Germanic worldview that, as we have seen, was concerned by instrumental causes and their production. Less able to grasp a more mystical understanding of the Eucharist, the Germanic peoples were concerned about how and when the objective (*dingliche*) presence of the Eucharist came about.[28] Paschasius's catechesis on the Eucharist emphasizes this presence and identifies those powerful words (like runes) that bring about the presence of the body and blood of the Lord: *Hoc est corpus meum* (This is my body) and *Hic est calix sanguinis mei*" (This is the cup of my blood). By considering the presence apart from its liturgical context, Paschasius is able to present the sacrament as an independent object and paves the way for such popular practices as the worship of the Eucharist outside of Mass. As Herwegen observed, "The Germanic imagination grasped the Eucharist in concrete, personal terms. Eucharistic liturgy was not intelligible as an ecclesial event, but rather as a means to individual experience of divine power."[29] Furthermore, "out of the Germanic desire to lay hands on, to grasp the spiritual at least with the eye, came the twelfth- and thirteenth-century ecclesiastical legitimation of ocular communion, with ostensoria for showing the host and for elevations of the host and chalice."[30]

Significantly, because of a very different liturgical history in the Oriental churches—one that was not influenced by the Germanic worldview—adoration of the Blessed Sacrament outside of Mass is unknown. It is also significant that the birth of the feast Corpus Christi in the thirteenth century took place in northern Europe (Liège, Belgium) and was brought to Rome by northerners. Despite the promulgation of the bull *Transiturus* in 1264 by Urban IV (a northerner from France) that made Corpus Christi a universal feast, it is not really accepted by the whole Church until the first decades of the 1300s, when the papacy

[27] Mary Collins, "Evangelization, Catechesis, and the Beginnings of Western Eucharistic Theology," *Louvain Studies* 23 (1998): 124.

[28] Ildelfons Herwegen, *Antike, Germantum, Christentum* (Salzburg: Verlag Anton Pustet, 1932), 51–52.

[29] Collins, "Evangelization," 138–39.

[30] Ibid., 136. See also the excellent synthesis on the "Germanization of the Liturgy: 750–1073" offered by Edward Foley in *From Age to Age: How Christians Have Celebrated the Eucharist* (Collegeville, MN: Liturgical Press, 2008), 133–83.

moved to Avignon.[31] The theological and pastoral origin, then, for our present practice of reservation and exposition of the Blessed Sacrament, unknown during the first millennium of the Church's existence, is arguably traceable to the Germanization of Christianity during the eighth and ninth century.

The Continuing Instrumentalization of the Holy

Further evidence for the ongoing Germanic intrumentalization of the holy with the Western Church is found in the Roman-Germanic Pontifical of the Tenth Century (PRG).[32] A pontifical is a liturgical book used by bishops that contains texts for those celebrations at which he is able to preside. The PRG contains diverse texts—from ordination and monastic profession to special prayers for the consecration of churches. This version of the pontifical served as the basis for subsequent pontificals, including the present Roman Pontifical.

One of the most striking features of this book is the sheer number of blessings illustrating the conviction that all of God's creation can be blessed and thus invested with divine power. In addition to the usual blessings that one would expect to find in such a book—the blessings of liturgical implements such as chalices, altar cloths, and vestments—it also contains special blessings and prayers for all kinds of agricultural activities and products: for seeds, for the crop's protection against worms, first fruits, apples, bread and cheese, grapes and beans, new vines, and soap.

Significantly, it also contains a series of blessings that were discontinued in subsequent pontificals because they were condemned by the Fourth Lateran Council in 1215.[33] These blessings had to do with

---

[31] For a detailed history of the feast see Miri Rubin, *Corpus Christi* (Cambridge, UK: Cambridge University Press, 1991), 164–85.

[32] *Le Pontifical romano-germanique du dixième siècle*, ed. C. Vogel and R. Elze, Studi e Testi (Città del Vaticano: Biblioteca Vaticana, 1963–1972), see vols. 226–27 (text), 266 (introduction and indices).

[33] Canon 18: "nec quisquam purgationi aquæ ferventis vel frigidæ seu ferri candentis ritum cuiuslibet benedictionis" ("Neither shall anyone in judicial tests or ordeals by hot or cold water or hot iron bestow any blessing"). *Conciliorum Oecumenicorum Decreta*, ed. Josepho Alberigo, J. A. Dossetti, Perikle-P. Joannou, Claudio Leonardi, Paulo Prodi (Bologna: Istituto per le Scienze Religiose, 1973), 265. See also Peter Brown, "Society and the Supernatural: A Medieval Change," *Daedalus* 104, no. 2 (Spring 1975): 133–51.

investing the implements of trial by ordeal with God's power. There is a blessing for hot irons used to determine guilt.[34] A suspect had to carry a bar of red-hot iron in his hands while walking a prescribed number of steps. If his hands did not suffer burns or if the burns healed cleanly without infection he was judged innocent. Otherwise he would be considered guilty. There are other blessings for flowing water where the accused would be thrown in, bound hand and foot.[35] If he floated, he was innocent. If he sank and drowned he was guilty (these criteria would be reversed in subsequent centuries when determining if a woman was a witch). Another ordeal involved boiling water. After a fully vested bishop or priest blessed boiling water in the atrium of a church, the accused (of theft or adultery) was forced to put his hand in the water. Again, if it was withdrawn unharmed or if the burns did not fester, the suspect was declared innocent.[36] Finally, there was the "ordeal by ingestion." The accused was forced to eat specially exorcised and blessed bread and cheese. If he choked he was guilty of theft.[37]

Other practices that paralleled the instrumentalization of the holy through the blessing of implements of trial were two customs called the "clamor" and the "humiliation" of relics of the saints. The clamor was done in the presence of the consecrated host. It became a custom at Mass celebrated in monasteries for monks to cry to God for help in answering particular intentions between the *Pater Noster* and the *Agnus Dei* while the priest held the consecrated host aloft and the monks prostrated themselves. The humiliation of relics was a practice whereby relics of saints of the monastery would be taken from their place of honor and placed on the ground before the altar until a favor was granted, at which time the relics would be restored to their place of honor.[38] This is not unlike the practice in our own day (at least in Chicago) of burying a statue of St. Joseph upside-down in the backyard to invoke his aid in selling a house. Once the house is sold, the statue is to be dug up and put in a place of honor in the new home.

[34] PRG 247, "Iudicium ferri ferventis," p. 380.

[35] PRG 248, "Benedictio aquae fluentis ad iudicium faciendum," pp. 393–94.

[36] PRG 247, "De iudicio aquae ferventis quomodo inventum sit," pp. 382–93.

[37] PRG 249, "Exorcismus et benediction panis et casei ad securitatem iudicii faciendum et ad inveniendum furtum," pp. 394–97; CCL, "Iudicium panis et casei," pp. 397–98.

[38] See Patrick Geary, "Humiliation of the Saints" and "Coercion of Saints in Medieval Religious Practice," in *Living with the Dead in the Middle Ages* (Ithaca, NY: Cornell University Press, 1994), 95–162.

The Roman-Germanic Pontifical, the *Heliand*, the writings of Paschasius Radbertus, and monastic customs of using the consecrated hosts and relics to obtain favors are all witnesses to the Germanic influence on popular religious beliefs and practices of the early Middle Ages. To conclude this chapter, we will now turn to an example of popular religious influence on the liturgy itself in the birth of liturgical drama in those areas of the Holy Roman Empire where the Roman Rite was imposed by imperial edict.

Liturgical Drama and the Roman Rite

Drama, as we saw in the second chapter, was one of the principal ways in which the Christian message celebrated in the liturgy was made accessible to the unsophisticated faithful who may not have been literate. The dramatic elements of the liturgies of Holy Week—processions with palms on Palm Sunday, washing of feet on Holy Thursday— illustrate the "representational" popular piety adopted from worship practices in the fourth-century Church of Jerusalem and incorporated into the Roman Rite. While these two "dramatic" elements are still part of our current liturgical practice today, it is important to note that in the Middle Ages many more such "dramatic" moments were added to the Roman liturgy during the ninth and tenth centuries. A good example is the *Quem Quaeritis* (Whom do you seek?) drama that preceded the reading of the gospel at Easter. Three young deacons, representing the three Marys, would come to the "tomb" and be met by the angel (played by another cleric) who would start the liturgical dialogue by asking, "Whom do you seek?"[39]

Where did such practices come from? Why did these additional moments of drama first appear in the Roman Rite outside of Rome between the eighth and tenth centuries and continue to develop into the high Middle Ages? While there is much scholarly debate as to the origins of liturgical drama, it is possible that this popular religious practice arose in the ninth century as a direct result of the imposition of the Roman Rite in areas of the empire that had practiced what is know as the "Gallican Rite."

It is important to remember that during the early Middle Ages, the Roman Rite was not the "standard" liturgical rite for all of western Eu-

---

[39] Aina Trotzig, "L'apparition du Christ ressucité à Marie Madeleine et le drame liturgique," *Revue de Musicologie* 86, no. 1 (2000): 83.

rope. There were many non-Roman local rites that naturally developed
in major cities that were influenced by the local culture. Although all
of these rites used Latin as the liturgical language (some more profi-
ciently than others), the style and organization of the liturgy (structure
of the eucharistic celebration, liturgical year, type of chant), and even
the way the Church itself was structured, varied a great deal from one
local rite to another. Two of these non-Roman Western rites are still
being practiced today: the Ambrosian Rite of the northern Italian city
of Milan and the so-called Mozarabic Rite that developed in the city
of Toledo in Spain. In addition to these rites were the "Celtic" rites
practiced in Ireland and in parts of the British Isles.

In present-day France (as well as parts of Switzerland and Germany), another family of rites commonly referred to as the Gallican
Rite was in use (the rite was named after Gaul, the Roman name for
France). Rather than a cohesive rite, it was in fact a family of variable
local liturgical practices that more or less resembled each other. All
Gallican liturgy was readily distinguishable from the more sober and
restrained Roman Rite. As the great liturgical historian Louis Duchesne noted, "It is well known by everyone that the Gallican Liturgy,
in features which distinguish it from the Roman use, betrays all the
characteristics of the Eastern Liturgies."[40] He goes on to comment that
some formularies, though in Latin, were translated word for word
from the Byzantine Rite. Another scholar describes Gallican liturgy
has having "a definite leaning toward splendor and ceremonial; there
is too a wide diversity of variable prayers exhibiting a strong Byzantine influence. . . . The prayers are often long and prolix, the rhetoric
exuberant and diffuse, the thought forms ornamental and involved."[41]
Joseph Jungmann described the drama inherent in the ceremonial side
of the Gallican liturgy:

> Take as an instance the dramatic build-up of the Mass-liturgy. . . .
> The high Mass in the Gallic area introduced a number of incen-
> sations. With censer swingings, the altar was encircled according
> to an elaborate and fixed plan, first at the beginning of the Mass
> proper, soon also at the beginning of the fore Mass. For the reading
> of the Gospel it was not enough that the incense envelop the book,

[40] Louis Duchesne, *Christian Worship: Its Origin and Evolution*, trans. M. L.
McClure (London: SPCK, 1903), 93.

[41] D. M. Hope, rev. G. Woolfenden, "The Medieval Western Rites," in *The
Study of Liturgy*, ed. Cheslyn Jones et al., rev. ed. (London: SPCK, 1992), 273.

but in conformity with a practice in vogue for quite a time, it was carried out into the midst of the assembled people, necessitating soon a multiplication of censers. Then the parade of Gospel-singing became Christ's triumphal march: to Christ resounds the *Gloria tibi Domine*, of which until then the Roman Mass knew nothing.[42]

It is hard to imagine a liturgical style more different from the restrained and sober classical Roman Rite. The Roman Rite, for example, was more fixed, knowing only one eucharistic prayer, while the Gallican rite knew several. The use of incense illustrates well the great difference between the two rites. Harkening to a customary feature of processions of the Roman emperor, incense was used in Rome during papal processions, but not during the liturgy itself. The Gallican liturgy, by contrast, favored mystery and drama. As Edmund Bishop remarked, "Mystery never flourished in the clear Roman atmosphere, and symbolism was no product of the Roman religious mind. Christian symbolism is not of pure Roman birth, nor a native product of the Roman spirit."[43]

It is no wonder, then, that there were at least two consequences to the imposition of this wildly different style of worship on the Frankish kingdom.[44] When Charlemagne imported the Roman liturgical books into his realm, his officials saw that they lacked prayers and celebrations judged essential by his imperial liturgists. It is for this reason that a supplement was written to provide for formularies for local saints but also to "improve" the sober Roman prayers that must have appeared overly laconic to the Franco-Germanic people who were so accustomed to a more expansive style of prayer.[45] These prayers later found their way back to Rome during the tenth century and were fused with the

---

[42] Joseph Jungmann, *The Mass of the Roman Rite: Its Origins and Development* (*Missarum Sollemnia*), trans. Francis Brunner, vol. 1 (New York: Benzinger, 1951), 77.

[43] Edmund Bishop, "The Genius of the Roman Rite," *Liturgica Historica: Papers on the Liturgy and Religious Life of the Western Church* (Oxford, UK: The Clarendon Press, 1918), 10.

[44] See Cyrille Vogel, "Les Échanges liturgiques entre Rome et les pays francs jusqu'à l'époque de Charlemagne," in *Le Chiese nei regni dell'Europa occidentale e I loro rapporti con Roma sino all'800*. Settimane di studio del centro italiano dis tudi sull'alto medioevo 7 (Spoleto: Presso la sede del centro, 1960), 185–295.

[45] See Cyrille Vogel, *Medieval Liturgy: An Introduction to the Sources*, trans. and rev. William Storey and Niels Rasmussen (Washington, DC: The Pastoral Press, 1986), 85–90.

original classic Roman Rite. It is the mixture, then, of the Roman and the Gallican that constitutes a large part of the sources for the texts in our present Roman liturgical books. One of the first compositions contained in this Franco-Germanic supplement, believed to have been redacted by Benedict of Aniane (+821), is the *Praeconium Paschale* or *Exultet* that is part of the Vigil of Holy Saturday in today's Roman Rite. Its fulsome poetry is a fine example of the Franco-Germanic style that could never have been produced in Rome of the eighth and ninth centuries:

> O wonder of your humble care for us!
> O love, O charity beyond all telling,
> to ransom a slave you gave away your Son!
> O truly necessary sin of Adam,
> destroyed completely by the Death of Christ!
> O happy fault
> that earned so great, so glorious a Redeemer.[46]

The second consequence of the "hybridization" of the Roman Rite with the Franco-Germanic poetic and dramatic sensibility is more speculative but also more intriguing. It is the contention of C. Clifford Flanagan that in order to cope with the new and sober rhetorical and ceremonial style of the Roman Rite, the Franco-Germanic liturgists also supplemented the austere Roman style of worship by creating dramatic liturgical moments like the *visitatio sepulchri* at Easter. These enrichments were added not simply to entertain but to engage the assembly in the ritual/liturgical moment. As Flanagan explains,

> We can now see that this ceremony is not a representational play, but an attempt to assert and make explicit the reality of the events which were believed to have been reactualized in the cult. It seeks neither to entertain nor to instruct in the usual sense of the word; instead it attempts to involve actively the entire cultic community in the events of the first Easter and therefore to apply the saving benefits of the once-for-all event to the tenth century congregation. . . . The "Quem quaeritis" question is not directed to a few "actors" but to the entire congregation because the congregation is thought to be caught up on the timelessness of the ritual act and

---

[46] *Roman Missal, Third Edition* (Collegeville, MN: Liturgical Press, 2011).

thus become identical with the Marys who were asked a similar question on the first Easter.[47]

If Flanagan's hypothesis is correct, it explains why these dramatic elements suddenly appear in the ninth and tenth centuries in the Roman Rite celebrated where the former Gallican Rite was practiced. It is important also to remember that this phenomenon does not appear in other classic historic liturgies. "Nowhere in any of the several Eastern rites do we find so much as a trace of liturgical drama. Even more striking is the fact that in the non-Roman Latin rites of the West there is likewise no liturgical drama."[48]

While the original intent of these dramatic interludes may have been to make clear the liturgical moment and involve the members of assembly in the historic events of salvation now made present before their eyes, it also opened the door to a new conception of the whole of Christian liturgy as a dramatic re-presentation of the events of salvation history, especially Christ's passion. It is significant that during this century the most famous Western liturgical commentator of the day, Amalarius of Metz (+850), proposed just such an allegorical interpretation of the Mass.[49] While not readily accepted by some of his contemporaries who saw his arbitrary linking of liturgical movement and gestures with moments in Christ's life (the singing of the "Gloria" with Christmas, the fraction of the host with the death of Christ on the cross) as highly problematic, this mystical and symbolic manner of connecting liturgical moments to Christ's life allowed a kind of popular participation in worship that was otherwise impossible due to the use of Latin and the growing clericalization of the celebration.[50]

This "move to the dramatic" in the ninth and tenth centuries, moreover, was accompanied by an abrupt physical separation of the assembly from the clerical celebrants of the Mass. As Jungmann points

[47] C. Clifford Flanagan, "The Roman Rite and the Origins of the Liturgical Drama," *University of Toronto Quarterly*, 43, no. 3 (1974): 281.

[48] Ibid., 278.

[49] On the relationship of Amalarius with liturgical drama see Donnalee Dox, "The Eyes of the Body and the Veil of Faith," *Theatre Journal* 56, no.1 (2004): 29–45.

[50] These reasons for the growth of the dichotomy between the liturgy and popular devotions are listed by the *Directory of Popular Piety and Liturgy*. The *Directory* also mentions a lack of biblical knowledge and the diffusion of apocryphal literature. See DPPL, 30.

out, "the altar was moved back to the rear wall of the apse" and the choir-gallery was redesigned and set between the priests and the laypeople. The liturgical focus shifted from the gathering of an assembly of believers around altar and word "to the mystery of God's coming to man, a mystery one must adoringly wonder at and contemplate from afar."[51] It was in this changed "stage" that new processions and dramas would be enacted both during and outside of the liturgy in the following centuries.[52] This development will be determinative of many of the evangelization strategies used by the first missionaries to the Americas.

Conclusion

The change of Christian religious imagination during the early Middle Ages is striking. It could be safely said that both the "public" and "private" levels of liturgical meaning were transformed. This change was the result of the meeting of two disparate religious worldviews—that of the Christian Mediterranean and the Germanic tribes—and it produced what we would come to know as the Western Church. In order for the Gospel to be understood and celebrated in the liturgy by the Franco-Germanic peoples a change was wrought in how the faith was presented and celebrated. Many of the distinctive features of the Roman Rite, in stark comparison with, say, the liturgical traditions of Byzantium or Egypt, are the result of what scholars call this "hybridization" of Roman and Franco-Germanic elements.

Popular piety in the Western Church was equally affected by this cultural shift. The belief that with the correct prayer, objects could become vessels containing both the presence and the power of God, refocused traditional Christian notions of sacraments. It also led to a kind of objectification of the Eucharist that had never been known in the first nine hundred years of Christianity.[53] In effect, the Eucharist is transformed from a memorial of Christ's sacrificial meal at which all

---

[51] Jungmann, *Mass of the Roman Rite*, vol. 1, 83–85.

[52] On the development of liturgical drama and mystery plays during the Middle Ages, see Aina Trotzig, "L'apparition du Christ ressucité," 83–104; Nicole Sevestre, "Le drame liturgique: théâtre du non-dit," *Revue de Musicologie* 86, no.1 (2000): 77–82; Norma Kroll, "Power and Conflict in Medieval Ritual and Plays: The Re-Invention of Drama," *Studies in Philology* 102, no. 4 (Fall 2005): 452–83.

[53] For a clear and insightful discussion of this entire topic, see Nathan Mitchell, *Cult and Controversy: The Worship of the Eucharist Outside of Mass* (Collegeville, MN: Liturgical Press, 1990).

present are called into communion with God present in the eucharistic elements and one another, to a singular focus on the body and blood of Christ in the elements of bread and wine offered in sacrifice, and in whose presence all must kneel and adore. It could be said that this shift of attitude and then the change of the rite itself to accommodate this shift (the elevation of the host and chalice prescribed in the thirteenth century as well as a new concern to reserve the Eucharist for private visits) made the Eucharist itself a popular devotion. The growth of the practice of celebrating votive Masses to obtain special favors in the thirteenth and fourteenth centuries further instrumentalized not just the eucharistic elements but the very liturgy itself. Masses of Saint Sebastian against the plague (*contra pestilentiam*), of St. Liborius against gallstones (*contra calculum*), of the Blessed Job against venereal disease (*contra morbum gallicum*), and others would have been unthinkable in the period prior to the Germanization of the Western Church.[54]

The introduction of drama into the liturgy compensated for a Roman Rite that seemed inadequate to express the religious sensibilities of the Franco-Germanic peoples and also paved the way for the exuberance of popular manifestations of piety and devotion that blossomed in the High Middle Ages (thirteenth to fifteenth centuries). The growth of sacred vernacular drama staged both inside and outside the church building answered the need for popular means of catechesis that complemented the iconography of Romanesque and Gothic cathedrals that presented the events and mysteries of the faith in sculpture, painting, and stained glass to a largely unlettered populace.

The popular concerns surrounding healing, exorcism, the power of relics, and the efficacy of going on pilgrimage (or crusade) to obtain forgiveness of sins are all aspects of popular religion that will continue to develop and grow stronger in western Europe during the Middle Ages. The birth of confraternities to provide charitable support for its members and promote eucharistic adoration is also an important development that shapes the medieval Church.[55] The Christianity of western Europe, both in its Catholic and Protestant varieties, would be transformed by both the Renaissance and the Reformation. It is important, though, not to retroject our twenty-first century understandings about what constitutes "superstition" versus "true religion." As Patrick Geary has said so well,

---

[54] Vogel, *Medieval Liturgy*, 163.
[55] See Mitchell, *Cult and Controversy*, 206–10.

Medieval religion was neither magic nor religion in the modern sense of these terms. More all-encompassing than modern, compartmentalized religion and less rationalized, codified, and articulated, medieval religion was an expression of a perception of the world, at times through joyous liturgical dance, at times through desperate physical abuse.[56]

It will be this essentially medieval practice of Christianity, with its popular forms of devotion existing alongside the official liturgical forms, that the first European missionaries will bring to the peoples of Africa, the Americas, and Asia during the so-called "age of discovery" of the fifteenth to seventeenth centuries.

[56] Geary, *Living with the Dead*, 127.

Chapter Six

The First Evangelization of the Americas

Worship and Popular Religion

The Spanish and Portuguese evangelization of the Americas in some ways echoes the Christianization of northern Europe during the early Middle Ages. The various aspects of the cultural and religious confrontation precipitated by the Spanish conquest of Central and South America are not unlike those of the conversion of the Germanic peoples in the ninth and tenth centuries at the hands of the Franks. Like the conversion of the Saxons accomplished predominantly by military force, the way in which Christianity "triumphed" among the native peoples of the Americas was partly due to coercion. While there were notable attempts to evangelize without force of arms,[1] it was the military dominance of the Spaniards coupled with a demoralization of a populace decimated by diseases brought by Europeans that produced a relatively swift religious transformation—at least superficially. As Orlando Espín points out:

> In a sacral world such as the sixteenth century's, where both the conquerors and the conquered believed that God was the ultimate explanation for every aspect of reality, to see the Amerindian world come to a humiliating defeat could easily be understood by the

---

[1] On attempts to peacefully evangelize the native peoples of the Americas, see Justo L. González, "Voices of Compassion," *Missiology: An International Review* 20, no. 2 (1992): 163–73.

vanquished in these religious categories the Spaniards also believed in. It must have been God's will to hand victory to Spain, and it must be that the Christian God is certainly mightier than all the traditional divinities. . . . Otherwise the conquest would not have been successful.[2]

While the new religion brought by the Europeans was gradually accepted by most of the native peoples of the Americas during the sixteenth century, it would be a mistake to think that these new converts did not interpret and transform the Christianity preached to them by the Franciscan, Dominican, and Augustinian friars charged by the Spanish crown to undertake this initial evangelization. Like the monks' preaching of the Gospel to the Saxons, the friars tried to make the faith intelligible to the peoples of the "New World" and in so doing helped produce a Christianity that not only reflected its immediate origin in Iberian Catholicism but also contained elements of Amerindian customs and traditions. In order to appreciate this *mestizaje* or "mixing" of Spanish and native elements, it is necessary to take a look at the kind of Catholicism that the Spaniards brought to the Americas and then consider the religious worldview of the peoples they evangelized.

Spanish Catholicism during the Age of Discovery

Spanish Christianity of the fifteenth and sixteenth centuries, while related to the Catholicism of western Europe, also differed from it in some important ways. Unlike the rest of the Latin Church, it knew a moment of real reform before Martin Luther nailed his Ninety-Five Theses to the door of the Wittenberg Castle church in 1517. Spanish Catholicism was especially inspired by religious orders such as the Franciscans. These orders exercised an important role in setting the spiritual standards for a period that was strongly marked by millennial expectations. The Spanish character was also shaped by centuries of armed struggle with the Moors, who were definitively defeated with the fall of Granada in 1492. The forced conversion of Moslems and Jews was a catalyst for developing catechetical approaches and materials that were later used in the New World, such as a brief revival of the

---

[2] Orlando Espín, "Trinitarian Monotheism and the Birth of Popular Catholicism: The Case for Sixteenth-Century Mexico," *Missiology: An International Review* 20, no. 2 (April 1992): 182.

ancient catechumenate. These aspects of the Spanish Church, prevalent before the reforms initiated by the Council of Trent at the end of the sixteenth century, characterize the particular medieval Catholicism that was brought to the Americas. It is helpful to take a closer look at these elements in order to understand better the faith that was brought by Spain to the Americas.

Prior to 1492, it would be difficult to imagine a less auspicious source for missionaries than Spain and the Spanish Church. After centuries of fighting against the Moors, and after a debilitating war with Portugal, Ferdinand of Aragon and Isabella of Castile (who would soon be monarchs of all of Spain) lamented in 1488 that "the Church has never been in such ruin and so badly ruled and governed as it is now; all the income that it should be spending on the poor and on charitable works is being wasted by the clergy on material matters, while the service of God and the good of the church are totally neglected."[3] For both reasons of state and a sincere desire to deal with the corruption of the Church, Queen Isabella especially promoted ecclesial reform.

The principal agent of this reform was Francisco Jiménez de Cisneros, a Franciscan who served as provincial of his order in Castile, and who later became archbishop of Toledo and primate of Spain from 1495 to 1517. He tried mightily to reform the diocesan clergy—many of whom lived lives that were far from edifying—but met with limited success. This was one of the reasons "for the progress of the religious orders, especially the mendicants, who came to form a spiritual elite to whom laymen looked as the true representatives of the Christian ideal."[4] It is not surprising, then, that both the Spanish crown and the Church would confide the evangelization of the world discovered by Columbus in 1492 to the reformed mendicant orders. After initial contact with the natives of the Caribbean islands, the evangelization of the American continent began in 1524 with the arrival of the "twelve Franciscan apostles," as they later became known. These twelve missionary Franciscans went to Mexico with a particular millennialist perspective. "They appear to have had millennial expectations, believing that the discovery and evangelization of the 'New World'—itself an eschatological term—was a sign of the approaching golden age of the Holy Spirit when the universal Church would be renewed in holy

---

[3] John Lynch, *New Worlds: A Religious History of Latin America* (New Haven, CT: Yale University Press, 2012), 1.

[4] Ibid., 3.

poverty and a way of life similar to that shared by the nascent church in the apostolic period."[5]

The Catholicism brought to the New World by the friars was essentially that of medieval Spain, influenced by the millennialism of Joachim of Fiore (+1202), a monk considered a prophet by many Franciscans who had predicted the conversion of the world by the preaching of new religious orders (later identified as the Franciscans and Dominicans). Many of the friars were convinced that the peoples of the New World were members of the lost tribe of Israel, who, once converted from their worship of idols, would be able to live a semimonastic life reminiscent of the reformers' image of the early Church. This presupposition about the "new order" made possible by the discovery of the New World would influence the approach to evangelization taken by these first missionaries who regarded many of the religious practices of the Amerindians as vestiges of the true faith that had been perverted by the devil.[6]

The Catholicism preached by the friars and conquistadores, however, was not only millennialist—it was also militant. Shaped by centuries of conflict with Islam, the fall of Granada in 1492 led to a revival of the crusading spirit and a desire to continue the reconquest of lands lost to the Moslems in North Africa. This new crusade was supported by both the Church and crown but soon lost steam after the discovery of the Americas. Expansion of the faith and colonization went hand-in-hand in the Spanish conquest of Central and South America. In the minds of many Spaniards, though, the conquest of these new lands was regarded as another kind of crusade. It was considered reasonable that the native peoples should submit to the political domination of the Spaniards since they came to bring the true religion (not to mention the other primary goal of the *conquista*: a search for gold).

Finally, this Catholicism shared the general characteristics of medieval Western Christianity. The vast majority of the people were marginally literate or illiterate. Theirs was a folk religion, based on

---

[5] Jaime Lara, "Roman Catholics in Hispanic America," in *The Oxford History of Christian Worship*, ed. Geoffrey Wainwright and Karen B. Westerfield Tucker (New York: Oxford University Press, 2006), 633.

[6] See Lara's more extensive discussion of the influence of Joachim of Fiore on the early missionaries in *City, Temple, Stage: Eschatological Architecture and Liturgical Theatrics in New Spain* (Notre Dame, IN: University of Notre Dame Press, 2004), 53–59.

custom and tradition rather than on the written word, and far from the more uniform Roman Catholicism that would later develop after the Council of Trent. "The Spanish people were inspired by a traditional religiosity accumulated from the past, as they flocked to mass, processions, shrines, and other popular devotions, unperturbed by the glaring abuses, dysfunctional clergy, and their own sinfulness. This was the *religiosidad popular* in which the conquerors of Mexico and Peru were also formed and which stirred their sense of mission."[7]

The practices of popular religion, a distinctive part of medieval, Iberian Christianity, would serve as the point of contact between the two worlds. Like the methods adopted by the first missionaries to evangelize the Germanic peoples of northern Europe, the Spanish missionaries imported celebrations practiced in Spain in light of the customs and mentality of the Amerindians. It was this adaptation that became crucial to native people's acceptance of the new faith. As Luis Weckman notes,

> Religious festivities, the holidays *par excellence* until the nineteenth century (and, to a certain extent, even today, especially in rural areas) combined in many instances Christian purposes and pagan ceremonies in a process of syncretism that the practical genius of the church fostered in Europe in the era that followed the Germanic migrations. The old practice of the church in medieval Europe of building Christian sanctuaries on the site of heathen sacred abodes, was repeated in Mexico, where many a church of today is built upon a pagan pyramid. Religious theater, especially that celebrated in the *atria* of churches—in many instances today, the *atrium* of the local church, is still the center of town life—is also remindful of medieval practices.[8]

This traditional religiosity—millennial, militant, and medieval—brought to the New World by the Spanish missionaries and soldiers in the sixteenth century and transformed by them and the peoples who embraced it shaped what will later be called Hispanic or Latino Catholicism.[9] This third reality came about by the fusion of religious

---

[7] Lynch, *New Worlds*, 4.

[8] Luis Weckman, "The Middle Ages in the Conquest of America," *Speculum* 26, no. 1 (January 1951): 138.

[9] See, for example, Virgilio Elizondo's classic work, *Christianity and Culture* (San Antonio, TX: Mexican American Cultural Center, 1975), 115–24; and Orlando Espín, "Trinitarian Monotheism," 177–204.

symbols and attitudes from Iberian medieval Catholicism with elements from Native American and, later, African provenance.[10] It seems clear to most observers that the religiosity that developed among the conquered people of the Americas, while related to the devotionalism of rural Spain, contains elements unique to the Americas.[11] It is to the religious worldview of the natives of the American continent that we now turn.

The Amerindian Religious World and Spanish Catholicism

In making a comparison between native religions—the Germanic religions encountered by Mediterranean Christian missionaries in the eighth to tenth centuries on the one hand, and the pre-Colombian religions of the Aztecs, Mayas, and Incas (to name the principal cultures) encountered by Iberian Catholics on the other—the native religions of the New World appeared closer to the religious vision of the evangelizers. Time and again, many of the friars noted that Christian practices and even symbols like the cross were mysteriously present in the Americas before the arrival of the missionaries. The friars attributed this to the native peoples being part of the lost tribe of Israel, or to the preaching of the apostles Thomas and Bartholomew who supposedly reached the shores of the Americas in the first century.[12] Virgil Elizondo has noted the striking similarities between the religions of the peoples of the New World and Spanish Christianity by listing the rites of the natives that were similar to sacraments of baptism, confession, and Communion.[13] The missionaries saw a natural affinity between the

---

[10] There are, of course, other elements in this *mestizaje*. The *conversos* (converted Jews) and *moriscos* (former Muslims) also came to the New World with distinct religious outlooks. The influence of the people of the Philippines needs to be considered as well because of the political and commercial connections between these islands and Mexico once they were conquered by Spain.

[11] See William Christian, "Spain in Latino Religiosity," in *El Cuerpo de Cristo: The Hispanic Presence in the U.S. Catholic Church*, eds. Peter Casarella and Raúl Gómez (New York: Crossroad, 1998), 325–30. Christian questions the uniqueness of much of Hispanic popular religion, positing more continuity with Spanish religious practices and worldview than is admitted by other authors. I find much of his argument unconvincing. See, for example, Orlando Espín, *The Faith of the People: Theological Reflections on Popular Catholicism* (Maryknoll, NY: Orbis, 1997).

[12] Lynch, *New Worlds*, 7.

[13] Elizondo, *Christianity and Culture*, 116–19.

native religion and many other Christian practices and beliefs, explaining the differences as a result of a later corruption introduced by people influenced by the devil.

There is, of course, no historical evidence for a pre-Colombian evangelization of the Americas. The religions of the peoples of Central and South America, while sharing characteristics of Iberian medieval Catholicism, were based on quite different presuppositions about the relationship of human beings to the divine and with the cosmos. These practices and beliefs, however, developed in a premodern, agricultural world that was not totally unlike that of Spain. Let us take the Nahua religion of Mesoamerica as our primary point of comparison.

The dominant ethnic group of Meso-America at the time of the conquest was the Nahuas. The term *Nahua* encompasses several different tribes present in Central America, the most famous of which was the war-like Mexica or Aztecs, whose center of power was Tenochtitlán (present-day Mexico City) from where they exacted tribute and prisoners for sacrifice from the surrounding peoples. At the time of the conquest, the Nahua were an extremely religious people worshiping a pantheon of gods and goddesses, many of whom demanded human sacrifice in order to maintain the world in its course and prevent catastrophe. The principal function of their complex calendar of ceremonies and festivals held through the year was to supply the gods with human blood and human lives in order to conserve the cosmos. "Eating" was the way in which both gods and human beings appropriated the sacrifices. Ritual cannibalism, then, was a logical and sanctioned part of the religious worldview.[14]

The numerous gods of the Aztecs, both male and female, personified the earth, the heavens, and natural forces such as rain, thunder, wind, fire, fertility, death, and war. They created and they also destroyed. They had to be appeased—by offerings of prayer, song, flowers—and human lives. There seems to have been an official, communal, and cultic level of the religion, overseen by the priests and the nobles, and a domestic or "popular" level that formed the belief system of the majority of the people who were commoners. Doctrine and other technical aspects of the religion do not seem to have been that important to the common people, and there was some diversity in the way the religion was practiced and explained.[15]

---

[14] See David Carrasco, "Cosmic Jaws: We Eat the Gods and the Gods Eat Us," *Journal of the American Academy of Religion* 63, no. 3 (Autumn 1995), 429–63.

[15] Lara, *City, Temple, Stage*, 3.

The lore concerning one god, in particular—Quetzalcóatl, the feathered serpent god associated with priests, artists, and merchants—is reputed to have played an important role in the conquest. We know many of the stories associated with this god through Bernardino de Sahagún's *General History of the Things of New Spain*, where the god is described as having been banished because of his opposition to human sacrifice and "as a hero who moved across time and space and was due to return from the east to Mexico in 1519, the year in which Hernán Cortés invaded the lands of the Mexica."[16] As Lara notes, he is the god that descended "from the summit Ometeotl, the heavenly mountain, resplendent beyond imagining, beyond thought . . . an incarnation of the Inconceivable [on] the axial ladder let down through an opening in the middle of the sky, as though from the golden sun-door of noon to the navel of the earth." Furthermore, in a striking parallel to Jesus, he is depicted wearing a crown of agave thorns and solemnly declaring at the moment of his self-sacrifice, "This is my blood."[17]

In addition to Quetzalcóatl, who was variously associated with both St. Thomas and the Conquistador Cortés, other Mexican gods and goddesses would be reinterpreted by subsequent generations as manifestations of Christian saints. The most famous example is the association between Tonantzin, the mother goddess, whose shrine was located on the hill of Tepeyac north of Mexico City, and the Virgin Mary, identified under the title of Our Lady of Guadalupe and venerated at the basilica that was eventually built on that very hill.

The Aztecs had basic commandments that paralleled the decalogue of the Hebrew Scriptures: to honor the gods, to honor fathers and mothers, not to kill, not to commit adultery or to steal. The Nahuas were used to the practice of elaborate religious processions. They had a complex calendar of feasts. They used water in rites of purification and even engaged in a kind of "communion" by eating bits of bread believed to be the flesh of a god. These and other practices convinced the friars that the peoples of Mesoamerica had received a revelation from the true God, however incomplete, before the coming of the Spaniards.

As James Lockhart and others have pointed out, while the content of Christianity was different from the polytheistic religions of the New World, the two religions shared many similar elements that must have

---

[16] Lynch, *New Worlds*, 9.
[17] Lara, *City, Temple, Stage*, 4.

made evangelization much easier than it had been centuries earlier in northern Europe.

> The friars had stepped into a situation already made for them. . . . The extent of their success depended precisely upon the acceptance and retention of indigenous elements and patterns which in many respects were strikingly close to those of Europe. Relatively few of the friars' innovations were entirely new to the Mesoamericans. It was because of such things as their own crafts and writing systems, their tradition of sumptuous temples as symbols of state and ethnic groups, their well developed calendar of religious festivities and processions . . . that they could quickly take to similar aspects of the Spanish heritage.[18]

Using the metaphor of language, Jaime Vidal has offered the helpful analogy to explain that while there were differences between the two religious views, the Christianity preached by the friars was foreign but comprehensible to the natives of Mexico. While the vocabulary or content of the two religions was different, according to Vidal, they both shared a common "grammar":

> In many respects, the native religions and Iberian popular Catholicism shared a common emotional and psychological "grammar" in which their different religious contents were expressed. Religious expressions were rooted in agricultural cycles, kinship relations and rituals expressing joy, grief, and other deeply felt human emotions; a sense of the special sacredness of certain times, places or persons, was found both in Iberian Catholicism and in the native religions. In the practice of their very different beliefs, both Spanish and native societies constructed meaning by ordering these experiences, like grammar is necessary to make coherent sense of nouns and verbs.[19]

It was undoubtedly true that at the beginning of the sixteenth century, just when the missionaries were convinced that the natives had sincerely embraced the new religion, they sometimes discovered that

---

[18] James Lockhart, "Some Nahua Concepts in Postconquest Guise," *History of European Ideas* 6, no. 4 (1985), 465–82.

[19] Jaime Vidal, "Towards an Understanding of Synthesis in Iberian Hispanic Popular Religiosity," in *An Enduring Flame: Studies on Latino Popular Religiosity*, ed. Antonio Stevens Arroyo and Ana María Díaz-Stevens (New York: Bildner Center, 1994), 71.

"at night the Indians continued to meet and call upon the devil and celebrate his feasts with many and diverse ancient rites."[20] This kind of "backsliding" and obvious syncretism most probably took place for several generations, yet it would be an error to conclude that the conversion of the Native Americans to Spanish Christianity was always deficient or insincere. The example of the veneration of the Virgin Mary as Our Lady of Guadalupe is a case in point. "Rather than *confusing* Mary with Tonantzin in a syncretism of content, the similar 'grammar' of religious expression allows the native to *replace* Mary for Tonantzin. I believe it is possible to limit syncretization to the 'grammar' of religious expression, while at the theological level a true *conversion* (i.e., change in the *object* of one's worship) occurs."[21] Vidal calls this process "synthesization," which he defines as "the eventual acceptance of religious content of theologically orthodox Spanish Catholicism on the part of the native population, mediated by the psychological acceptability of the religious forms of Mediterranean Catholicism (popular and/or institutional) to this population."[22]

How did this "synthesization" work itself out in terms of popular religious practices and liturgy? It is here that it is helpful to abandon our sharp distinction between liturgy and popular devotion in order to more completely understand how Christianity was first appropriated by the people of the Americas. As we saw with the birth of the Roman Rite in the fourth and fifth centuries occurring alongside the older and deeply popular *refrigeria* meals, a parallel popular form of Christianity developed in New Spain alongside the liturgy and the other religious practices directly overseen by the Church authorities. This "popular church" is the direct result of the kind of Catholicism imported to the New World and the way it was received by the native peoples.

The First Period of Evangelization: Liturgy and Popular Religion

There is a general consensus among historians that the evangelization of the Americas can be divided into two distinct periods. As we have noted, the first period, characterized by the leadership of the Franciscans, Dominicans, and Augustinians, essentially preached a medieval Christianity. Before the Council of Trent mandated a greater

---

[20] Lynch, *New Worlds*, 13.
[21] Vidal, "Toward an Understanding of Synthesis," 71.
[22] Ibid., 73.

standardization of the liturgy at the end of the sixteenth century, it was only natural that the friars would have brought to the New World much more "flexible" medieval worship practices—some of which would be later condemned by the Council of Trent and consequently banned in the Americas. The Rite of Mass itself, celebrated in Latin, may not have been terribly compelling to the native peoples, but the elements that surrounded its celebration—art, music, movement, drama—attracted the religious sympathy of the new converts. Fray Juan de Zumárraga, first archbishop of Mexico, commented in a letter to Emperor Charles V, for example, that "music had made more converts than preaching had."[23]

Local medieval customs such as the use of a "liturgical dragon" carried on a pole in penitential processions that originally came from Salisbury (Sarum) in England were introduced into Mexico by friars who had experienced them locally in Spain.[24] The friars also brought the widespread medieval practice of the "Missa sicca" or "dry Mass" to the Americas. This was the practice of celebrating a Mass with all of its elements except for the consecration of the bread and wine. In place of the host and chalice a cross or a relic was elevated at that moment of the liturgy. This was a practice that developed for long sea voyages where there was a fear that the consecrated wine would be spilled. Jaime Lara notes, though, that there is evidence to suggest that the friars "taught their lay leaders or catechists to celebrate dry Masses when there were no priests available. There are reports of indigenous laymen donning alb and chasuble for the ceremony. Later Church councils condemned the practice more than once, a fact that indicates that it was very popular and not so easily suppressed."[25] It was also a common practice to stage dramas within the liturgy to illustrate the biblical readings and keep the attention of the native peoples—again, not unlike the dramatic elements introduced in the Roman Rite by the Franco-Germanic liturgists.

Other distinctive liturgical practices imported by the friars were elements of the liturgical rite of Spain called the Visigothic or Mozarabic

---

[23] Quoted in Robert Ricard, *The Spiritual Conquest of Mexico* (Berkeley: University of California Press, 1974), 168.

[24] Jaime Lara, "The Liturgical Roots of Hispanic Popular Religion," in *Misa, Mesa y Musa: Liturgy in the U.S. Hispanic Church*, ed. Kenneth G. Davis (Chicago: World Library Publications, 1997), 27.

[25] Ibid., 29.

Rite.[26] This distinctive way of worship, not unlike the Gallican Rite we saw in the previous chapter, differed from the Roman Rite that was imposed on Spain during the eleventh century at the insistence of Pope Gregory VII. While the Roman Rite became the standard rite for Spain, several churches in Toledo and a chapel in the cathedral were permitted to continue to use the Mozarabic Rite. Local usages based on this rite were retained even in those areas that were forced to adopt the Roman Rite. In particular, liturgical elements of the Mozarabic rite of marriage were popular and were included in the *Manual de adultos*[27] for priests (a ritual book containing the celebration of marriage and baptism). The *Manual* was used until the 1560s by the first missionaries in Mexico. In addition to rites of betrothal, during the rite of marriage the custom of giving arras (thirteen coins) by the groom to the bride to indicate his pledge of material support, the use of the lazo (cord or rope to unite the couple), the solemn handing over of the bride, and the veiling of the bride and the groom's shoulder all became common parts of the marriage rite in New Spain, even though they were not part of the Roman Rite. Ironically, although considered today as "popular religious expressions," they have their origin in the formal liturgical practices of the Mozarabic Rite.[28]

The *Manual* was also inspired by the *Liber Sacerdotalis* (priests' handbook) of the Dominican Albert Castellani. The *Liber Sacerdotalis* had been prepared for mass conversion of Muslims and Jews in southern Europe and contained rites for an adult catechumenate. The *Manual* specified that the catechumenate would begin in mid-Lent (or mid-Eastertide when baptism was scheduled for Pentecost). It went beyond Castellani in that it contained directives that the texts used should be translated into the vernacular languages, and that the catechumens be welcomed with great warmth. Exorcisms and rites of dismissal of

---

[26] Both names are somewhat inadequate. The term "Visigothic" is misleading since many elements of the Rite antedate the coming of the Visigoths to Spain. "Mozarabic" refers to the Christians who lived under the yoke of the Muslims after the Arab conquest of Spain in the eighth century.

[27] This ritual book was commissioned by the three mendicant orders of Vasco de Quiroga, bishop of Michoacán, and published in 1540.

[28] See the useful pastoral reference by Raúl Gómez, Heliodoro Lucatero, and Sylvia Sánchez, *Gifts and Promise: Customs and Traditions in Hispanic Rites of Marriage* (Portland, OR: Oregon Catholic Press, 1997); and Mark Francis and Arturo Pérez-Rodriguez, *Primero Dios: Hispanic Liturgical Resource* (Chicago: Liturgy Training Publications, 1997), 95–118.

the catechumens during Mass were provided and adapted for the large number of converts who were assembled in the many open-air evangelization centers set up by the three mendicant orders throughout Mexico, many examples of which are still extant.[29]

In their evangelizing activities, the friars attempted to "translate" Christian concepts and truths of the faith in a manner that would make sense to the native peoples. For example, in trying to convey the centrality and importance of the Eucharist, the missionaries drew on the pagan Mesoamerican sacral relationship of the sun god Tecatlipoca feeding on the blood of sacrificial victims in order to maintain the stability of the world to explain Christ's sacrifice celebrated in the Mass liturgy and his blood shed for the redemption of humankind. The crosses, erected in the open-air evangelization centers, were adorned not only with the instruments of the passion but with an obsidian mirror in the central axis, a sign of the old sun god. "Such mirrors on crosses could not but be read by the indigenous populations as the solar symbols whose vital liquid was, in the Christian dispensation, the blood of the voluntary victim of Golgotha.[30]

Probably the most popular and enduring of these adaptations was the introduction of drama, music, and dance as a means of both worship and instruction. Two major examples are the Christmastime traditions of *las posadas* and the *pastorelas*. The Augustinian invention of *las posadas*—a dramatic reenactment held during the days before Christmas in which "Mary" and "Joseph" seek lodging for a place to give birth to Jesus at the houses in the neighborhood—is a prime example of how the Gospel was literally brought to the people. While related to the medieval Spanish *Officium Pastorum* or "office of the shepherds"—a play used at Christmas—the Mexican *pastorelas* were also accepted with enthusiasm by the newly converted natives who were already accustomed to religious drama. They were then reinterpreted to reflect their own particular cosmology.[31] For these reasons they continue to be popular to this day in many parts of the Hispanic world.

---

[29] On both the (temporarily) restored Catechumenate in the *Manual* and the architecture employed for mass conversions, see Jaime Lara, *City, Temple, Stage,* 17–39.

[30] "The Sacramented Sun: Solar Eucharistic Worship in Colonial Latin America," in *El Cuerpo de Cristo: The Hispanic Presence in the U.S. Catholic Church,* ed. Peter Casarella and Raúl Gómez (New York: Crossroad, 1998), 272–73.

[31] See Alejandro García-Rivera, "The Whole and the Love of Difference: Latino Metaphysics as Cosmology," in Orlando Espín and Miguel Díaz, *From the*

Corpus Christi processions, usually accompanied by costumed actors playing personages from salvation history with music and dancing, became a staple in celebrating the period after Easter. These were often accompanied by entertaining mock battles danced between the "Christians" and "Muslims" (or angels and demons). Palm Sunday and Holy Thursday processions, with their inherent dramatic moments, as well as the *Via Crucis Viviente* (Living Way of the Cross) or reenactment of the suffering and death of Jesus, have long been among the central events of Holy Week. This "Jesus of the Triduum," as Roberto Goizueta has named him, is both central and pervasive in the religious imagination of Hispanics, aided by the yearly drama that involves the whole community in his suffering and death.[32]

Thus, the friars did not limit themselves to the strictly "liturgical" celebrations such as the Rite of Mass and the celebration of the other sacraments in their efforts at evangelization. Drawing on their experience back in Spain of a Christianity that permeated all of life, they were able to present to the Amerindians celebrations and observances that were omnipresent, sacralizing every moment of life. In some ways, it was the more "popular" Spanish practices, duly adapted to the New World, that offered the best and easiest form of what we today would call "inculturation." As Lara notes, "liturgical celebrations of the church year were supplemented by events and practices of a more popular nature, which nevertheless had the task of gradually permeating the life of new communities with a new Christian identity. These practices included, among others, a flourishing veneration of the saints, various prayers to the Name of Jesus and to the Holy Cross, and the late medieval innovations of the Stations of the Cross and the rosary."[33]

It is important to note that while some efforts of the friars and their native collaborators would be suppressed at the end of the

---

Heart of Our People (Maryknoll: Orbis, 1999), 67–74. See also Miguel Arias, Mark Francis, and Arturo Pérez, *La Navidad Hispana: Christmas at Home and at Church* (Chicago: Liturgy Training Publications, 2000). Another example of drama incorporated into worship was the development of the Christmas *Posadas* by the Augustinians in the sixteenth century. See a wonderful reflection on this Christmas devotion by Virgilio Elizondo, "Living Faith: Resistance and Survival," in *Mestizo Worship: A Pastoral Approach to Liturgical Ministry* (Collegeville, MN: Liturgical Press, 1998), 5–12.

[32] See Roberto S. Goizueta, *Caminemos con Jesús: Toward a Hispanic/Latino Theology of Accompaniment* (Maryknoll, NY: Orbis, 1995), 32.

[33] Lara, "Roman Catholics in Hispanic America," 642.

sixteenth century after the enforcement of more rigid principles of the Counter-Reformation, their attempts at inculturation were done with discernment and with the participation of the native peoples themselves. The people were not just passive recipients of the Christian faith but actively engaged in the new religion's interpretation and transmission. Like the missionaries to the Germanic peoples before them who were challenged to interpret the faith to a different culture, the mendicants operated out of two general principles: dynamic equivalence and ritual substitution. After thoroughly learning the native languages and working with Nahua *literati*, they purposely sought pre-Columbian rites and religious objects which were not objectively tied to idolatry and which could be given a new Christian interpretation without too much catechesis. "Thus, feathers, flowers, mirrors, jewelry, dances, musical instruments, poetic expressions, geography were reworked to accommodate them to the new religion. In short, a resacralization of Mesoamerican space and time had occurred by the end of the sixteenth century when the new religion began to think out loud in the Amerindian culture."[34]

It could however be argued that while elements of the faith were inculturated for catechetical purposes through popular religious practices during this period, the eucharistic liturgy as the central rite of the Church remained only acculturated—simply juxtaposed to native cultural elements—especially after the canons and decrees of the Council of Trent were implemented at the end of the sixteenth century. Performed in Latin with only clerical celebrants actively engaged in the rite, the native peoples sometimes participated in the rite itself with song and dances, but increasingly after the 1560s, their actions were progressively moved to the periphery of the liturgy itself. In the Hispanic world of the Western Hemisphere, the later century of the *colonia* saw only a superficial dialogue between the local cultures and the core of the Catholic *liturgical* tradition. Much like the *matachines* or groups of Native American sacred dancers who still dance outside the church building in many parts of Mexico and the southwestern United States at special celebrations, the culture of indigenous America never penetrated the rubrical wall set up by the Tridentine reforms intended to protect the Rite of Mass from abuses and errors. The Roman Rite, as it was presented, was a form of worship performed largely by Europeans and regulated by rubrics that rendered it impervious to the influence of the surrounding culture(s).

---

[34] Jaime Lara, *Christian Texts for Aztecs: Art and Liturgy in Colonial Mexico* (Notre Dame, IN: University of Notre Dame Press, 2008), 260.

Planting the Seeds of a Church Sustained by Popular Religion

It is useful to return at this point to our previous distinction between the levels of "official" and "public" meaning. Highlighting this distinction is especially important when one cultural group among many has the authority to control what is "official." This was clearly the case in colonial Spanish America, where the European evangelizers determined "correct" and "orthodox" expressions of the faith, while the Amerindian who were "evangelized" did not have an "official" say in this determination. During the first hundred and fifty years of the conquest of the Americas, after an initial optimism voiced by the friars that after due instruction the natives would be spiritually mature enough to be ordained, the promotion of an indigenous priesthood was abandoned. At the end of the sixteenth century the Franciscan Jerónimo de Mendieta voiced a commonly held belief among the Spaniards that "the majority of the Indians are of a strange nature, different from that of other nations (although I do not know if some of the Greeks share this same quality), which is that they are not good for leading and ruling but rather for being led and ruled."[35]

Mendieta's opinion of the spiritual maturity of the native peoples reflects decisions made by Mexican Church councils in 1555 and 1585 and affirmed by a royal decree to deny major orders to both natives and those of mixed European and Indian blood (*castas*). Stafford Poole states that "in 1585 the bishops of New Spain clearly intended to exclude all Indians and *castas* from the priesthood without any qualification whatever. This exclusion was based on social reality and social prejudice. Indian, mestizo, and mulatto priests would not have been acceptable in most parts of New Spain and would not have fitted the hierarchical conceptions of the priestly state at that time."[36] While the Holy See was not in agreement with this categorical exclusion, because of the right of the Spanish crown to govern in Church affairs (*Patronado Réal*) this decision held sway for many centuries, thereby denying the native and mestizo population "official" religious power.

---

[35] "[U]n natural extraño que tienen por la mayor parte los indios, diferente del de otras naciones (aunque no sé si participan de él algunos de los griegos) que no son buenos para mandar ni regir, sino para ser mandados y regidos" (Mendieta, *Historia ecclesiástica Indiana*, 4.23; 3.103, quoted in Osvaldo F. Pardo, *The Origins of Mexican Catholicism* [Ann Arbor: University of Michigan Press, 2006], 50).

[36] Stafford Poole, "Church Law on the Ordination of Indians and *Castas* in New Spain," *Hispanic American Historical Review* 61, no. 4 (November 1981): 649–50.

What was the consequence of this decision? The Mass was something done by the *padres*, and the *padres* by definition were not of the people during the colonial period. Over the course of the decades and centuries, the number of priests—who had to be either *peninsulares* (Spaniards born in Spain) or *criollos* (men of "pure" Spanish blood born in the New World)—were never sufficient to meet the pastoral needs of the population. It is for this reason that the sacramentals and popular religious practices assumed an even greater importance in the spiritual lives of the people of New Spain, since these religious expressions did not depend on the leadership of a priest. This is not to say that the people did not hold the Mass and sacraments ministered by the priest in high esteem and attend Mass when it was periodically available—especially in remote rural areas. But, as Virgilio Elizondo points out, it was their involvement in expressions of popular religion, and especially for Mexicans their veneration of Our Lady of Guadalupe, that safeguarded the faith of generations.[37] As Elizondo reminds us, "The deepest identity of the people is expressed in those expressions of faith which are celebrated voluntarily by the majority of the people, transmitted from generation to generation by the people themselves, and go on with the Church, without it, or even in spite of it."[38]

The Church in Latin America, in some ways, is a Church that was lay-led for centuries. In the early centuries the local caciques or chiefs and later the mayors and officials of small towns were the ones to finance and organize processions and other public religious observances—especially if there was not a resident priest. Among the Maya, their "elite dominated both the organization of processions, rituals, and feast days, and funded the expenses through the income derived from communal lands set aside for that purpose. The same men, descendants of pre-conquest rulers and priests, led their people in the new religion as majordomos of confraternities and caciques of their villages."[39]

---

[37] See Virgilio Elizondo, "Popular Religion as Support of Identity: A Pastoral-Psychological Case-Study Based on the Mexican American Experience in the U.S.A.," *Concilium: Popular Religion*, vol. 186, ed. Norbert Greinacher and Norbert Mette (Edinburgh: T&T Clark, 1986): 36–43; and *La Morenita: Evangelizer of the Americas* (San Antonio: Mexican American Cultural Center, 1976).

[38] Virgilio Elizondo, "Popular Religion as the Core of Cultural Identity Based on the Mexican American Experience in the United States," in *An Enduring Flame: Studies on Latino Popular Religiosity*, ed. Antonio Stevens Arroyo and Ana María Díaz-Stevens (New York: Bildner Center, 1994), 117.

[39] Lynch, *New Worlds*, 18.

Conclusion

In this chapter we have seen how Christianity was again transformed so as to speak to the peoples of the Americas. Because of the manner of the evangelization promoted by the friars who substituted popular Christian religious expressions for similar pre-Columbian Nahua customs and beliefs, our modern distinctions between liturgy and popular piety would probably not have been readily understood by either the Spanish missionaries or the Amerindians. It was the "popular" elements used by the friars and their native collaborators—in both their catechesis on the sacraments of baptism, Eucharist, and penance and in their more general Christian explanation of space and time—that made the message of the Gospel understandable to the Nahuas. These popular elements were a part of their larger worldview that sacralized the Amerindian universe. While the various definitions of popular religious expressions made by the *Directory on Popular Piety and Liturgy* are helpful, they cannot be taken as absolutes. The holistic sense of the sacred is still part of the spiritual heritage of the Hispanic/Latino peoples that needs to be accounted for in order for pastoral and liturgical ministry to be effective.

Much more could be said of the first evangelization of the Maya, Incas, and other indigenous peoples who were evangelized by the Spanish and the Portuguese in the sixteenth century. It would be fascinating to parallel the experience of the Spanish missionaries in the Americas with what they encountered in the Philippine Islands, since many of the same Iberian customs were imported and transformed in a parallel fashion by the peoples of East Asia, reflecting the genius of their cultures.[40] The "synthesis" of beliefs and customs that occurred in places such as Haiti, Cuba, and Brazil with their large number of Africans makes the *mestizaje* of peoples and beliefs all the more complex.[41] In a real sense, the popular religious expressions that were born of this

---

[40] One example is the Advent *Misa de Aguinaldo* that becomes the *Simbang Gabi* series of votive Masses in honor of the Blessed Virgin shared by both Hispanic America and the Philippines. See Dennis Estrella, "A Historico-Critical Evaluation of the Philippine Simbang Gabi Liturgical Custom" (license thesis, Pontifical Liturgical Institute of Saint Anselm, Rome, 2009).

[41] It is important to note the continued dynamism of syncretic religions such as Umbanda and Candomblé in Brazil, Santería in Cuba, and Voudún in Haiti—all of which represent examples of cultural resistance to the Christianity imposed by the Europeans.

confrontation of cultures of the sixteenth century continued to develop in the succeeding centuries and help to explain why Hispanic (and Filipino) Catholicism has understood itself using different "public" and "private" meanings than the Catholicism of the European immigrants who came to the shores of North America several centuries later with related but different expressions of popular religiosity.

Chapter Seven

The Transformation of Popular Religion after the Council of Trent

This chapter will explore the relationship of liturgy and popular religion in the nineteenth and early twentieth centuries. However, in order to understand how the relationship between liturgy and popular religion was transformed, it is essential to first examine how the Council of Trent (1545–1563) significantly changed the spiritual and liturgical landscape during the period of the Counter-Reformation. Indeed, those who call into question an intentional "discontinuity" of Church practice and discipline brought about by the Second Vatican Council would probably be surprised at the extent of the disciplinary and pastoral "discontinuities" that were mandated by Trent. We have already noted some of the changes in the liturgy celebrated in New Spain once the more strict liturgical decrees of the Counter-Reformation were implemented after the 1560s.

It is important to remember how the reforms launched by the Council of Trent changed the relationship between the liturgical life of the Church and lay people in Europe—and their descendants in the United States. We will examine the nineteenth-century renaissance of popular devotional practice encouraged by Church authorities that occurred simultaneously with the massive European immigration to the United States. Euro-Catholic devotional life served as an important way in which the new immigrants maintained their identity and coped with the challenges posed by an often hostile Protestant majority. The devotional life of Catholics in the nineteenth and twentieth centuries was also influenced by the concern of the papacy to both promote and control the "extra-liturgical" life of the faithful.

We will then discuss various attempts at reforming the liturgy itself (as well as popular religious practices) that took place during the centuries that followed the Council of Trent. The Synod of Pistoia at the end of the eighteenth century and the birth of the classic liturgical movement in the nineteenth century will both attempt to place the liturgy, not devotions, as the focus of lay participation in worship—with limited success.

The chapter will conclude by speaking about the liturgical movement and its critique of Catholic devotional life and how this movement serves as an important backdrop to how the Constitution on the Sacred Liturgy of the Second Vatican Council will eventually regard popular religious practices.

The Council of Trent: Liturgy and Popular Religion

The state of worship in the years before the Council of Trent is a subject of divergent scholarly opinions. Historians of worship generally describe the liturgical situation of the late Middle Ages as being rather chaotic. The chaos was caused by not only the diversity of liturgical customs from diocese to diocese and from country to country but also questionable worship practices like the *missa sicca* described in the previous chapter. Although the Roman Rite was imposed in many places in Western Europe during the reign of Gregory VII (+1085) and his successors, most Church authorities did not consider local variations terribly problematic. Many dioceses in France and religious orders such as the Benedictines, Dominicans, and Carthusians had their own liturgical "uses" that continue into the present century. The possibility of a greater uniformity of liturgical life in the whole Latin Church was never considered before the fifteenth century, for the simple reason that such standardization would have been impossible without the new technology of printing and movable type pioneered by Gutenberg in 1450.

The growth of spiritual movements during the late Middle Ages such as the *devotio moderna* tended to encourage a more individualistic piety. While acknowledging the importance of the sacraments, these movements neglected the importance of the liturgy itself as a source for spirituality.[1] This lack of a more communal, spiritual perspective is not surprising because the medieval organization of the Church—the reform of which was to be a major theme at the Council of Trent—was

---

[1] See DPPL, 34.

much more diffuse. As John Bossy points out, there was a simple but crucial distinction between the late medieval experience of Church and that of the post-Tridentine period. "The Church of the last medieval centuries was not in actual fact a parochially grounded institution."[2]

Liturgical historians such as Marcel Metzger and Theodor Klauser and social historian Philippe Ariès echo many other scholars by emphasizing that at the end of the Middle Ages, the religious life of most people was not sustained by parishes. In reality, most people expressed their faith on two very distinct levels. For lay people, especially in rural areas, processions, pilgrimages, and the cult of the relics were at least as important as the sacraments. There were more elite religious movements around monasteries and cities where smaller numbers of Christians—lay and clerical—were inspired by a more interior and personal piety that often centered around the suffering Christ.[3] The parish church was not really the primary point of reference for either group of Christians.

Other historians, however, notably Eamon Duffy and John Bossy, while acknowledging that parishes may not have been central to the religious expression of medieval Christians, challenge the assumption that the liturgy was marginalized as a source for the religious imagination of the late Middle Ages. In his examinations of documents such as prayer books and other records that have survived from late medieval and Reformation England, Duffy states rather categorically that "the liturgy was in fact the principal reservoir from which the religious paradigms and beliefs of the people were drawn."[4]

How can we make sense of these very different historical interpretations of the liturgy's influence on the religious imagination of the late Middle Ages? The key is found by looking at the central place in the piety and practice that the Eucharist occupied just before the Reformation. Miri Rubin, in fact, regards the Eucharist itself, and not the parish, as an organizing "institution" for the whole of medieval society

[2] John Bossy, "The Counter-Reformation and the People of Catholic Europe," *The Past and Present Society* 47 (1970): 53.

[3] See Marcel Metzger, *History of the Liturgy: Major Stages* (Collegeville, MN: Liturgical Press, 1997), 133; Theador Klauser, *A Short History of the Western Liturgy: An Account and Some Reflections* (Oxford, UK: Oxford University Press 1979), 120; Philippe Ariès, "Religion Populaire et Réformes Religieuses," *La Maison Dieu* 122 (1975): 84–97.

[4] Eamon Duffy, *The Stripping of the Altars: Traditional Religion in England 1400–1580* (New Haven, CT: Yale University Press, 1992), 2.

that both described and prescribed basic societal relationships. "Power defined the center of the discussion: the sacrament was a central symbol or test of orthodoxy and dissent throughout the later Middle Ages. Christ's presence in the sacrament, the need for sacerdotal mediation, the practice of gazing at the sacrament, the notion of certain inherent magical properties of the host, the body of Christ: all these could be crucial tests. And we find them conducted by people across the social spectrum."[5] Moreover, there is real evidence to suggest that even though the late medieval Mass was attended by many of the faithful outside of the structure of local parishes, it was more participatory than some historians of the liturgy would usually allow. Bossy maintains that "if we take the late medieval mass on its own terms, not as a service of instruction nor a liturgical fossil but a contemporary and evolving social ritual, we may agree that it involved a good deal of participation."[6]

What was the nature of this participation? Nathan Mitchell clarifies the way lay people entered into the celebration of the Mass. "It might be said . . . that medieval laypersons participated in the eucharist not so much by 'understanding' the words and rites but by 'observing proper demeanor toward its Lord and his acts.' " Taking the medieval Mass on its own terms, as Bossy suggests, leads Mitchell to assert,

> The mass meant what it did to lay participants at least in part because it was conducted in a ritual language of gestures and symbols they knew from secular life. Some of these gestures and symbols were learned from family and village life, some from the marketplace, some from the royal court. In effect, medieval lay participants "understood" the liturgy with their bodies, and so their connection to the ritual flowed from a rich layering of associations, of social relationships and rituals expressing those relationships.[7]

This "kinesthetic" or "bodily" participation is very much the way the majority of Christians engaged in popular religious customs as well—more through ritual action and emotions than purely cerebral

---

[5] Miri Rubin, *Corpus Christi: The Eucharist in Late Medieval Culture* (New York: Cambridge University Press, 1991), 9.

[6] John Bossy, "The Mass as a Social Institution," *The Past and Present Society* 100 (1983): 36.

[7] Nathan D. Mitchell, "Reforms, Protestant and Catholic," in *The Oxford History of Christian Worship*, ed. Geoffrey Wainwright and Karen Westerfield Tucker (Oxford, UK: Oxford University Press, 2005), 308.

contemplation. In fact, it is likely that the "public" level of meaning during the late Middle Ages made little distinction between the liturgy proper and popular religious practices since they tended to blend together. It was precisely this *mélange* that would be severely criticized by the Protestant Reformers and become the object of "purification" by the Council fathers of Trent.

By the end of the fifteenth century, the educational level of Europe had been improved by the printing press and the availability of printed material that led to ever-higher levels of literacy throughout European society. This in turn led to an anxiety on the part of Church authority to "purify" the practice of the faith. Concern for doing away with superstitious practices and inculcating orthodox belief will produce—in both Protestantism and Catholicism—a new genre of publication called a "catechism." Martin Luther himself originated this new questions-and-answer form of catechesis, and Catholics, not to be outdone, developed their own catechism based on the teachings of the Council of Trent. This same concern influenced Trent's program of liturgical reform.

It was this sixteenth-century concern for the faithful's right understanding of doctrine that, Nathan Mitchell argues, led both the Protestant Reformers and the Council fathers and their successors to embrace a guiding principle of a liturgical reform that equated lay participation with "well-informed cognitive access." Mitchell states:

> The approach to [liturgical] reform adopted by the Council of Trent had more in common with a Protestant emphasis on "doctrinally informed lay participation" than with medieval notions of lay involvement in the mass. Both Trent and the Reformers pursued a goal that can be described as "modern"—informed, educated, well-catechized people who understand, intellectually, the significance of the Church's public, ritual actions. At the end of the day, both Protestant and Catholic leaders of the sixteenth century found themselves agreeing that the proper solution to the liturgical "problem" was "intellectually informed participation by lay folk." The Reformers sought to achieve this goal through the use of vernacular languages, the restoration of the word to its rightful place in public worship, and frequent evangelical preaching. Similarly, the bishops present at Trent's twenty-second session (17 September 1562) . . . admitted that the mass "contains much instruction for the people," and so "the holy council commands pastors and all who have the *cura animarum* that they, either themselves or through others, explain frequently during the celebration of the mass some of the things read during the mass, and

that among other things they explain some mystery of this most
holy sacrifice, especially on Sundays and festival days.[8]

The Council fathers of Trent, in emphasizing the cognitive dimension of worship, departed in a significant way from how most of the
faithful participated in the liturgy before the Reformation. Although the
Council ultimately rejected the possibility of liturgy in the vernacular,
this "modern," "official" interpretation of participation promoted by
Trent made the layperson's experience of the celebration of the Mass
quite different from their experience during the late Middle Ages. While
in practice catechetical explanations were usually not given by the
clergy during Mass, the necessity of providing a uniform liturgical book
cleansed of errors and superstition to serve as the basis for such solid
instruction became imperative. This purified *editio typica*, or standard
edition of the Mass rite, was made possible by the new technology of
the printing press. This task was entrusted to liturgical scholars of the
period who, although lacking the necessary historical resources at our
disposal today, were mandated to produce a book that returned "to
the pristine norm and rites of the ancient Fathers."[9]

The principal inspiration for what would become the Missal of Pius
V issued in 1570 was the late medieval *Missale secundum consuetudi-
nem Romanae Curiae*, the first printed missal at use by the papal court,
published in 1474. The ceremonial directives (or rubrics) attached to
this version of the Roman Rite were drawn up by John Burchard of
Strasbourg, master of ceremonies of Pope Alexander VI. It is important
to note that in his *ordo missae* of 1501, the laity is directed to stand
on Sundays and during Eastertide, to answer the prayers at the foot
of the altar along with the acolytes, and to bring up the offerings.[10]
However, in the *Ritus servandus* (introductory instruction), and in
the *Rubricae generalis missalis* of the 1570 Missal of Pius V, all refer-

---

[8] Ibid., 310. Quoting *The Canons and Decrees of the Council of Trent*, trans.
H. J. Schroeder (St. Louis, MO, and London: B. Herder, 1941), 148.

[9] "*ad pristinam . . . Patrum normam ac ritum restituerunt*" (*Missale Roma-
num*, 33).

[10] *Ordo servandus per sacerdotum in celebratione Missae sine cantu et sine
ministris secundum ritum S. Romanae Ecclesiae*, cited by Burkhard Neunheuser,
"The Liturgies of Pius V and Paul VI," in *Roles of the Liturgical Assembly* (New
York: Pueblo, 1977), 208; John K. Leonard and Nathan Mitchell, *The Postures
of the Assembly during the Eucharistic Prayer* (Chicago: Liturgy Training Publications, 1994), 72–74.

ence to participation by lay people has been dropped. The concern to defend the legitimacy of "private Masses" against the attacks of the Reformers seems to have led the Council of Trent to disregard what was considered a nonessential to a validly celebrated Mass: the assembly.[11] It was not until the end of the nineteenth century that lay people were encouraged by the Holy See to follow the Mass in translation. Before that time some vernacular translations of the Mass were even placed on the "Index of Forbidden Books." It was only under Pope Leo XIII (1878–1903) that the publication of such resources for lay people was regularized.[12]

Most scholars agree that it was the decrees of the Council of Trent that enabled people to make hard and fast distinctions between the liturgy and popular devotions. As Carl Dehne has observed, "The category of popular devotions in the strictest sense arose in the Roman Catholic Church as a result of the codification of rites ordered by the Council of Trent. The limits of the official liturgy were definitely set, so that eventually specific official authorization came to be considered an indispensable element constituting a form of worship as part of the official liturgy of the Church."[13] The decrees of the Council of Trent also organized the spiritual and liturgical life of Christians around parishes in a way unknown in the period before the Council. This organizational and spiritual "clarity" will be a hallmark of the Counter-Reformation Church.

While this ability to distinguish between popular religious expression and the official rites of the Church was especially evident in Europe and North America, this distinction was far less apparent to many Catholics in Latin America who maintained a more "medieval" approach to liturgy. The chronic lack of priests, especially in the rural areas of the old Spanish Empire, made it difficult to implement many of the Tridentine decrees and to catechize in the spirit of the Counter-Reform. It

[11] Adrien Nocent, *La Messa prima e dopo San Pio V* (Casale Monferrato: Piemme, 1985), 45–52.

[12] On the vicissitudes of liturgical translations and the vernacular see Keith F. Pecklers, *Dynamic Equivalence: The Living Language of Christian Worship* (Collegeville, MN: Liturgical Press, 2003), 1–41. See also Mark Francis, "Liturgical Participation of God's People," in *With One Voice: Translation and Implementation of the Third Edition of the Roman Missal* (Washington, DC: Federation of Diocesan Liturgical Commissions), 55–86.

[13] Carl Dehne, "Roman Catholic Popular Devotions," *Worship* 49, no. 8 (1975): 449.

is not surprising, then, that the religious practices of Hispanics, when compared to those of the Euro-Americans, were found wanting by nineteenth-century U.S. Church leaders. This judgment created tension. It also provoked a disenfranchisement of Hispanics in the life of the Church in places like the American Southwest and California, where Euro-American Catholics imposed a clericalized form of popular piety and devotionalism that was very different from their more lay-initiated, centuries-old popular religious practices.[14] It should be noted, though, that the dominant Irish and German clergy directed this same suspicion toward southern Italians and Sicilians, who themselves presented a strikingly different "variant" of Catholicism.[15]

Liturgy as Devotion

Since the direct participation by lay people in the clerically centered liturgy of Trent was not encouraged—and at times even discouraged by Catholic authorities as a kind of crypto-Protestant inclination—it was quite natural that the development of devotional and popular religious practices would serve as an outlet for the faith expressions of lay Catholics. Devotional methods of "hearing Mass" became the norm and were promoted. The Mass was transformed as an occasion for "pious exercises." Praying the rosary and other devotions were to occupy lay people who were excluded from direct participation in the celebration of the Mass. Various forms of eucharistic adoration outside of Mass, already present in the medieval Church, were further developed and became even more important in the worship life of Catholics. This is especially true of the elaborate annual *Corpus Christi* procession, with its solemn exposition of the Blessed Sacrament and dramatic reenactments of episodes in the life of Christ or events from the Old Testament. Linked also to the Eucharist was the growing importance of the devotion to the Sacred Heart of Jesus after Pope Pius IX designated its feast, celebrated on the Friday after Corpus Christi as a feast of the universal Church in 1856. The version of this medieval

[14] See Michael E. Engh, "From Frontera Faith to Roman Rubrics: Altering Hispanic Religious Customs in Los Angeles, 1855–1880," *U.S. Catholic Historian* 12, no. 4 (Fall 1994): 85–105.

[15] See Michael P. Carroll's nuanced insight of appreciating the "variants" of Catholicism presented by the different immigrant ethnic groups in "Popular Catholicism in Pre-Famine Ireland," *Journal for the Scientific Study of Religion* 34, no. 3 (1995): 354–65.

devotion that was promoted was that of the Visitadine nun Margaret Mary Alacoque (1647–1690). It focused on meditation of the love of Jesus for humankind in his sacred heart and the need for reparation for the sins of humanity. It centered on observing the feast and receiving Communion at nine consecutive first Fridays.[16]

Devotion to the Blessed Virgin Mary under her various titles became another hallmark of Counter-Reformation Catholicism. This is exemplified by Pius V's attribution of the Christian victory over the Turks to Mary's intervention at the battle of Lepanto in 1571, and to apparitions of Mary, especially in nineteenth-century France: Our Lady of the Miraculous Medal, Pellevoisin, and Lourdes. While the Council of Trent culled the feast days of many of the historically doubtful saints of the Middle Ages from the liturgical calendar, more and more new names were added to the sanctoral to the point that, once again, saints' days eclipsed the main seasons of the liturgical year.[17]

Scholars have also observed a change in other popular devotions after Trent. Many, although not all, of the devotions practiced prior to the sixteenth century were associated with traditional places of pilgrimage such as healing springs, caves, village boundaries, or the relics of local saints venerated in sanctuaries or chapels apart from parish churches. This kind of popular religion was often associated with and limited to specific sites that were often regarded as sacred in pre-Christian times. These practices were tolerated by the clergy and sometimes even promoted by them. The devotions harked back to the Germanic spiritual sensibility. They were "instrumental" in the sense that many of these devotions were practiced for specific outcomes such as healing and fertility. This focus changes with the implementation of the Tridentine reforms that emphasized the mediating role of the priest and the local parish as the basic point of contact between the layperson and the Church. After Trent, more universal devotions not having a direct relationship to the natural world begin to take center stage. The Sacred Heart devotion and other devotions to Mary under her more general titles would be examples of these new "universally" focused devotions. The clergy actively promoted "universal" devotions

---

[16] On the history and theology of this devotion, see Jeanne Weber, "Devotion to the Sacred Heart: History, Theology and Liturgical Celebration," *Worship* 72, no. 3 (May 1998): 236–54.

[17] See Enrico Cattaneo, "L'Éta del Barocco," in *Il culto cristiano in Occidente* (Roma: Edizione Liturgiche, 2003), 328–51.

since they tended to focus on redemption and the ethical and spiritual life and could be transported from one place to another in an organization of Church that found its principal point of reference in parishes.[18]

In many ways, the development of more "general" devotions paralleled the shift to uniformity and standardization that was happening at the same time in the liturgy. While some may have originated as local devotions, "they were approved by the pope for promotion in standardized form throughout the church. Because they were standardized, general devotions required both printing and literacy for their dissemination."[19] We will now see that during the nineteenth century, conditions in Europe and America will become extraordinarily favorable to the diffusion of more "universal" devotions standardized in Rome and promoted by the clergy.

The Clericalization and Romanization of European and Euro-American Popular Piety

The middle of the nineteenth century witnessed a phenomenon of what historian Emmet Larkin has dubbed the "devotional revolution."[20] While this development was particularly striking in Ireland due to its linkage with Irish nationalism, Catholicism in general—in both Europe and North America—was dramatically transformed through the practice of devotions that answered very deep spiritual and emotional needs of Catholics on both continents coping with the turbulent social conditions caused by industrialization and immigration. It also responded to the attacks on the authority of the Church in modern society launched by the secularist "free thinkers" who sought to diminish the influence of the Church in society. The characteristics of this "revolution" changed European popular religion in several fundamental ways. Devotions became not only more "generalized" in that the objects of devotion were less focused on particular localities or nations, but they also became more clerically controlled and dependent on the papacy. This shift took place due to two new developments: the possibility of cheaply

---

[18] See Ann Taves's discussion of the work of Marie Hélène Froeschlé-Chopard and William Christian on local and general devotions in *The Household of Faith: Roman Catholic Devotions in Mid-Nineteenth Century America* (Notre Dame, IN: University of Notre Dame Press, 1986), 90–94.

[19] Ibid., 93.

[20] Emmet Larkin, "The Devotional Revolution in Ireland," *The American Historical Review* 77, no. 3 (June 1972): 625–52.

produced manuals of piety and the growing level of literacy among the Catholic underclass.[21]

This "devotional revolution" cannot be understood without taking into account the movement within the Catholic Church known as "ultramontanism." Literally meaning "beyond the mountain," ultramontanism was especially strong in many parts of Western Europe where Catholics saw the authority of the pope (who lived on the other side of the mountain—at least if one lived in France or Germany) and the centralization of ecclesial power in Rome as a powerful counterbalance to the rationalism of the Enlightenment and persecution of the Church unleashed by the French Revolution. This movement saw its crowning achievement in the declaration of the dogma of papal infallibility by the First Vatican Council in 1870. It also reflected the concern of the papacy to promote and control the growing variety of popular religious practices through the granting of indulgences: a prerogative of the pope.

Pope Pius IX (+1878), more than any other pope of the nineteenth century, saw the granting of indulgences—the remission of temporal punishment due to one's sins—as a way of heightening his spiritual power. At the moment that the nationalist forces were unifying Italy and severely reducing the temporal power of the pope by wresting the Papal States from his political control, Pius "sought ways to consolidate his power amid the fury of the nineteenth-century attacks on the papacy" and "he promoted indulgences with renewed vigor, aided by the Vatican's well-organized bureaucracy."[22]

In her history of Catholic devotions during the nineteenth century, Ann Taves has observed that the focus of these devotions supported by the papacy tended to link them to the Eucharist. As she points out, "Ultramontane devotionalism not only centralized and standardized practice, but also subordinated devotions to Mary and the saints to devotion to Jesus in the Blessed Sacrament. Saints were played down relative to Jesus and Mary; Mary was subordinated, at least in theory, to Jesus; and sacramentals were subordinated, again at least in theory, to the sacraments."[23] This focus on the Blessed Sacrament and the other

---

[21] The Irish give a striking example of the dramatic growth of literacy. It is estimated that in 1861, over 45 percent of the Irish were illiterate. By 1900, only 16 percent of adults were unable to read or write. Ibid., 651.

[22] James P. McCartin, *Prayers of the Faithful: The Shifting Spiritual Life of American Catholics* (Cambridge, MA: Harvard University Press, 2010), 28.

[23] Taves, *The Household of Faith*, 102.

sacraments enhanced the role of the clergy, since it was the priest's special power to consecrate the bread and wine (and celebrate most of the other sacraments) that made these devotions possible. Devotions to Mary (the rosary) and the Sacred Heart (the First Friday devotion) were promoted in the presence of the Blessed Sacrament, thereby "clericalizing" them. Peter Williams sums up the irony of "popular devotions" becoming clericalized. He notes that this phenomenon "in the sense that it was severely clerical in its orientation and control . . . was not 'popular in the strict sense of its originating among the people.' Rather, it was more of a *tertium quid*, an emergent 'clerico-popular' culture controlled by an elite caste of celibates but aimed at and drawing broad support from a poorly educated constituency."[24]

Devotions were also seen as a way of catechizing the faithful, keeping them safe from the errors of Protestantism, and promoting a new, emotional attachment to the pope. One of the most famous exponents of ultramontanism, Frederick Faber (+1863), a convert from Anglicanism, linked the very notion of the papal indulgences attached to devotions with Catholic orthodoxy. He explained that Catholics find the presence of Christ in three ways: in the Eucharist, in sacrificing their lives for the poor and children, and in the pope. He wrote that "the Sovereign pontiff is a third visible presence of Jesus among us. . . .The Pope is the Vicar of Jesus on earth. . . . By divine right he is subject to none . . . he is a monarch. He is the visible shadow cast by the Invisible Head of the Church in the Blessed Sacrament." [25]

Faber also insisted that special devotions were "essentially doctrinal devotions," underlining the differences between Catholics and non-Catholics. As Taves explains, "Virtually all Catholic devotions, including novenas, scapulars, and devotions to the saints and their relics, presupposed the Catholic understanding of the communion of saints and the spiritual economy of merits and satisfactions. The use of indulgences to promote devotions was simply a higher-level manifestation of the same phenomenon."[26] The exponents of devotions,

---

[24] Peter W. Williams, *Popular Religion in America: Symbolic Change and the Modernization Process in Historical Perspective* (Englewood Cliffs, NJ: Prentice-Hall, 1980), 75.

[25] Frederick W. Faber, *Devotion to the Pope* (Baltimore: John Murphy, 1860), 20, 23. Cited by Taves, *The Household of Faith*, 105.

[26] Taves, *The Household of Faith*, 106. See also Ann Taves, "Context and Meaning: Roman Catholic Devotion to the Blessed Sacrament in Mid-Nineteenth Century America," *Church History* 54, no. 4 (December 1985): 486.

then, presented to the faithful a comprehensive worldview—one that was coherent and made sense of their new surroundings—especially for the many Catholic immigrants to the United States who naturally felt culturally uprooted and dislocated. These devotions also made it easier to establish clerical control and discipline over an ethnically diverse flock that sought to forge a new identity in their new country. Taves neatly sums up how devotionalism was an important part of the Church in the United States pastoral strategy.

> The devotional practices promoted during the mid-nineteenth cen-
> tury were thus promoted by the hierarchy to standardize practices
> in the parish church internationally; to relocate the devotional
> practices of the parish church under the control of the priest; to
> distinguish Catholics from non-Catholics; and to rally the laity
> to the church and its hierarchy in the face of perceived dangers
> from without. In so doing, they directly and indirectly enhanced
> the hierarchy's control over the laity, while fostering a distinctively
> Catholic identity with international as opposed to national or
> ethnic overtones.[27]

Clearly, the co-opting of much of popular religion by Church authorities in the nineteenth century in Europe and North America created a very different relationship between "popular" expressions of the faith and the official Church. In many ways, it is this particular variation of popular religion, with its neat distinctions between liturgy and popular religion, that will be the principal point of reference for official treatment of popular piety in the documents of Vatican II and in the 2001 *Directory of Popular Piety and Liturgy* issued by the Roman Congregation for Worship.

Notwithstanding this clericalization of much of the devotional life of European Catholics in the nineteenth century, it is important to note that this process was never complete. Devotion to the rosary, popularized by the clergy, never required the presence of a priest. Other pious customs surrounded the wearing of the brown scapular of our Lady of Mt. Carmel. The scapular was believed to guarantee being freed from the suffering of purgatory the Saturday after one's death. In a certain sense, these devotions sidestep the sacramental system of the Church and promise grace and salvation through the intercession of the Blessed Virgin. This belief is graphically illustrated by Michelangelo

---

[27] Taves, *The Household of Faith*, 111.

in his fresco of the Last Judgment in the Sistine Chapel. Mary, seated next to Christ the Judge, looks down at angels pulling up two of the faithful to heaven by means of a rosary.

Popular Piety and the Liturgical Movement

In order to complete our discussion of popular religion in the nineteenth century, it is important to note that the various movements for reform of the liturgy that began in the eighteenth century developed a highly critical relationship to Catholic "popular piety." Although ultimately condemned by Pope Pius VI, the Synod of Pistoia (1786) convoked by Bishop Scipione de' Ricci (+1810) and under the patronage of Leopold, the Grand Duke of Tuscany, attempted a real reform of Church structure and liturgical life. Concerned with lay participation in the liturgy, the synod drew upon the growing collection of historical studies on the liturgy by advocating a return to patristic practices such as having only one altar in a church, the reception of the eucharistic bread consecrated at that Mass and not from hosts reserved in the tabernacle, a revision of the saints calendars and more control over processions and other popular religious practices such as the presence of relics on altars. Importantly, it also called for the use of the vernacular at worship.

Because of its association with Jansenism, its "top down" attempt at curtailing popular religious practices—such as its condemnation of the devotion to the Sacred Heart of Jesus—and its pursuit of more local independence in Church governance, the synod was ultimately a failure. The decision of the synod was rejected by the people and condemned by the pope in his bull *Auctorem Fidei* of 1794.[28]

Apart from the "failed" Synod of Pistoia, most historians credit the French Benedictine monk Prosper Guéranger (1805–1875), as being the pioneer of what would become the "liturgical movement" of the nineteenth and early twentieth centuries. He sought to restore Benedictine life in France by buying back the Priory of Solesmes in northern France and becoming its first abbot in 1837. Like so many religious figures in France after the Revolution, he sought to revitalize the Church that had been severely weakened by both the rationalism of the Enlightenment and the political forces that consistently attempted to limit the power and influence of the Church in French

---

[28] Keith F. Pecklers, "The Jansenist Critique and the Liturgical Reforms of the Seventeenth and Eighteenth Centuries," *Ecclesia Orans* 20, no. 3 (2003): 332–36.

society. Cuthbert Johnson neatly sums up Guéranger's basic insight. "Religious practice in post-Revolutionary France was at a low level. Guéranger believed that renewal in the Church could be achieved through a renewal of the liturgy."[29]

Guéranger's quest to renew the liturgy was through the *restoration* of the Roman Rite. As André Haquin points out, "He wished to reconnect with the past and to come as close as possible to Roman doctrine and liturgy from before the times of Gallicanism and Jansenism; he fought effectively in favor of abandoning 'neo-Gallican' liturgies and the return of the French dioceses to the pure Roman liturgy."[30] Like many French Catholic leaders of his generation, Guéranger was a liturgical ultramontanist and saw the Roman liturgy, linked to the pope, as a guarantor of orthodoxy and a bulwark against the depredations of the secularism infecting French society. He is considered the "founder" of the liturgical movement because he proposed the liturgy as the principal source for an ecclesial spirituality for both ordained and nonordained that went beyond looking at Catholic liturgy as only a series of rites whose rubrical directives had to be followed. In his 15-volume work, titled *L'année liturgique* (the liturgical year), he encouraged a real liturgical spirituality. In line with the nineteenth century's fascination with the Middle Ages, Gueranger's promotion of both monasticism and the liturgy was influential among a certain group of educated Catholics who were able to understand Latin. Such Catholics tended to view most popular religious practice with indifference or even suspicion as a form of prayer influenced by superstition and a lack of education.

What Guéranger initiated in focusing on the liturgy as a source of real spirituality for the whole Church was embraced and developed in other Benedictine monasteries in Germany and Belgium. The liturgical movement went beyond its monastic origins through the work of the Belgian Dom Lambert Beauduin (+1960) who is identified as the founder of the contemporary liturgical movement. In reflecting on his Catholic training at the end of the nineteenth century, he wrote about how popular piety regarding the Eucharist was more important than the celebration of the Mass.

---

[29] Cuthbert Johnson, *Prosper Guéranger (1805–1875): A Liturgical Theologian*, Analecta Liturgica 9 (Rome: Studia Anselmiana, 1984), 424.

[30] André Haquin, "The Liturgical Movement and Catholic Ritual Reform," in *The Oxford History of Christian Worship*, ed. Geoffrey Wainwright and Karen Westerfield Tucker (Oxford, UK: Oxford University Press, 2005), 687–98.

You'll excuse my frankness, but the missal was for me a closed
and sealed book. And this ignorance extended not only to the
variable parts of the Mass, but even to the unchanging parts and
principally to the canon. . . . Even the great and perfect acts of
worship, the principal ends of the Mass, of participation in the
sacrifice of communion with the body of the Lord, the spiritual
offering of good acts . . . in short, none of the great realities that
the Eucharistic liturgy constantly puts into act, not one dominated
my Eucharistic piety. . . .Visits to the Blessed Sacrament had a
more vital role in my piety than the act of sacrifice itself.[31]

He shared with Guéranger the insistence that the liturgy, not
popular religious practice, should be the focus of every Christian's
prayer, but he also sought to make the liturgy more accessible to the
ordinary Catholic. His work as a diocesan priest ministering to working
class people of the diocese of Liège, influenced by the Catholic social
teaching contained in Pope Leo XIII's *Rerum Novarum* (1891), dis-
posed him to see the liturgy as a real force for social good. He further
developed this relationship after becoming a monk of the Monastery
of Mont César in 1906. His address given at the Congress of Catholic
Works at Malines in 1909 titled *"La vraie prière de l'Eglise"* (The real
prayer of the Church), spoke of restoring the liturgy to the people
through translation into the vernacular languages. This was to be done,
not necessarily to displace popular religious practice, but to offer to
all the baptized the possibility of making the liturgy a real source of
their Christian spirituality.

Other leaders in the movement also saw the liturgy as a source
for social regeneration during the first decades of the twentieth century. Dom Virgil Michel (+1938) of Saint John's Abbey in Collegeville,
Minnesota, was the most famous American exponent of the liturgical
movement at the beginning of the last century. He saw the liturgy as
the principal way of regenerating a society fractured by the greed of the
gilded age, the First World War, and the suffering of the Great Depres-
sion because the worship of the Church, in his view, steered a midcourse
between the two "pagan extremes" of exaggerated individualism on
one hand and the tyranny of collectivism (Fascism and Communism)
on the other. Influenced by the European liturgical movement in both
Belgium and Germany, Michel drew upon the authority of Pope Pius

---

[31] Sonya Quitslund, *Beauduin: A Prophet Vindicated* (New York: Newman
Press, 1973), 10–11.

X to support an integral relationship between liturgy and social justice. It is the "Christian spirit" alone that can regenerate society, and that spirit is found in the liturgy. In an article titled "The Liturgy, the Basis of Social Regeneration," he stated that "Pius X not only called [the Mass] the indispensable source of the true Christian spirit, but added that the faithful must derive this spirit from the Church's worship by active participation."[32]

Because the liturgical pioneers were so convinced that placing the liturgy of the Church at the center of Christian spirituality and imagination would be able to transform not only the Church but society, they often viewed popular religious practices at best as a distraction and at worst an obstacle to this crucial social regeneration. William Busch, another American liturgical pioneer, voiced this concern in 1925 in a letter he wrote to the editors of *Commonweal* magazine:

> Undoubtedly there is something amiss in the present quality of Catholic spirituality. Our devotional life and hence our whole mentality as Catholics, is individualistic, and the chief reason for this is to be found in an examination of our prayer books. The individualistic character of modern prayer literature cannot fail to impress itself upon our life and dim our social vision. But the official liturgical prayers of the church, which we do not use, or which we use so privately and mechanically as not to count, are filled through and through with that very spirit for which you are so justly pleading. We have lost that sense of Christian neighborliness and of the kingdom of God on earth which the liturgy teaches.[33]

Proponents of the liturgical movement sometimes juxtaposed Catholic devotional practices made popular in the nineteenth century to the liturgical prayer of the Church—the devotional practices were almost always found wanting. Judged as being superficial, sentimental, individualistic, inattentive to social solidarity, Catholic popular piety

---

[32] Virgil Michel, "The Liturgy the Basis of Social Regeneration," *Orate Fratres* 9 (1935): 540. On this historic theme of the modern liturgical movement, see also Margaret M. Kelleher, "Liturgy and Social Transformation: Exploring the Relationship," *U.S. Catholic Historian* 16, no. 4 (1998): 58–70; and Keith F. Pecklers, *The Unread Vision: The Liturgical Movement in the United States of America: 1926–1955* (Collegeville, MN: Liturgical Press, 1998).

[33] William Busch, letter to the editor, *Commonweal*, 1925, quoted in *How Firm a Foundation: Voices of the Early Liturgical Movement*, comp. and intro. Kathleen Hughes (Chicago: Liturgy Training Publications, 1990).

was challenged by the members of the liturgical movement. It is this antipathy that finds its way into the treatment of popular religion by the Constitution on the Sacred Liturgy of Vatican II and in official documents on the liturgy published after the Council.

Conclusion

This chapter has traced the transformation of both popular religion and liturgy (and their relationship to one another) in Europe and North America. This transformation occurred within the context of dramatic changes that came about in the relationship between the Church and European society through the Reformation, Counter-Reformation, the Enlightenment, and the French Revolution. In some ways these changes came about as European culture moved from a premodern to modern worldview as social change and technology (printing) radically altered the average believer's experience of religion in general and worship in particular. The challenge of Protestantism to the authority of the Church made possible by printing and more common literacy promoted more precise distinctions to be made between official (liturgical) worship and popular religious practice. It also produced a real change in the way in which people (both Catholics and Protestants) were engaged with at worship. No longer was the "kinesthetic" or "bodily" participation in the rites of the Church and in popular devotions the key mode of participation. After the Reformation and Trent, much more official concern was placed on purifying worship and devotional life from superstition and error. This resulted in a reorganization of the Christian life around parishes supervised more carefully by priests. A less kinesthetic and more passive stance of the faithful toward the official liturgy now completely dominated by clerics was promoted. At the same time, though, popular religious customs such as devotion to the Sacred Heart and rosary were encouraged, as was a heightened emphasis on eucharistic devotion that linked many of these devotions to the reserved Eucharist.

"Clerico-popular" European devotional life became a key point of reference for developing the identity of Euro- American Catholics who immigrated in great numbers to the United States. With the exception of Hispanic and possibly some Italian Catholics, these devotions, printed and linked to indulgences granted by the pope, served to unite disparate Euro-American Catholic cultural groups as the Church entered the twentieth century. They were linked to an ultramontane notion of ecclesiology that saw the pope as the one guarantor and defender of

Catholic orthodoxy. Proponents of the liturgical movement, though, challenged nineteenth- and early twentieth-century Catholic devotional practice. Wishing to restore the liturgy as the chief source of spiritual life and catalyst for social transformation, many of the movement's ardent supporters developed an antipathy to the individualism and lack of social consciousness they saw in devotionalism. Their desire to subordinate these practices to the official worship of the Church will be reflected in the documents of Vatican II and in subsequent documents issued by the Roman Congregation for Worship. We will now look at liturgy and popular devotions after the Second Vatican Council in order to propose a way forward where both these forms of prayer are enabled to enrich each other.

Chapter Eight

Liturgy and Popular Religion before and after Vatican II

Among the many changes set in motion by the Second Vatican Council was a reevaluation of the place of popular religion vis-à-vis the official liturgy of the Church. This reevaluation affected both the official and public meaning of the liturgy, since it was now the official expectation that all present at worship would "pray the liturgy" and not engage in popular religious practices during the celebration. This chapter will first consider the consequences of this change—both desired and inadvertent—especially among Euro-American Catholics. We will then discuss how this changed relationship between liturgy and popular religious practice was received in the largest "minority" group of Catholics in the United States—the Hispanic community. Mention will also be made of the ongoing interpretation of the Constitution on the Sacred Liturgy's treatment of popular religion and liturgy as found in official documents issued by the Roman Congregation for Worship. Finally, we will describe a decided turn toward both centralization in liturgical affairs on the part of the Congregation for Divine Worship and Discipline of the Sacraments reflected in two recent documents: *Liturgiam Authenticam* (2001)[1] and the revised *General Instruction on the Roman Missal* (2002).[2]

---

[1] *Liturgiam Authenticam*, Instruction on the Use of Vernacular Languages in the Publication of the Books of the Roman Liturgy, March 28, 2001.
[2] *Institutio Generalis Missalis Romani*, General Instruction on the Roman Missal, *Editio Typica Tertia*, 2002, 2010.

Popular Religion and Liturgy Prior to Vatican II

As we saw in the previous chapter, several attempts had been made to restore the official worship of the Church to lay people before Vatican II. The liturgical movement—both at its inception and later in the twentieth century—sought to make the liturgy of the Church the central source of spirituality for laypeople as well as clerics. In doing so, the movement drew a line between those who were able to engage in the rites as active participants and those who, for whatever reason, continued to engage in pious exercises such as the rosary and novena prayers during the celebration. This dilemma is clearly alluded to in what came to be known as the "magna carta" of the liturgical movement, Pope Pius XII's encyclical of 1947, *Mediator Dei*. The pope embraced many of the goals of the movement, but he made it very clear that he did not subscribe to the movement's suspicion of and lack of enthusiasm for popular devotions. While the pope supported the emphasis on what he termed the "objective" piety of the liturgy, he adamantly argued in defense of public devotions, denouncing the fact that the liturgical movement had relegated them to an inferior category by disdainfully referring to them as "subjective" or "personal" piety.

> 28. . . . We desire to direct your attention to certain recent theories touching a so-called "objective" piety. While these theories attempt, it is true, to throw light on the mystery of the Mystical Body, on the effective reality of sanctifying grace, on the action of God in the sacraments and in the Mass, it is nonetheless apparent that they tend to belittle, or pass over in silence, what they call "subjective," or "personal" piety.

> 29. It is an unquestionable fact that the work of our redemption is continued, and that its fruits are imparted to us, during the celebration of the liturgy, notable in the august sacrifice of the altar. Christ acts each day to save us, in the sacraments and in His holy sacrifice. . . . From these profound considerations some are led to conclude that all Christian piety must be centered in the mystery of the Mystical Body of Christ, with no regard for what is "personal" or "subjective," as they would have it. As a result they feel that all other religious exercises not directly connected with the sacred liturgy, and performed outside public worship should be omitted.

> 30. But though the principles set forth above are excellent, it must be plain to everyone that the conclusions drawn from them respecting two sorts of piety are false, insidious and quite pernicious.

Later in the document Pope Pius makes it clear that there were factors that legitimately impede the kind of active participation of the laity in the Mass called for by those in the liturgical movement. Therefore, it was unrealistic to expect that everyone would be able to participate in the same way.

> 108. Many of the faithful are unable to use the Roman missal even though it is written in the vernacular; nor are all capable of understanding correctly the liturgical rites and formulas. So varied and diverse are men's talents and characters that it is impossible for all to be moved and attracted to the same extent by community prayers, hymns and liturgical services. Moreover, the needs and inclinations of all are not the same, nor are they always constant in the same individual. Who, then, would say, on account of such a prejudice, that all these Christians cannot participate in the Mass nor share its fruits?

Despite the great advance promoting lay participation in worship enunciated in this encyclical, Pope Pius XII simply accepted the fact that the liturgy, even in translation, was not able to be the prayer of all the baptized. The pope went on to suggest that these lay people can participate in the Mass and obtain its spiritual fruits through other means such as devotional prayers—as long as such prayers are in harmony with the sacred rites: "They can adopt some other method which proves easier for certain people; for instance, they can lovingly meditate on the mysteries of Jesus Christ or perform other exercises of piety or recite prayers which, though they differ from the sacred rites, are still essentially in harmony with them" (*MD* 108).

Popular Religion and the Euro-American Church after Vatican II

While much of what was contained in *Mediator Dei* was reiterated by the Constitution on the Sacred Liturgy of Vatican II, as Patrick Malloy has commented, "Only sixteen years after [Pius XII] championed subjective piety, Vatican II made a decisive move against it."[3] Article 13 of the Constitution sums up the new relationship between popular devotions and liturgy established by the Council and then repeated by subsequent authoritative documents issued by the Congregation for Divine Worship.

---

[3] Patrick L. Malloy, "The Re-Emergence of Popular Religion among Non-Hispanic American Catholics," *Worship* 72, no. 1 (1998): 3–4.

Popular devotions of the Christian people are to be highly commended, provided they accord with the laws and norms of the Church, above all when they are ordered by the Apostolic See.

Devotions proper to individual Churches also have a special dignity if they are undertaken by mandate of the bishops according to customs or books lawfully approved.

But these devotions should be so drawn up that they harmonize with the liturgical seasons, accord with the sacred liturgy, are in some fashion derived from it, and lead the people to it, since, in fact, the liturgy by its very nature far surpasses any of them.

It is clear that the Council, following the initiative of many of the advocates of the liturgical movement, intended to subordinate both devotions in particular and popular religion in general to the approved liturgical books. Given the Council's openness to the vernacular and its obvious desire to relax the rigidity of the Tridentine Rite, many thought that popular religious practices—especially during the celebration of Mass—were now a distraction and unnecessary. In effect, the symbiosis between liturgy and popular devotions, between the official and the popular described by *Mediator Dei*, was rejected by Vatican II. It is important to note the kind of "devotions" that are being described by the Constitution in article 13. They are those that "accord to the law and norms of the Church," undertaken by the mandate of the bishops according to "customs or books" that have been lawfully approved; and "they are in harmony with" and "lead the people to the liturgy" that "by its very nature surpasses any of them." It is here that the Council establishes the principle that the official liturgy must be *the* point of spiritual reference for all the baptized: a principle long held by the leaders of the liturgical movement who championed this position based on their reading of liturgical history.

The kind of popular religion described by the Council, however, is the European devotionalism that we examined in the preceding chapter, aptly characterized by Williams as "clerico-popular." It was a devotionalism approved and promoted by ecclesiastical authority that constituted a *tertium quid* between religious practices generated by the people and those controlled by the hierarchical Church. This very focused allusion to European devotionalism, with its presumption of a symbiosis between the official liturgy and popular devotions, never really encompassed all popular religious practices, since many had developed well outside of the purview of official ecclesiastical authority.

This is especially true of non-European popular religion such as the Hispanic and Filipino that maintained an independence from clerical oversight.

Ironically, the popular devotions described by the Liturgy Constitution were in the process of being disconnected from the authority of the institutional Church by the Council itself. The way in which devotions to the Sacred Heart or novenas to the Sorrowful Mother were validated in the nineteenth century—through papal indulgences—was criticized during the conciliar debates as a problematic practice based on a deductive theology that grew up in medieval Western Europe. Both Eastern Christians and many of the *periti* at the Council questioned the theological rationale for indulgences.[4] This indirectly undermined the *raison d'être* of much devotional performance for many Euro-Americans, weakening the link between devotions and the authority of the Church.

Scholars have advanced other reasons why the clerical connection to devotions was weakened after the Council. Some identify the erosion of Church authority and credibility due to the ongoing scandal of priestly pedophilia and the way the bishops mishandled this betrayal of trust. Others attribute the growing lack of confidence in devotions to U.S. Catholics leaving the Catholic ghetto of the 1950s and entering into the American mainstream, thus succumbing to secularization. Yet others contend that the cultural dynamic working against the coherence of the Church and its message in the United States is not secularization as such. The vast majority of Americans are still believers. Rather, it is what has been called "deregulation" of religious authority. In an insightful study of the effect of U.S. culture on religion and religious sensibilities, Vincent Miller has persuasively argued that while the vast majority of Americans still claim belief in God and identification with Christianity, the authority of what is regarded as "institutional religion" has steadily eroded.

> The decline once described in terms of an all-encompassing secularization appears, rather, to have been a decline in the social and cultural power of religious institutions. The symbols, practices, and myths that they once stewarded continue to inform people's lives, but religious authorities and institutions exercise less control over how these are used. Some writers employ metaphors drawn from

---

[4] On this debate see John O'Malley, *What Happened at Vatican II?* (Cambridge, MA: Belknap Press, 2008), 280–82.

economics to describe this shift. They speak of the "deregulation" of religion or the decline of religious institutional monopolies.[5]

This insight helps to explain the oft-heard assertion of people in the United States and other places that they are "spiritual" but not "religious." It also takes devotional and other popular religious observances out from under the aegis of the institutional Church where it had rested for Euro-Americans since the middle of the nineteenth century.[6]

It could also be argued that the liturgical reform itself inadvertently contributed to the break between Euro-American popular devotions and the institutional Church. Just as the Council of Trent mandated a less "external" kinesthetic and a more cognitive way of being present at worship through better knowledge of the catechism and approved prayers, Vatican II raised the stakes even higher by mandating lay liturgical involvement based on "full, conscious, and active" participation.[7] In some places this led to a "take no hostages" approach when the liturgical renewal was implemented. Popular religious expressions, because were not by nature "liturgical," needed to be suppressed. This was nowhere more evident than in the aniconic approach taken in the art and environment prescribed for renewed churches. While perhaps overly severe, Salvador Ryan describes the result. "Although some initial efforts at the re-ordering of churches were a success, many others failed dismally. The decrease of emphasis on visual stimulation that was ubiquitous in the medieval period leads, in certain cases, to the replacement of biblical scenes on stained glass windows by amorphous multi-coloured designs that only individuals with a PhD in postmodernism might begin to interpret." He goes on to note that the outcome of well-intentioned simplification has sometimes led to creating a void that the new liturgy was incapable of filling. "The dispensing of 'clutter' of all sorts, including various statues and images, may have been intended to focus the worshipper's mind more fully on the various movements within the liturgy itself, but it also succeeded in creating an atmosphere of sterility in what, for many, was as familiar a building as their own

---

[5] Vincent Miller, *Consuming Religion: Christian Faith and Practice in a Consumer Culture* (New York: Continuum, 2003), 92.

[6] *Keith* Pecklers, "Issues of Power and Access in Popular Religion," *Liturgical Ministry* 7 (Summer 1998): 136–40.

[7] See Philippe Ariès, "Religion Populaire et Réformes Religieuses," *La Maison Dieu* 122 (1975): 84–97.

home."[8] This explains why for some, the liturgical renewal was more alienating than engaging.

Therefore, despite the undeniably positive aspects of the liturgical reforms of Vatican II, one of the common complaints directed against the new liturgy was that Catholic worship was emptied of both its visual impact and its "mystery." To be fair, much of this criticism is not so much based on the reform articulated by the liturgical documents but stems from partial and admittedly superficial implementation of the new liturgical directives. For example, the restoration of the liturgy to the assembly, while a good thing in itself, sometimes focused the attention of the assembly on itself rather than on God. Some priests also misunderstood the art of liturgical presiding as an opportunity to draw attention to themselves rather than to facilitate the people's entering into God's presence in ritual and prayer. The concern for intelligibility sometimes led to a flattening out of the presidential prayers, now voiced in the vernacular and understood by those present, but prayed in a way that scarcely evoked the presence of the Holy One. Carl Dehne, writing what has become a classic article on popular religion and liturgy, went even further in questioning some of the underlying principles that marked Vatican II's liturgical reform: ". . . the principles we tend to assume to be good without further justification: simplification, dignity-serenity-moderation, lexical intelligibility, discomfort with ritual unless it is rendered safe by verbalization, emphasis on a personal style for leaders and on monolithic response by followers, and—above all—variety."[9]

It seems to me that Dehne's critique, while partially valid, is describing a rather "fundamentalistic" approach to implementing the liturgical reform that does not take into account the people present at worship. In blindly imposing this set of abstract qualities drawn from the classic Roman Rite and valued by Vatican II's liturgical reform (dignity, serenity, moderation, intelligibility) without taking into account the cultural context and ritual history of the people of the assembly, it is no wonder that at times the reform of the liturgy was resented or simply ignored. At the same time, however, the solution to this problem can scarcely be found in a wholesale borrowing of the language of prayer

---

[8] Salvador Ryan, "Resilient Religion: Popular Piety Today," *The Furrow* 56, no. 3 (2005): 136.

[9] Carl Dehn, "Roman Catholic Popular Devotions," *Worship* 49, no. 8 (1975): 448.

and ritual patterns common to the preconciliar devotions. As Anscar Chupungco has pointed out, the discursive style of devotional prayer along with its frequent use of repetitive and litanic petitions makes it particularly difficult to transform into liturgical prayer.[10]

This is not to say that the reformed liturgy of Euro-American Catholics has nothing to learn from popular religious forms of prayer. As Patrick Malloy points out, devotions among Euro-Americans have reemerged and become more popular decades after the close of the Council. It is important for liturgical ministers to understand why.

> If the devotional re-emergence is in part an embodied protest against the liturgical *status quo*, then it is a voice . . . not to be ignored or silenced. Where modern liturgy is anthropocentric, the devotions are centered on Christ, his Mother, and other heavenly personages; where modern liturgy neglects the transcendent, the devotions move the worshiper into a network of personal relationships beyond the self; where modern liturgy is cerebral, the devotions are ceremonial and embodied; where modern liturgy is hesitant to give voice to the negative experiences of human life, the devotions express without apology all of the conflicting emotions of being both human and Christian. The cross has no less place than the crown.[11]

The scholarship of Robert Orsi has helped clarify our understanding of the Catholic devotional culture that held sway before the Council. He has explored how this culture supported religious experience and gave meaning and identity to a Catholic worldview—and why some people even today yearn for at least part of it to return. In his three principal books, *The Madonna of 115th Street, Thank You, St. Jude,* and *Between Heaven and Earth*,[12] Orsi introduces us to the premodern worldview of preconciliar American Catholic culture that took divine intervention in human affairs as commonplace. It was through the

---

[10] Anscar J. Chupungco, *Liturgical Inculturation: Sacramentals, Religiosity, and Catechesis* (Collegeville, MN: Pueblo, 1992), 110–19.

[11] Malloy, "The Re-emergence of Popular Religion," 23.

[12] *The Madonna of 115th Street* (New Haven, CT: Yale University Press, 1985); *Thank You, St. Jude: Women's Devotion to the Patron Saint of Hopeless Causes* (New Haven, CT: Yale University Press, 1996); and *Between Heaven and Earth: The Religious Worlds People Make and the Scholars Who Study Them* (Princeton, NJ: Princeton University Press, 2004).

practice of devotions that religious sensitivity permeated Catholic life, revealing the presence of Jesus, Mary, and the saints. Devotions helped give meaning to the most difficult aspects of human existence such as sacrifice for family, terrible suffering, and death. The experience of the presence of God in all aspects of life, presupposed and celebrated in the devotional life of Euro-American Catholics, created a religious world that supported and constantly reinforced the conviction of God acting in the sacraments. At the same time, it provided an alternate way of accessing the holy that was not totally dependent on the official Church.

The ongoing challenge of the liturgical reform was to invite lay Catholics to "full, conscious, and active participation" in the liturgy at the precise moment when the "sacred canopy" of Catholic institutions began to break down. Moving out of the old ethnic Catholic neighborhoods to the suburbs during the 1960s changed the "spiritual geography" of many Catholics. Reaction to Pope Paul VI's encyclical *Humanae Vitae* (1968), reiterating the Church's opposition to artificial birth control, did much to shake the confidence of some in the credibility of the Church and its authority over their moral and spiritual lives. This erosion of confidence only continued in subsequent decades, reaching crisis stage in the early 2000s when the clerical pedophilia scandal was fully exposed. The authority of the official Church over extra-liturgical spiritual practices has been severely compromised among many Catholics who now seek spiritual connections outside of the institution in traditions other than Christianity.[13]

Popular Religion and the Hispanic/Latino Church after Vatican II

The same kind of break between preconciliar devotionalism and the official liturgy did not happen among many non-European Catholic cultural groups such as Hispanics or Filipinos after the Council—mainly because these groups never experienced the secularizing effects of the Enlightenment in the same way as Euro-Americans, nor were they as exposed to the ultramontane "clerico-popular" version of devotionalism imposed in the nineteenth century. The chronic lack of clergy—especially of native clergy as opposed to those of pure European blood—also set up a dichotomy in many places between the

---

[13] On this transformation see James McCartin, *Prayers of the Faithful: The Shifting Spiritual Life of American Catholics* (Cambridge, MA: Harvard University Press, 2010), 174–83.

official religion of the "empowered" and the religion of the people. In a very real sense, popular religion remained "popular" for the people of Latin America and continued to represent an alternative set of religious practices in addition to the official liturgy promoted by the Church. Popular practices such as home altars, pilgrimages, veneration of suffering Jesus, and recourse to Mary under her various titles were never primarily based on written documents or promoted by papal indulgences. Rather, they were handed on from generation to generation by word of mouth, primarily by lay people—especially women—rather than the clergy. Orlando Espín and Sixto Garcia present a more adequate definition of popular religion from a Latin American perspective that takes into account its truly "popular" nature. They describe popular religion as:

> the set of experiences, beliefs and rituals which more-or-less peripheral human groups create, assume and develop (within concrete socio-cultural and historical contexts, and as a response to these contexts) and which to a greater or lesser degree distance themselves from what is recognized as normative by church and society, striving (through rituals, experiences and beliefs) to find an access to God and salvation which they feel they cannot find in what the church and society present as normative.[14]

This definition underscores the aspect of popular religion in Latin America that is characterized by resistance to a cultural oppression in which the Church itself participated. While also present in some aspects of Euro-American devotionalism—the prominence of women in leading novenas and other devotional practices comes to mind—Hispanic popular religion involves society's voiceless who find God and celebrate the inherent dignity of those without institutional power by circumventing the usual or normative channels of grace such as the sacraments. Although once disdained by liberation theologians and Marxist thinkers like Antonio Gramsci as a social "opiate" that helped promote a fatalistic acceptance by poor people of their inferior status in society, more recent Latin American theologians have regarded popular religion as a means of cultural, even political, resistance and empowerment.[15]

---

[14] Orlando O. Espín and Sixto J. García, "Hispanic-American Theology," in *Catholic Theological Society of America Proceedings* 42 (1987): 115.

[15] See Michael Candelaria, *Popular Religion and Liberation: The Dilemma of Liberation Theology* (Albany, NY: SUNY Press, 1990).

The official documents of the Latin American Church—especially the statements by CELAM (the Episcopal Conference of Latin America) meeting in Medellin, Colombia (1968), Puebla, Mexico (1979), Santo Domingo, Dominican Republic (1992), Aparecida, Brazil (2007) have all taken up the theme of popular religion as a necessary context for both evangelization and inculturation of the faith. The most extensive treatment of popular religion is found in the document from the 1979 Puebla meeting. While calling for a purification of popular religious practices, the document frankly acknowledges the important place that the "people's Catholicism" enjoys in the minds and hearts of believers in Latin America—especially the poor and the marginalized. Specifically in regard to the liturgy, *Puebla* famously argues for a cross-fertilization (*mutua fecundación*) between liturgy and popular piety in order to better evangelize and proclaim the faith in South America and the Caribbean. It is helpful to quote the entire article since it describes one of the urgent pastoral tasks identified by the bishops surrounding popular religion:

> to promote the cross-fertilization between Liturgy and popular piety giving lucid and prudent direction to the impulses of prayer and charismatic vitality that are evident today. Moreover, the religion of the people, with its great symbolic and expressive richness, can give to the liturgy a creative dynamism. This, duly discerned, can serve to more and better incarnate the universal prayer of the Church in our culture.[16]

In reality, this cross-fertilization has already happened and continues to happen and is part of the liturgical patrimony of the peoples of Latin America. The celebration of the sacraments, for example, while following the basic outline of the Roman Ritual, is presented and contextualized by means of expressive elements drawn from popular religious practices. We have already seen how explanatory rites such as the lasso, the giving of the arras, and the veiling came into the Hispanic Rite of Matrimony. The heightened role of *padrinos* (godparents/spon-

---

[16] Puebla, 465 (III, c) Favorecer la mutua fecundación entre Liturgia y piedad popular que pueda encauzar con lucidez y prudencia los anhelos de oración y vitalidad carismática que hoy se comprueba en nuestros países. Por otra parte, la religión del pueblo, con su gran riqueza simbólica y expresiva, puede proporcionar a la liturgia un dinamismo creador. Éste, debidamente discernido, puede servir para encarnar más y mejor la oración universal de la Iglesia en nuestra cultura.

sors) in the various rites of passage—from baptism to marriage, and even funerals—all emphasize the social relationships that the faith is expected to nurture. Processions, prayer vigils, and dramatic enactments like posadas and ways of the cross all provide profound expressions of faith that are often conjoined to the liturgy itself. In their National Pastoral Plan for Hispanic Ministry (1987), the U.S. bishops echo the concern of the Latin American bishops for an appropriate integration of popular religious practices in celebrating the faith. The bishops describe popular religion as the place where Hispanic spirituality is incarnated: a home of living relationships, a family, a community.[17] It is for this reason that the liturgical reforms of Vatican II, in simplifying the official rites, did not necessarily displace the popular religious customs that accompany the Hispanic interpretation of the Roman Rite. Rather, it is precisely these elements, drawn from popular traditions and often led by lay people that the bishops of both Latin America and the Hispanic bishops of the United States regard as an important basis for the inculturation of the liturgy.

Liturgy, Popular Religion, and the Congregation for Worship: A Guarded Openness

The official documents dealing with liturgy and popular religion issued after the Council by the Congregation for Worship seem to presuppose a Eurocentric experience of devotions and do not quite "fit" the experience outside of Europe or North America. Echoing the Constitution on the Sacred Liturgy (13), subsequent documents of the Holy See draw the line at incorporating elements of popular piety in the liturgy itself. For example, the 1994 instruction of the Congregation for Worship, *Varietates Legitimae* (Inculturation and the Roman Liturgy), when mentioning devotional practices makes it clear they should not replace or be integrated in what are properly liturgical celebrations.

> Alongside liturgical celebrations and related to them, in some particular Churches there are various manifestations of popular devotion. These were sometimes introduced by missionaries at the time of the initial evangelization, and they often develop according to local custom. The introduction of devotional practices into

---

[17] On the place of Hispanic popular religion in liturgy, see Mark R. Francis and Arturo J. Pérez-Rodríquez, *Primero Dios: Hispanic Liturgy Resource* (Chicago: Liturgy Training Publications, 1997), 10–13.

liturgical celebrations under the pretext of inculturation cannot be allowed "because by its nature, (the liturgy) is superior to them." It belongs to the local ordinary to organize such devotions, to encourage them as supports for the life and faith of Christians, and to purify them when necessary, because they need to be constantly permeated by the Gospel. He will take care to ensure that they do not replace liturgical celebrations or become mixed up with them. (VL 45)

The *Directory on Popular Piety and the Liturgy* (2002), another document of the Congregation for Worship, reiterates the distinction between Liturgy and pious exercises by citing a line from a document of the Italian Bishops' Conference.

Careful attention to these principles should lead to a real effort to harmonize, in so far as possible, pious exercises with the rhythm and demands of the Liturgy, thereby avoiding any "mixture or admixture of these two forms of piety." This in turn ensures that no hybrid, or confused forms emerge from mixing Liturgy and pious exercises, not that the latter, contrary to the mind of the Church, are eliminated, often leaving an unfilled void to the great detriment of the faithful. (DPPL 74)

Both documents presuppose that liturgy and popular religious practices are easily distinguishable. They also presuppose that the local bishop will be able to regulate these practices. One wonders if it would really be possible for bishops and other clergy to "control" the popular religious practice now tied to the celebration of the liturgy in the Hispanic community. Much like the custom of the Advent Wreath or "the unity candle" at weddings in many North American parishes—practices that are not "liturgical" and do not appear as such in any liturgical books—in the Hispanic Church there are dramatic elements juxtaposed to the Rite of Mass and celebration of the sacraments that are clearly "extra" liturgical—but now considered standard and an expected part of the celebration. Examples such as the *"acostada del niño"* at Christmas Midnight Mass (placing the statue of baby Jesus in the manger as Mass begins); beginning Mass on Easter morning with the ritual "meeting" of the statues of the Risen Jesus and the Sorrowful mother (called the *Santo Encuentro,* or in the Tagalog of the Philippines, the *Salubong*); after the birth of a child and before the baptism, celebrating a *presentación del niño* at Sunday Mass where the newborn is presented to the community after the homily and then consecrated to Mary at the end of the celebration. All of these are popular practices, not contained in the official Roman ritual books, yet widely practiced in the Hispanic world. There are also, of course, the many Hispanic symbols used during the Rite of Marriage, such as the lazo/rosary, the arras, and veiling, that, as we saw, came from the Mozarabic Rite but are not featured in the official Roman Rite—thus making them "popular" as opposed to "official."

Therefore, it is easy to see why a Catholic from Latin America would be confused after reading some of the official documents from Rome regarding "mixing up" popular religious practices with the liturgy. It is something that is constantly done. The *Via Crucis Viviente* (the dramatic reenactment of the way of the cross—a "passion play") on Good Friday is also an example of how a popular religious practice has overshadowed the official liturgy in some parts of the Hispanic world. Again, this clearly seems to go counter to the spirit of the documents—yet it would be disastrous for the local bishop to intervene by canceling the way of the cross and telling the faithful that they should be content with only the liturgy of the Solemn Commemoration of the Passion during the afternoon of Good Friday, using the official explanation that the *Via Crucis* is a mere "representation" while the liturgy of Good Friday is "*anamnesis*, or mysterious presence of the redemptive event of the Passion" (DPPL 144). The same kind of disaster would ensue if the bishop insisted on an exclusive celebration of the Third Sunday of Advent during a year when the feast of Our Lady of Guadalupe (December 12) happened to fall on that Sunday.

The point does not need to be belabored, but many popular religious practices are not easily separable from the liturgy and, in fact, have long been incorporated into the celebration. The documents, though, rightly point out a hierarchy of celebration. The Eucharist is the preeminent celebration of the mystery of our redemption—the paschal mystery. It is the central celebration of the Christian life and the rest of the sacraments and sacramentals are rightly ordered to it. There are, of course, examples of inserting popular religious elements that are hard to justify theologically: Marian shrines that block the assembly's view and overwhelm the altar so that the celebration of the Mass cannot be seen; a celebrant ending the prayers of the faithful with a "Hail Mary" rather than a concluding prayer addressed to God in Christ and through the Spirit. I remember attending a Saturday evening Mass in Ireland that was a concatenation of devotional prayers: since Mass began at 5:00 p.m., we started Mass by kneeling for the recitation of the Angelus. After Communion we were led in the *Anima Christi* prayer, and before the final blessing we all recited the prayer to the guardian angel. All of these are examples of hard-to-defend insertions of popular religious elements in the liturgical celebration.[18]

The Supraregional Roman Rite?

The question of the relationship of popular piety and liturgy, as well as the wider issue of the inculturation of the liturgy, has become more complicated with the publication of two documents by the Congregation for Divine Worship and the Discipline of the Sacraments. The first, the instruction *Liturgiam Authenticam,* "On the use of vernacular languages in the publication of the books of the Roman Liturgy,"[19] offered new principles of translating the Latin *editio typica* into vernacular languages. It was this document that guided the latest translation of the third edition (*editio tertia*) of the Roman Missal issued in 2002. In addition to changes and additions to prayer texts in the Missal, the *editio tertia* added a whole chapter to the General Instruction of the Roman Missal that speaks about culture, inculturation, and the Roman Rite.

The new ninth chapter of the revised General Instruction asserts that because of the process of inculturation it had already undergone, the Roman Rite has acquired "a certain supraregional character." The text reads as follows: "Over the course of the centuries the Roman Rite has not only conserved liturgical usages that had their origin in the city of Rome, but has also, in a deep, organic and harmonious way incorporated into itself certain others, which were derived from the customs and genius of different peoples and of various particular Churches of both West and East, thus acquiring a certain supraregional character" (GIRM 397).[20] This is an echo of a statement in *Liturgiam*

---

[18] On the challenge of determining the appropriate relationship between liturgy and popular religion see Peter E. Fink, "Liturgy and Popular Piety in the Church's Magisterium," in *Directory on Popular Piety and Liturgy: A Commentary,* ed. Peter Phan (Collegeville, MN: Liturgical Press, 2005), 45–57; James Empereur, "Popular Religion and the Liturgy: The State of the Question," *Liturgical Ministry* 7 (Summer 1998): 105–20.

[19] *Liturgiam Authenticam,* Instruction on the Use of Vernacular Languages in the Publication of the Books of the Roman Liturgy, March 28, 2001.

[20] Translation mine. The original text: "Ritus ille saeculorum decursu non solum usus liturgicos ex urbe Roma oriundos servavit sed etiam profundo, organico et harmonico modo alios quosdam in se integravit, qui e consuetudinibus et ingenio

Authenticam that speaks of the Roman Rite as a "precious example and an instrument of true inculturation" because of its ability to assimilate liturgical usages from diverse origins "into a harmonious unity that transcends the boundaries of any single region." These documents, then, seem to be saying that because the Roman Rite has done its work of inculturation (in its formative period, from the fourth to the eleventh century) it no longer needs any further inculturation or enrichment since it has become transcultural. Article 398 describes well the attitude of the current CDW regarding inculturation: "Inculturation requires a necessary amount of time, lest in a hasty and incautious manner the authentic liturgical tradition suffer contamination." The choice of adjective is important here since it betrays an attitude of caution. Thus, the Congregation's starting point is the "pure" Roman Rite that needs to be protected from corruption as an absolute good—as an end in itself.

It could be argued that these documents build a kind of firewall between the Roman Rite and the various cultural contexts in which it is celebrated. Despite strong statements by national conferences of bishops before the continental synods of Africa, Asia, and Oceania that literal translations of the Latin texts were severely compromising the ability of the liturgy to evangelize their people, the current policy seems to reject out of hand "dynamic equivalence" in translation; a method that would grant a greater leeway in rendering Latin texts into languages used by cultures extremely removed from Rome.

Needless to say, if this attitude reflecting resistance to cultural variation in translation is apparent, the influence of popular religious practices seems to be precluded. While *Varietates Legitimae* as well as numerous documents on liturgy and pastoral life issued by national bishops' conferences speak of the need for inculturation and a real dialogue with the popular religious practices of their people, the dialogue with new cultural influence from outside the very circumscribed and static description of the Roman Rite presented by *Liturgiam Authenticam* and the ninth chapter of the General Instruction can only discourage the "cross-fertilization" between liturgy and popular piety desired by the Latin American bishops in their Puebla document.

---

diversorum populorum variarumque Ecclesiarum particularium sive Occidentis sive Orientis derivabantur, indolem quandam supraregionalem sic acquirens."

Conclusion

This chapter has examined the complex and changing relationship of liturgy and popular religious practices before and after Vatican II. From actively encouraging devotions during Mass (at least for those who were not able to follow in translation) to Vatican II's desire for every baptized person to participate in liturgical prayer to the exclusion of devotional activity, the Church profoundly changed the relationship between lay people and its official worship. Popular religious practices were relegated to the periphery as liturgy in the vernacular became the centerpiece of the liturgical reform. While this was a positive development, there was also a loss in the various ways that popular religion supported Catholic identity and spirituality and helped make the sacred present throughout the life of a Catholic. The changes after the Council also severed the authoritative underpinning established in the nineteenth century of popular devotions for the Euro-American Church. Because of their very different and independent relationship between popular piety and the institutional Church, Hispanics did not experience the liturgical change in the same way as Euro-American Catholics did. Many of the leaders in the Hispanic world see in popular religion a key to the inculturation of the Roman Rite among their people, calling for a cross-fertilization between popular religion and the official liturgy. This same valorization of popular religion is much less pronounced in the most recently issued documents of the Congregation for Divine Worship regarding the Roman Missal, who see the Roman Rite as "supraregional" and already an intercultural form of prayer able to cross cultural divisions without problems. For that reason they seem to see the influence of popular religion as a threat to what they regard as the purity of the Roman Rite.

Conclusions

The previous pages have borne witness to the exceedingly complex relationship that has existed between popular religion and the official liturgy of the Church. It is important to note that this study was far from exhaustive. There are many other fascinating examples of the intersection between popular religious practices and the Roman Rite, many of which underscore the presupposition that to become a Christian, people of non-Western cultures had to first become "Europeans." For example, a case study in cultural insensitivity is the amazing story of the fifteenth-century voluntary conversion of the sub-Saharan African Kingdom of the Kongo and the subsequent charges by Portuguese missionaries that neither their Christianity in general or their worship in particular were "pure" enough (read: European enough).[1] The sad account of the Holy See's ultimate rejection of the possibility of Chinese Catholics' participation in rites that venerated their ancestors was essentially a controversy about the acceptability of popular religious custom and its place in Christian worship. As Anscar Chupungco has remarked, the consequence of this rejection in 1742 "spelled the loss of China and Indochina to the Church."[2] Similar missionary experiences in India and with other non-Western cultures present us with both positive models of evangelization and cautionary tales that recount missed opportunities for proclaiming the Gospel more effectively.[3] These stories could easily be the object of another book.

[1] See John Thornton, "The Development of an African Catholic Church in the Kingdom of the Kongo, 1491–1750," *The Journal of African History* 25, no. 2 (1984): 147–67.

[2] Anscar Chupungco, *Cultural Adaptation and the Liturgy* (Mahwah, NJ: Paulist Press, 1982), 38. See also George Minamiki, *The Chinese Rites Controversy* (Chicago: Loyola Press, 1985); Peter Phan "Culture and Liturgy: Ancestor Veneration as a Test Case," *Worship* 76, no. 5 (2002): 403–29.

[3] M. Amaladoss, "Relaunching the Indian Liturgy—Some Reflections on our Experiments," *Vidyajyoti Journal of Theological Reflection* 49 (1985): 435–45;

The previous pages, then, offer just a glimpse of the varied interaction between liturgy and popular religion down through the centuries. By centering on several key examples of that history, I believe it is possible to draw some conclusions regarding this relationship. Liturgy and popular religion can be envisioned as two streams flowing alongside each other, both emptying into the same sea. At times these streams unite, their waters intermingling and often indistinguishable; at other times they flow at quite a distance from each other in channels that easily demarcate one from the other. Both streams ultimately flow, however, in the same direction and have the same goal—celebrating the transforming presence of the Holy One in our midst.

Conclusion One: We Need to Enlarge Our Categories Describing Popular Religion

The categories that Catholics have traditionally employed to distinguish liturgy from popular religion are in need of revision. The terms "popular religion," "pious exercise," "popular piety" often overlap and at times blind us to the way the majority of Christians have experienced and celebrated their faith. While the Council of Trent may have distinguished more clearly between liturgy and popular piety, the European "symbiosis" arrived at in the nineteenth century between the liturgy and "clerico-popular" pious practices has broken down and needs to be understood in a more inclusive and broader fashion. This understanding must include elements that have already been present in the history of the liturgy.

The resurgence among Catholics in the global South of the dimension of charismatic prayer in a liturgical context mirrors what we read about worship in the pages of the New Testament. Any "public" description of worship in Africa, India, and South America must take into account this dimension that goes beyond the rather staid constraints of "classical" Roman ritual, since these gifts of the Spirit introduce the expectation that is active in their lives in spontaneous and miraculous ways: through faith healing, exorcism, speaking in tongues, and other manifestations of the Spirit that may appear to some Church authorities as dangerously uncontrolled. The fact that many peoples today—especially from the global South—experience altered

---

and Paul M. Collins, *Christian Inculturation in India* (Aldershot, UK / Burlington, VT: Ashgate Publishing, 2007).

states of consciousness in much the same way as those described in the pages of the New Testament challenges those of the Global North who tend to be skeptical of such religious experience. The presence of immigrant Catholics in the traditionally Christian countries in the Global North, most of whom go to church convinced of the power of prayer to make a difference in their lives, is a dimension of "popular religion" that needs to be taken seriously, especially when preparing liturgy in a multicultural community.[4]

Conclusion Two: The Common People's Liturgical Observance Has Been Different down through History

Despite the contention of many in the liturgical movement that the liturgy—especially the eucharistic celebration—has been the center of the Christian life from the beginning of the Church, the historical record indicates that in practice this ideal was not always the case. The great liturgical historian Joseph Jungmann insightfully noted that

> in the present-day liturgical movement, primitive Christianity is often held up before our eyes as a model, an exemplar of liturgical observance. We are to believe that Christians of old, contrary to the tendency of modern individualism, know of no other, or scarcely any other, form of prayer than liturgical prayer. It is a mistake to palm this off as reality. . . . The idea that the life of the primitive Christians revolved exclusively around the liturgy is not correct. And it cannot be correct simply because it would be unnatural.[5]

When looking at the Christian past, we have a tendency to project our own experiences and points of reference on previous generations. Some eras are idealized depending on what we want to see. As Jungmann pointed out, the liturgical movement tended to focus on the early patristic period as the golden age of liturgy. Members of the movement saw this era as a time when the adult catechumenate formed converts

---

[4] For a fascinating view of the revitalization of the Church in many Latin American countries due to the growth of charismatic Catholicism, see Edward L. Cleary, *The Rise of Charismatic Catholicism in Latin America* (Gainesville: University Press of Florida, 2011); on the effect of charismatic Christians from India on churches in the British Isles, see Kristina Cooper, "Feel the Spirit," *The Tablet* 267 (May 18, 2013): 4–5.

[5] Joseph Jungmann, *The Early Liturgy* (Notre Dame, IN: University of Notre Dame Press, 1959), 97.

in a faith centered around the liturgy, and when the initiatory sacraments of baptism, confirmation, and Eucharist were celebrated in such a way as to lead new Christians into a worshiping assembly where all were encouraged to participate. The Church before Constantine was held up by many in the movement as the lodestar for Church reform since it had not yet become compromised by the money and power that came with being the official religion of the empire. Even once the Church triumphed over paganism, the gradual Christianization of the empire was seen as a time when the liturgy constituted the principal point of participation in the life of the Church.

At the same time the liturgical movement was looking to the patristic age to authenticate its vision of a renewed liturgy, other early twentieth-century Catholics looked back to the Middle Ages and saw a "golden age" of European Christianity. A good example of this idealization is found in a book by James Walsh, titled *The Thirteenth, Greatest of Centuries,*[6] propagated by the Knights of Columbus at the beginning of the last century. The appeal of this century lies in that it was seen by some Catholics as an "Age of Faith," a moment when the Church held its appropriate place in the social and political life of Europe. It was a time when the Gothic cathedrals were built and scholastic theology reached its apogee within the universities that had sprung up throughout western Europe. Christianity was an integral part of the culture, and participation in society automatically meant participation in the life of the Church and the liturgy.

The idealization of these past "golden ages" obscures the fact that common people approached the official liturgy of the Church in ways that are not always reflected in the "official interpretations" of history. We have seen through archaeological evidence that while large crowds frequented the strictly eucharistic celebration in the basilicas, it is most probable that the principal contact that the majority of the faithful may have had with ritual of the Church was more informal and based on celebrating *refrigeria* in the large *martyria* or covered cemeteries located outside of the city walls in the Greco-Roman world. While the *refrigeria* may or may not have included a eucharistic celebration, it seems clear that there was much popular enthusiasm for eating and drinking at the tombs of the martyrs and loved ones. Later, the Germanization of Christianity set the stage during the Middle Ages and

---

[6] James Walsh, *The Thirteenth, Greatest of Centuries* (New York: Catholic Summer School Press, 1907).

Counter-Reformation for a different notion of lay participation at the Mass. Although the Eucharist itself ordered medieval society, the focus on the elements of the sacrament rather than its celebration led to a disassociation of the worshiping community from the liturgical celebration. Consequently, popular devotions surrounding the Eucharist increasingly substituted for direct participation in liturgical prayer. This was especially true after the Council of Trent, when a new emphasis was placed on a more interior, cognitive approach to lay participation in worship. It was precisely this situation that the liturgical reforms of Vatican II sought to address. We must be careful not to allow our own prejudices to blur our vision of the Church's past experience of worship; otherwise we fall into an exercise in nostalgia rather than history.

Conclusion Three: The Roman Rite Is a Cultural Expression of the Faith That Needs Adaptation

In reviewing the history of the Roman Rite, it is very obvious that it has been influenced by the various cultural contexts within which it developed. This is notably true of the culture that gave it birth, famously described by Edmund Bishop as the "genius of the Roman Rite." It is clear that during the fourth century, when the liturgy in Rome shifted from Greek to Latin, decisions were made as to what kind of cultural context was to be used for shaping the Roman Rite. We saw that the literary style and ritual language spontaneously chosen by Church authorities, especially Pope Damasus, was that of the pagan Roman cultus and the imperial court, rather than language more directly influenced by the Bible. This choice was almost inevitable given that Christianity was proposed to occupy the place of the old Roman civil religion as a sustainer of the empire after the conversion of the Emperor Constantine. The hieratic language as well as court address and ceremonial adopted into the liturgy from the Roman pagan religion and court protocol was meant to heighten the sense of the sacred and make Christianity more acceptable to the élite of Roman society. One of the secondary results of this development, however, was to create a greater distance between the official liturgy of the Church and the understanding of the common faithful. While the official liturgy (like its pagan antecedent) was supported by the people, they also naturally sought to find alternate forms of prayer and connection with the sacred.

Both the positive and the negative aspects of the "Roman genius" are very much with us today. While the simplicity and practicality of the rite are still obvious, an element that has been restored (in translation)

is the pagan cultic language and the literary conventions of the imperial
court, despite the contention by the Congregation for Worship and the
Discipline of Sacraments that the Roman Rite has been able to adopt
other cultural usages in "a deep, organic, and harmonious way."[7] It is
this language, as well as the convoluted syntax that slavishly reflects the
grammatical idiosyncrasies of the Latin text that seem to be the source
of much of the dissatisfaction with the new translation. "Obsequious
and distracting" are common adjectives used by many respondents in
polls taken to evaluate the reception of the new translation.[8] One can
legitimately wonder why this aspect of "the Roman Genius" seems to
be considered an intrinsic part of "the substantial unity of the Rite"
desired by the Constitution on the Sacred Liturgy.[9]

Unfortunately, this approach to translation is again widening the
distance between the liturgy and most of the faithful at worship (including many priest-celebrants) who have a difficult time understanding
the prayer texts. Instead of promoting a cross-fertilization between
popular religion and the official liturgy of the Church, this translation
is widening the gap. While liturgical language clearly needs to be in
a different "register" than ordinary speech, this heightened "register"
does not necessarily demand that our prayer be voiced in a style that
does not respect the grammar and rhetoric of the English language. It
can also be assumed that since, according to the GIRM, the Roman Rite
has been able to adopt in "a deep, organic and harmonious way" from
the cultures in which it has been celebrated, the Rite would not have an
insurmountable problem in adapting its language to the mentality and
genius of modern English speakers. This kind of adaptation was done
when the Franco-Germanic peoples revised the rather laconic style of
prayer they received from the Roman Rite during the eighth and ninth
centuries. If we are to promote a more productive dialogue between
liturgy and popular religion, the insightful provision contained in the

---

[7] GIRM, 397.

[8] See the obvious dissatisfaction with the new translation reflected in the results
of two polls; one conducted by the *Tablet* of London in January 2013 (http://www
.thetablet.co.uk/blogs/468/26) and the other by the Godfrey Diekmann, OSB,
Center for Patristics and Liturgical Student of St. John's University in Collegeville,
Minnesota, May 21, 2013 (http://www.csbsju.edu/SOT/Programs/Diekmann-Center
/New-Roman-Missal-Survey-of-US-Priests.htm).

[9] SC, 38. See also Rita Ferrone's insightful analysis of the new translation in
"It Doesn't Sing: The Trouble with the New Roman Missal," *Commonweal* 138,
no. 13 (July 15, 2012).

first instruction on liturgical translation issued in 1969 (*Comme le Prévoit*) should also not be forgotten: "Texts translated from another language are clearly not sufficient for the celebration of a fully renewed liturgy. The creation of new texts will be necessary."[10]

Popular Religion: Giving Life to the Liturgy

The interaction between popular religion and liturgy continues. While a core of the liturgy is not subject to change,[11] neither the liturgy nor popular religion is static and unchangeable (despite the best efforts of some to pretend otherwise). We have seen how the Roman liturgy has been adapted to and influenced by the many cultures with which it has come into contact. We have also seen how popular religious practices have had a decisive role in these adaptations. One of the ways liturgy has "come to life" for many people was by the introduction of dramatic elements that help focus the attention of the assembly on a particular moment or incident proclaimed in the Scriptures or celebrated during the course of the liturgical year. We saw the introduction of dramatic elements into the celebration of the Holy Week liturgy in Jerusalem in the patristic period. This popular strategy to capture the imagination of the faithful at worship was also employed when the sober Roman Rite was imposed on the Franco-Germanic peoples in the ninth century under Charlemagne.

One of the dramatic additions to the rites of Holy Week during the ninth century was the washing of the feet on Holy Thursday.[12] This practice arose in medieval monasteries. After the homily, the presider would doff his chasuble and kneel to wash the feet of twelve monks who represented the twelve apostles. This dramatic illustration of the humble service Jesus commanded all his disciples to emulate was quickly adopted by monasteries as well as in cathedrals and other

[10] *Comme le Prévoit*, Instruction on the Translation of Liturgical Texts for Celebrations with a Congregation, Consilium for Implementing the Constitution on the Sacred Liturgy (January 25, 1969), par. 43.

[11] See SC 21: "For the liturgy is made up of immutable elements divinely instituted, and of elements subject to change. These not only may but ought to be changed with the passage of time if they have suffered from the intrusion of anything out of harmony with the inner nature of the liturgy or have become unsuited to it."

[12] Theodor Klauser, *A Short History of the Western Liturgy: An Account and Some Reflections*, 2nd ed. (New York: Oxford University Press, 1979), 81.

churches on Holy Thursday. The practice of washing feet fell into disuse—especially in parishes—after the Council of Trent but was reproposed in the restoration of Holy Week under Pius XII in 1955 and continues to be part of the rite prescribed for the Evening Mass of the Lord's Supper on Holy Thursday found in the Missal of Paul VI.

A controversy around the Catholic world broke out in 2013 when Pope Francis, presiding at his first Holy Thursday Eucharist as pope (March 28, 2013), went to a juvenile prison in the outskirts of Rome and washed the feet of twelve of the inmates, two of whom were young women and two of whom were Muslims. Several traditionalist commentators expressed their consternation that the pope was not following liturgical law. The rubrics call for twelve chosen men (*viri selecti*) to come forward to have their feet washed. One head of a national liturgy office went so far as to say that, while the pope could reinterpret the rubrics, no one else was allowed to make this kind of change since what the rite was about was a "mimesis" (or reenactment) of what Jesus did at the last supper.

In an interesting way, this incident raises an important conviction that has been at the heart of this book. Popular religious practice and liturgy, while different, are meant to enrich each other along the lines called for by the Latin American bishops at Puebla. This is apparent when we consider the originally "extra-liturgical" gesture that is the foot washing at Holy Thursday. While some popular religious practice would be strictly "mimesis"—a reenactment of a past event such as the famous Passion Play of the Bavarian city of Oberammergau or the Hispanic *Via Crucis Viviente* (living way of the cross)—the foot washing is not necessarily in that category. To offer a strict reenactment, one needs costumes and staging. In most parts of the Catholic world, twelve men do not dress like the first-century followers of Jesus to have their feet washed. Therefore, this gesture is something more than mere mimesis; it celebrates what theologians call an *anamnesis* of the event. *Anamnesis* (remembering) is at the heart of the liturgy. But it is a remembering that is not a mere mental operation. *Anamnesis* takes place through word and gesture that summons to mind (and heart) an important past event in order to make his transformative power present to those participating in the rite. Christian liturgy is predicated on an *anamnesis* of Christ's paschal mystery that makes present to us the way in which his passion, death, and resurrection have forever changed our relationship to God, to one another, and to the world. As Richard McCall has pointed out in relation to the more dramatic elements of our Holy Week celebration, "What is the *dramatic* impetus of the liturgy but the *enactment* of narrative event through liturgical praxis? That praxis, as in this case, need not be mimetic. To fast and to feast is not to playact Jesus. It is to enact one's involvement with, and incorporation into, the unfolding narrative. It is to enter into anamnesis."[13]

Pope Francis, following the interpretation of the liturgical tradition of Holy Week that he had long practiced as archbishop of Buenos Aires, included both men and women in the foot washing. In so doing, he powerfully set before the world a true *anamnesis* of the meaning of Jesus' action at the Last Supper meant to underline that charity and humble service is a constitutive part of the Eucharist. He went beyond a legalistic equation of a popular religious symbol with an "unchangeable" part of the liturgy. Through this popular religious gesture the pope has reminded us that our love and service in the name of Christ is to be offered to all of humankind, whatever their gender or religion. It takes seriously the new context in which we live and worship. It is a context that must include women and men, people of all ages and religious faiths. In short, his action spoke a profound word to all believers in a way that the liturgy could not by itself accomplish as easily.

Popular religion and the liturgy both constitute indispensable parts of our common religious expression as Catholics. They will continue to be marked by both continuity and change since the world in which we live is in constant evolution. As we experience the presence of the Risen One, nourished by both the official worship of the Church and enriched popular religious practices that celebrate this presence, our spiritual lives rest within the best of Catholic tradition.

---

[13] Richard D. McCall, "Anamnesis or Mimesis: Unity and Drama in the Paschal Triduum," *Ecclesia Orans* 13, no. 2 (1996): 319. See also Martin Connell, *Eternity Today: On the Liturgical Year*, vol. 2 (New York: Continuum, 2006), 131–34.

Selected Bibliography

Magisterial Documents

Congregation for Divine Worship and Discipline of the Sacraments. *Directory on Popular Piety and the Liturgy: Principles and Guidelines.* Vatican City: Libereria Editrice Vaticana, 2002.

————. *Liturgiam Authenticam* (On the Use of Vernacular Languages in the Publication of the Books of the Roman Liturgy), Fifth Instruction for the Right Implementation of the Constitution on the Sacred Liturgy of the Second Vatican Council. Vatican web site. http://www.vatican.va/roman_curia/congregations/ccdds/documents/rc_con_ccdds_doc_20010507_liturgiam-authenticam_en.html, 2001.

————.*Varietates Legitimae* (Inculturation and the Roman Liturgy), Fourth Instruction for the Right Implementation of the Constitution on the Sacred Liturgy of the Second Vatican Council. Vatican City: Libereria Editrice Vaticana, 1994.

Consejo Episcopal Latinoamericano (CELAM). *La Evangelización en el presente y en el futuro de América Latina* (Puebla: Conclusiones de la III Conferencia General del Episcopado Latinoamericano). Bogotá: CELAM, 1983.

Consilium for Implementing the Constitution on the Sacred Liturgy. *Comme le Prévoit* (On the Translation of Liturgical Texts for Celebrations with a Congregation). Libereria Editrice Vaticana, 1969.

Institutio Generalis Missalis Romani (General Instruction of the Roman Missal). Editio Typica Tertia (2002/2010). Vatican web site. http://www.vatican.va/roman_curia/congregations/ccdds/documents/rc_con_ccdds_doc_20030317_ordinamento-messale_en.html.

John Paul II, Pope. *Redemptoris Missio* (Encyclical on the Permanent Validity of the Church's Missionary Mandate). 1990.

Paul VI, Pope. *Evangelii Nuntiandi* (Apostolic Exhortation on Evangelization in the Modern World). 1975.

Pius XII, Pope. *Mediator Dei* (Encyclical on the Sacred Liturgy). AAS 39 (1947): 521–95.

The Roman Missal, Third Edition. Study Edition. Collegeville, MN: Liturgical Press, 2011.

Vatican Council II. "Dignitatis Humanae" (Declaration on Religious Freedom). In *Vatican Council II: The Sixteen Basic Documents*, edited by Austin Flannery, OP, 551–68. Northport, NY: Costello, 1996.

———. "Gaudium et Spes" (Pastoral Constitution on the Church in the Modern World). In *Vatican Council II: The Sixteen Basic Documents*, edited by Austin Flannery, OP, 163–282. Northport, NY: Costello, 1996.

———. "Lumen Gentium" (Dogmatic Constitution on the Church). In *Vatican Council II: The Sixteen Basic Documents*, edited by Austin Flannery, OP, 1–95. Northport, NY: Costello, 1996.

———. "Sacrosanctum Concilium" (Constitution on the Sacred Liturgy). In *Vatican Council II: The Sixteen Basic Documents*, edited by Austin Flannery, OP, 117–61. Northport, NY: Costello, 1996.

Books and Articles

Amar, Joseph. "The Loss of Syria: New Violence Threatens Christianity's Ancient Roots." *Commonweal* 139, no. 17 (October 12, 2012): 13–15.

Ariès, Philippe. "Religion Populaire et Réformes Religieuses." *La Maison Dieu* 122 (1975): 84–97.

Bamat, Thomas, and Jean-Paul Wiest, eds. *Popular Catholicism in the Two-Thirds World: Changes and Challenges for the Churches*. Maryknoll, NY: Center for Mission Research and Study, 1999.

Benavides, Gustavo. "Resistance and Accommodation in Latin American Popular Religiosity." In *An Enduring Flame: Studies on Latino Popular Religiosity*, edited by Anthony M. Stevens-Arroyo and Ana María Díaz-Stevens, 37–68. New York: PARAL, 1994.

Berger, Peter, Grace Davies, and Effie Fokas. *Religious America, Secular Europe? A Theme and Variations*. Aldershot, UK: Ashgate Publishing, 2008.

Bossy, John. "The Counter-Reformation and the People of Catholic Europe." *Past and Present Society* 47 (1970): 51–70.

———. "The Mass as a Social Institution 1200–1700." *Past and Present Society* 100 (1983): 29–61.

Botte, Bernard. *From Silence to Participation: An Insider's View of Liturgical Renewal*. Translated by John Sullivan. Washington, DC: The Pastoral Press, 1988.

Bowes, Kim. *Private Worship, Public Values, and Religious Change in Late Antiquity*. Cambridge, UK: Cambridge University Press, 2008.

Boyarin, Daniel. "Martyrdom and the Making of Christianity and Judaism." *Journal of Early Christian Studies* 6, no. 4 (1998): 577–627.

Bradshaw, Paul F. *Reconstructing Early Christian Worship*. Collegeville, MN: Liturgical Press, 2009.

Bradshaw, Paul F., and Maxwell E. Johnson. *The Origins of Feasts, Fasts, and Seasons in Early Christianity*. Collegeville, MN: Liturgical Press, 2011.

Brown, Peter. *The Cult of the Saints: Its Rise and Function in Latin Christianity.* Chicago: University of Chicago Press, 1981.

———. "Society and the Supernatural: A Medieval Change." *Daedalus* 104, no. 2 (1975): 133–51.

———. *The World of Late Antiquity: AD 150–750.* London: Harcourt Brace Jovanovich, 1971.

Brown, Raymond Edward. "Not Jewish Christianity and Gentile Christianity but Types of Jewish/Gentile Christianity." *Catholic Biblical Quarterly* 45 (1983): 74–79.

Bruce, F. F. *Peter, Stephen, James and John: Studies in Early Non-Pauline Christianity.* Grand Rapids MI: Eerdmans Publishing Co., 1979.

Candelaria, Michael R. *Popular Religion and Liberation: The Dilemma of Liberation Theology.* Albany, NY: State University of New York Press, 1990.

Cardoza-Orlandi, Carlos. "Drum Beats of Resistance and Liberation: Afro-Caribbean Religions, the Struggle for Life and the Christian Theologian." *Journal of Hispanic/Latino Theology* 3 (1995): 50–61.

Carrasco, David. "Cosmic Jaws: We Eat the Gods and the Gods Eat Us." *Journal of the American Academy of Religion* 63, no. 3 (1995): 429–63.

Carroll, John T. "Sickness and Healing in the New Testament Gospels." *Interpretation* 49, no. 2 (1995): 130–32.

Carroll, Michael P. "Popular Catholicism in Pre-Famine Ireland." *Journal for the Scientific Study of Religion* 34, no. 3 (1995): 354–65.

Cattaneo, Enrico. *Il culto cristiano in occidente: note storiche.* 2nd ed., Ristampa. Roma: Edizioni Liturgiche, 2003.

Christian, William. "Spain in Latino Religiosity." In *El Cuerpo de Cristo: The Hispanic Presence in the U.S. Catholic Church,* edited by Peter Casarella and Raúl Gómez, 325–30. New York: Crossroad, 1998.

Cleary, Edward L. *The Rise of Charismatic Catholicism in Latin America.* Gainesville: University Press of Florida, 2011.

Clottes, Jean, and David Lewis Williams. *The Shamans of Prehistory: Trance and Magic in the Painted Caves.* Translated by Sophie Hawkes. New York: Harry N. Abrams, Inc., 1996.

Collins, Mary. "Devotions and Renewal Movements: Spiritual Cousins of the Liturgy." In *Called to Prayer: Liturgical Spirituality Today,* edited by Lawrence J. Johnson, 47–68. Collegeville, MN: Liturgical Press, 1986.

———. "Evangelization, Catechesis, and the Beginnings of Western Eucharistic Theology." *Louvain Studies* 23 (1998): 124–42.

Collins, Mary, and David Power, eds. *Concilium: Liturgy, A Creative Tradition.* Vol.162. Edinburgh: T&T Clark, 1983.

Collins, Roger. *Early Medieval Europe 300–1000.* New York: St. Martin's Press, 1999.

Connell, Martin. *On the Liturgical Year. Vol.2 of Eternity Today*. New York: Continuum, 2006.

Cooper, Kristina. "Feel the Spirit." *The Tablet* 267 (May 18, 2013): 4–5.

Dehn, Carl. "Roman Catholic Popular Devotions." *Worship* 49, no. 8 (1975): 446–60.

———. "Devotions, Popular." In *The New Dictionary of Sacramental Worship*, edited by Peter Fink, 331–40. Collegeville, MN: Liturgical Press, 1990.

Delameau, Jean. "Official and Popular Religion in France during the Reformation and Counter Reformation." In Greinacher and Mette, *Concilium: Popular Religion*, 3–11.

Dever, William G. "The Silence of the Text: An Archaeological Commentary on 2 Kings 23: The Contribution of Archaeology to the Study of Canaanite and Early Israelite Religion." In *Scripture and Other Artifacts: Essays on the Bible and Archaeology in Honor of Philip J. King*, edited by M. D. Coogan, C. J. Exum, and L. E. Stager, 160. Louisville, KY: Westminster John Knox, 1994.

Díaz-Stevens, Ana María. "Analyzing Popular Religiosity for Socio-Religious Meaning." In *An Enduring Flame: Studies on Latino Popular Religiosity*, edited by Anthony M. Stevens-Arroyo and Ana María Díaz-Stevens, 17–36. New York: PARAL, 1994.

Doeve, J. W. "Official and Popular Religion in Judaism." In *Official and Popular Religion: Analysis of a Theme for Religious Studies*, edited by Pieter Henrik Vrihof and Jacques Waardenburg, 325–39. The Hague: Mouton Publishers, 1979.

Dolan, Jay P. *In Search of an American Catholicism: A History of Religion and Culture in Tension*. Oxford: Oxford University Press, 2002.

Duchesne, Louis. *Christian Worship: Its Origin and Evolution*. Translated by M. McClure. London: SPCK, 1903.

Duffy, Eamon. *The Stripping of the Altars: Traditional Religion in England 1400–1580*. New Haven, CT: Yale University Press, 1992.

Dunn, James G. D. *Unity and Diversity in the New Testament: An Inquiry into the Character of Earliest Christianity*. London: SCM Press, 1977.

Duquesne, J. "Un débat actuel: La religion populaire." *La Maison Dieu* 122 (1975): 7–19.

Dussel, Enrique. "Popular Religion as Oppression and Liberation: Hypotheses on Its Past and Its Present in Latin America." In Greinacher and Mette, *Concilium: Popular Religion*, 82–96.

Eliade, Mircea. *From Gautama Buddha to the Triumph of Christianity. Vol. 2 of A History of Religious Ideas*. Translated by Willard R. Trask. Chicago: University of Chicago Press, 1982.

Elizondo, Virgilio. *Christianity and Culture*. San Antonio: Mexican American Cultural Center, 1975.

————. *La Morenita: Evangelizer of the Americas.* San Antonio: Mexican American Cultural Center, 1976.

————. "Popular Religion as Support of Identity: A Pastoral-Psychological Case-Study Based on the Mexican American Experience, in the U.S.A." In Greinacher and Mette, *Concilium: Popular Religion*, 36–43.

Empereur, James. "Popular Religion and the Liturgy." *Liturgical Ministry* 7 (1998): 105–20.

Engh, Michael E. "From *Frontera* Faith to Roman Rubrics: Altering Hispanic Religious Customs in Los Angeles, 1855–1880." *U.S. Catholic Historian* 12, no. 4 (Fall 1994): 85–105.

Espín, Orlando. *The Faith of the People: Theological Reflections on Popular Catholicism.* Maryknoll, NY: Orbis, 1997.

Espín, Orlando. "Trinitarian Monotheism and the Birth of Popular Catholicism: The Case of Sixteenth-Century Mexico." *Missiology* 20, no. 2 (1992): 177–204.

Farhadian, Charles E., ed. *Christian Worship Worldwide: Expanding Horizons, Deepening Practices.* Grand Rapids, MI: Eerdmans Publishing Company, 2007.

Fassberg, Steven E. "Which Semitic Language Did Jesus and Other Contemporary Jews Speak?" *Catholic Biblical Quarterly* 74 (2012): 263–80.

Ferrone, Rita. "It Doesn't Sing: The Trouble with the New Roman Missal." *Commonweal* 138, no. 13 (July 15, 2012).

Filotas, Bernadette. *Pagan Survivals, Superstitions and Popular Cultures in Early Medieval Pastoral Literature.* Toronto, Canada: Pontifical Institute of Medieval Studies, 2005.

Fitzmyer, Joseph E. "The Languages of Palestine in the First Century AD." *Catholic Biblical Quarterly* 32 (1970): 501–31.

Flanagan, C. Clifford. "The Roman Rite and the Origins of the Liturgical Drama." *University of Toronto Quarterly* (1974): 263–84.

Foley, Edward. *From Age to Age: How Christians Have Celebrated the Eucharist.* Revised and expanded edition. Collegeville, MN: Liturgical Press, 2008.

Francis, Mark. "Building Bridges between Liturgy, Devotionalism and Popular Religion." *Assembly* 20 (April 1994): 636–38.

————. "Liturgical Inculturation: The State of the Question." *Liturgical Ministry* 6 (1997): 97–107.

————. "Liturgical Participation of God's People." In *With One Voice: Translation and Implementation of the Third Edition of the Roman Missal*, 55–86. Washington, DC: Federation of Diocesan Liturgical Commissions, 2010.

————. "Popular Piety and Liturgical Reform in a Hispanic Context." In *Dialogue Rejoined: Theology and Ministry in the United States Hispanic Reality*, edited by Ana María Pineda and Robert Schreiter, 162–77. Collegeville, MN: Liturgical Press, 1995.

————. *Shape a Circle Ever Wider: Liturgical Inculturation in the United States.* Chicago: Liturgy Training Publications, 2000.

Francis, Mark, and Arturo Pérez-Rodriguez. *Primero Dios: Hispanic Liturgical Resource*. Chicago: Liturgy Training Publications, 1997.

Geary, Patrick. *Living with the Dead in the Middle Ages*. Ithaca, NY: Cornell University Press, 1994.

Gittins , Anthony J. "Beyond Liturgical Inculturation: Transforming the Deep Structures of Faith." *Irish Theological Quarterly* 69 (2004): 47–72.

Gogolok, Osmar Erwin. "Pastoral Aspects of Popular Religion in Brazil." In Greinacher and Mette, *Concilium: Popular Religion*, 105–12.

Goizueta, Roberto. *Caminemos con Jesús: Toward a Hispanic/Latino Theology of Accompaniment*. Maryknoll, NY: Orbis, 1995.

Gomes, Jules. "Popular Religion in Old Testament Research: Past Present & Future." *Tyndale Bulletin* 54, no. 1 (2003): 31–50.

Greinacher, Norbert, and Norbert Mette, eds. *Concilium: Popular Religion*. Vol. 186. Edinburgh: T&T Clark, 1986.

Haquin, André. "The Liturgical Movement and Catholic Ritual Reform." In *The Oxford History of Christian Worship,* edited by Geoffrey Wainwright and Karen Westerfield Tucker, 687–98. Oxford: Oxford University Press, 2005.

Henau, Ernest. "Popular Religiosity and Christian Faith." In Greinacher and Mette, *Concilium: Popular Religion*, 71–81.

Hengel, Martin. *The "Hellenization" of Judaea in the First Century after Christ*. Translated by John Bowden. London: SCM Press, 1989.

Herwegen, Ildelfons. *Antike, Germantum, Christentum*. Salzburg: Verlag Anton Pustet, 1932.

Hidal, Sten. "Evidence for Jewish Believers in the Syriac Fathers." In *Jewish Believers in Jesus: The Early Centuries,* edited by Oskar Skarsaune and Reidar Hvalvik, 568–80. Peabody, MA: Hendrickson Publishers, 2007.

Hope, D. M. "The Medieval Western Rites." In *The Study of Liturgy,* revised edition, edited by Cheslyn Jones, et al., revised by G. Woolfenden, 264–85. London: SPCK, 1992.

Jenkins, Philip. *The Lost History of Christianity: The Thousand-Year Golden Age of the Church in the Middle East, Africa, and Asia—and How it Died*. San Francisco: HarperOne, 2008.

———. *The New Faces of Christianity: Believing the Bible in the Global South*. Oxford, UK: Oxford University Press, 2006.

Johnson, Cuthbert. *Prosper Guéranger (1805–1875): A Liturgical Theologian*. Analecta Liturgica 9. Rome: Studia Anselmiana, 1984.

Johnson, Luke Timothy. *Among the Gentiles: Greco-Roman Religion and Christianity*. New Haven, CT: Yale University Press, 2009.

Judd, Stephen. "Fashioning a Vital Synthesis: Popular Religion and the Evangelization Project in Southern Peru." In Greinacher and Mette, *Concilium: Popular Religion*, 113–21.

Jungmann, Joseph. *The Early Liturgy*. Notre Dame, IN: University of Notre Dame Press, 1959.

————. "The Defeat of Teutonic Arianism and the Revolution in Religious Culture in the Early Middle Ages." In *Pastoral Liturgy*, translated by Ronald Walls. New York: Herder and Herder, 1962.

————. *The Mass of the Roman Rite: Its Origins and Development*. Translated by Francis Brunner. New York: Benzinger, 1951.

Karras, Ruth Mazo. "Pagan Survivals and Syncretism in the Conversion of Saxony." *The Catholic Historical Review* 72, no. 4 (October 1986): 553–72.

Kelleher, Margaret Mary. "Liturgy, Culture, and the Challenge of Catholicity." *Worship* 84, no. 2 (March 2010): 98–120.

Kelleher, Margaret Mary. "Liturgy and Social Transformation: Exploring the Relationship." *U.S. Catholic Historian* 16, no. 4 (1998): 58–70.

Kilmartin, Edward. *The Eucharist in the West: History and Theology*. Collegeville, MN: Liturgical Press, 1998.

Kroll, Norma. "Power and Conflict in Medieval Ritual and Plays: The Re-Invention of Drama." *Studies in Philology* 102, no. 4 (2005): 452–83.

Laferty, Maura K. "Translating Faith from Greek to Latin: Romanitas and Christianitas in Late Fourth-Century Rome and Milan." *Journal of Early Christian Studies* 11, no. 1 (Spring 2003): 21–62.

Lara, Jaime. *Christian Texts for Aztecs: Art and Liturgy in Colonial Mexico*. Notre Dame, IN: University of Notre Dame Press, 2008.

————. *City, Temple, Stage: Eschatological Architecture and Liturgical Theatrics in New Spain*. Notre Dame, IN: University of Notre Dame Press, 2004.

————. "Precious Jade Green Water: A Sixteenth-century Adult Catechumenate in the New World." *Worship* 71 (1997): 415–28.

————. "The Liturgical Roots of Hispanic Popular Religiosity." In *Misa, Mesa y Musa: Liturgy in the U.S. Hispanic Church*, edited by Kenneth G. Davis, 25–33. Schiller Park, IL: World Library Publications, 1997.

————. "The Sacramented Sun: Solar Eucharistic Worship in Colonial Latin America." In *El Cuerpo de Cristo: The Hispanic Presence in the US Catholic Church*, edited by Peter Casarella and Raúl Gómez, 261–91. New York: Crossroads, 1998.

————. "Roman Catholics in Hispanic America." In *The Oxford History of Christian Worship*, edited by Geoffrey Wainwright and Karen Westerfield Tucker, 633–50. New York: Oxford University Press, 2006.

Larkin, Emmet. "The Devotional Revolution in Ireland." *The American Historical Review* 77, no. 3 (1972): 625–52.

Leonard, John K., and Nathan Mitchell. *The Postures of the Assembly during the Eucharistic Prayer*. Chicago: Liturgy Training Publications, 1994.

Lockhart, James. "Some Nahua Concepts in Postconquest Guise." *History of European Ideas* 6, no. 4 (1985): 465–82.

Lynch, John. *New Worlds: A Religious History of Latin America*. Bodmin, Cornwall, UK: Yale University Press, 2012.

McCall, Richard D. "Anamnesis or Mimesis: Unity and Drama in the Paschal Triduum." *Ecclesia Orans* 13, no. 2 (1996): 315–22.

McCartin, James P. *Prayers of the Faithful: The Shifting Spiritual Life of American Catholics*. Cambridge, MA: Harvard University Press, 2010.

McCreevy, John. *Catholicism and American Freedom: A History*. New York: Norton, 2003.

McGowan, Andrew. *Ascetic Eucharists: Food and Drink in Early Christian Ritual Meals*. Oxford, UK: Clarendon Press, 1999.

MacMullen, Ramsay. "Christian Ancestor Worship in Rome." *Journal of Biblical Literature* 129, no. 3 (2010): 597–613.

———. *Christianizing the Roman Empire (AD 100–400)*. New Haven, CT: Yale University Press, 1984.

———. *The Second Church: Popular Christianity AD 200–400*. Atlanta: Society of Biblical Literature, 2009.

Maldonado, Luis. "Popular Religion: Its Dimensions, Levels and Types." In Greinacher and Mette, *Concilium: Popular Religion*, 3–11.

———. *Religiosidad Popular*. Madrid: Ediciones Cristiandad, 1975.

Malherbe, Abraham. *Social Aspects of Early Christianity*. Philadelphia: Fortress Press, 1983.

Malloy, Patrick. L. "The Re-Emergence of Popular Religion among Non-Hispanic American Catholics." *Worship* 72, no. 1 (1998): 2–25.

Matovina, Timothy. "Liturgy, Popular Rites and Popular Spirituality." *Worship* 63 (1989): 351–61.

Meeks, Wayne. *The First Urban Christians: The Social World of the Apostle Paul*. New Haven, CT: Yale University Press: 1983.

Metzger, Marcel. *History of the Liturgy: The Major Stages*. Translated by Madeleine Beaumont. Collegeville, MN: Liturgical Press, 1997.

Michel, Virgil, OSB. "The Liturgy the Basis of Social Regeneration." *Orate Fratres* 9 (1935): 536–45.

Miller, Vincent. *Consuming Religion: Christian Faith and Practice in a Consumer Culture*. New York: Continuum, 2003.

Mitchell, Nathan. *Cult and Controversy: The Worship of the Eucharist Outside of Mass*. Collegeville, MN: Liturgical Press, 1990.

———. "Reforms, Protestant and Catholic." In *The Oxford History of Christian Worship*, edited by Geoffrey Wainwright and Karen Westerfield Tucker, 307–50. Oxford: Oxford University Press, 2005.

Mohrmann, Christine. "Les origines de la latinité chrétienne à Rome." *Vigiliae Christianae* 3 (1949): 67–106.

———. *Liturgical Latin: Its Origins and Character*. Washington, DC: Catholic University of America Press, 1957.

———. "Quelques observations sur l'évolution stylistique du canon de la messe romaine." *Vigiliae Christianae* 4 (1950): 1–19.

Murphy, G. Ronald. "Magic in the *Heliand*" *Monatshefte* 83, no. 4 (1991): 386–97.

———. *The Saxon Savior: The Transformation of the Gospel in the Ninth-Century Heliand*. Oxford, UK: Oxford University Press, 1989.

Neuenheuser, Burkhard. "The Liturgies of Pius V and Paul VI." In *Roles of the Liturgical Assembly,* 207–20. New York: Pueblo, 1977.

———. *Storia della liturgia attraverso le epoche culturali.* Terza edizione ampliata e rinnovata. Roma: Edizioni Liturgiche, 1999.

Nocent, Adrien. *La Messa prima e dopo San Pio V.* Casale Monferrato: Piemme, 1985.

O'Malley, John. *What Happened at Vatican II?* Cambridge, MA: Belknap Press, 2008.

Orsi, Robert. *The Madonna of 115th Street: Faith and Community in Italian Harlem, 1880–1950.* New Haven, CT, and London: Yale University Press, 1985.

Pardo, Osvaldo. *The Origins of Mexican Catholicism: Nahua Rituals and Christian Sacraments in Sixteenth-Century Mexico.* Ann Arbor: University of Michigan Press, 2004.

Parker, Christian. "Popular Religion and Protest against Oppression: The Chilean Example." In Greinacher and Mette, *Concilium: Popular Religion,* 28–35.

Pecklers, Keith F. *Dynamic Equivalence: The Living Language of Christian Worship.* Collegeville, MN: Liturgical Press, 2003.

———. "Issues of Power and Access in Popular Religion." *Liturgical Ministry* 7 (1998): 136–40.

———. "The Jansenist Critique and the Liturgical Reforms of the Sixteenth and Eighteenth Centuries." *Ecclesia Orans* 20, no. 3 (2003): 325–38.

———. *The Unread Vision: The Liturgical Movement in the United States of America: 1926–1955.* Collegeville, MN: Liturgical Press, 1998.

Perez, Arturo. "Mestizo Liturgy: A *Mestizaje* of the Roman and Hispanic Rites of Worship." In *Misa, Mesa, y Musa, Volume 2: Liturgy in the U.S. Hispanic Church,* edited by Kenneth G. Davis, 2–16. Franklin Park, IL: World Library Publications, 2008.

Phan, Peter. "Multiple Religious Belonging: Opportunities and Challenges for Theology and Church." *Theological Studies* 64 (2003): 495–519.

———. "Speaking in Many Tongues: Why the Church Must Be More Catholic." *Commonweal* 134, no. 1 (January 12, 2007).

Pietri, Charles. "Liturgy, Culture and Society at the End of the Ancient World (Fourth-Fifth Centuries)." In Collins and Power, *Concilium: Liturgy, a Creative Tradition,* 38–46.

Pilch, John J. *Visions and Healing in the Acts of the Apostles: How Early Believers Experienced God.* Collegeville, MN: Liturgical Press, 2004.

Piwowarski, Wladyslaw. "The Guarantor of National Identity: Polish Catholicism." In Greinacher and Mette, *Concilium: Popular Religion,* 20–27.

Reid, Barbara E. *Taking up the Cross: New Testament Interpretations through Latina and Feminist Eyes.* Minneapolis, MN: Fortress Press, 2007.

Rose, Els. *Ritual Memory: The Apocryphal Acts and Liturgical Commemoration in the Early Medieval West (c. 500–1215)*. Leiden: Brill, 2009.

Rubin, Miri. *Corpus Christi*. Cambridge: Cambridge University Press, 1991.

Ruggieri, Giuseppe. "Ecclesiastical Strategy and Religious Needs." In Greinacher and Mette, *Concilium: Popular Religion*, 97–104.

Russell, James C. *The Germanization of the Early Medieval Christianity: A Sociohistorical Approach to Religious Transformation*. Oxford: Oxford University Press, 1994.

Ryan, Salvador. "Resilient Religion: Popular Piety Today." *The Furrow* 56, no. 3 (2005): 131–41.

Sanneh, Lamin. *Disciples of All Nations: Pillars of World Christianity*. Oxford, UK: Oxford University Press, 2008.

Sanneh, Lamin. *Whose Religion Is Christianity? The Gospel beyond the West*. Grand Rapids, MI: Eerdmans, 2003.

Schreiter, Robert J. *The New Catholicity: Theology between the Global and the Local*. Maryknoll, NY: Orbis Books, 1997.

Semporé, Sidbe. "Popular Religion in Africa: Benin as a Typical Instance." In Greinacher and Mette, *Concilium: Popular Religion*. 44–51.

Sevestre, Nicole. "Le drame liturgique: theater du non-dit." *Revue de Musicologie* 86, no. 1 (2000): 77–82.

Shorter, Arlward. *Toward a Theology of Inculturation*. Maryknoll, NY: Orbis Books, 1988.

Skarsaune, Oscar. "The Ebionites." In *Jewish Believers in Jesus: The Early Centuries*, edited by Oskar Skarsaune and Reidar Hvalvik, 419–62. Peabody, MA: Hendrickson Publishers, 2007.

Stegmann, Wolfgang, Bruce J. Malina, and Gerd Theissen, eds. *The Social Setting of Jesus and the Gospels*. Minneapolis, MN: Augsburg Fortress, 2002.

Stevens-Arroyo, Anthony, and Ana María Díaz-Stevens. *An Enduring Flame: Studies on Latino Popular Religiosity*. New York: Bildner Center Publications, 1994.

Suess, Paulo. "The Creative and Normative Role of Popular Religion in the Church." In Greinacher and Mette, *Concilium: Popular Religion*, 122–32.

Taft, Robert F. "Mass without the Consecration?" *America* 188, no. 16 (May 12, 2003): 7–11.

———. *Through Their Own Eyes: Liturgy as the Byzantines Saw It*. Berkeley, CA: InterOrthodox Press, 2006.

Taves, Ann. "Context and Meaning: Roman Catholic Devotion to the Blessed Sacrament in Mid-Nineteenth Century America," *Church History* 54, no. 4 (1985): 482–895.

———. *The Household of Faith: Roman Catholic Devotions in Mid-Nineteenth-Century America*. Notre Dame, IN: University of Notre Dame Press, 1986.

Trotzig, Aina. "L'apparition du Christ ressucité à Marie Madeleine et le drame liturgique." *Revue de Musicologie* 86, no. 1 (2000): 83.

Twelftree, Graham H. "In the Name of Jesus: A Conversation with Critics." *Journal of Pentecostal Theology* 17 (2008): 157–69.

Vidal, Jaime. "Towards an Understanding of Synthesis in Iberian and Hispanic American Popular Religiosity." In *An Enduring Flame: Studies on Latino Popular Religiosity*, edited by Anthony M. Stevens-Arroyo and Ana María Díaz-Stevens, 69–96. New York: PARAL, 1994.

Vogel, Cyrille. "The Cultic Environment of the Deceased in the Early Christian Period." *Temple of the Holy Spirit: Sickness and Death of the Christian in the Liturgy*, translated by Matthew J. O'Connell, 259–76. New York: Pueblo Publishing Co., 1983.

———. "Les Échanges liturgiques entre Rome et les pays francs jusqu'à l'époque de Charlemagne," in *Le Chiese nei regni dell'Europa occidentale e i loro rapporti con Roma fino all'800*. Settimane di studio del centro italiano di studi sull'alto medioevo 7 (Spoleto: Presso la sede del centro, 1960): 185–295.

———. *Medieval Liturgy: An Introduction to the Sources*. Translated and revised by William Storey and Niels Rasmussen. Washington, DC: The Pastoral Press, 1986.

Vorländer, Hermann. "Aspects of Popular Religion in the Old Testament." In Greinacher and Mette, *Concilium: Popular Religion*, 63–70.

Ward, Anthony. "The Future Roman Liturgy, How Roman?" *Worship* 52, no. 2 (1978): 146–54.

Walls, Andrew. *The Cross-Cultural Process in Christian History*. Maryknoll, NY: Orbis Books, 2002.

Weaver, Dorothy Jean. "'Wherever This Good News Is Proclaimed': Women and God in the Gospel of Matthew." *Interpretation* 64, no. 4 (October 2010): 390–400.

Weber, Jeanne. "Devotion to the Sacred Heart: History, Theology, and Liturgical Celebration." *Worship* 72, no. 3 (1998): 236–54.

Weckmann, Luis. "The Middle Ages in the Conquest of America." *Speculum* 26, no. 1 (1951): 130–41.

———. *The Medieval Heritage of Mexico*. New York: Fordham University Press, 1992.

Williams, Peter. *Popular Religion in America: Symbolic Change and the Modernization Process in Historical Perspective*. Englewood Cliffs, NJ: Prentice-Hall, 1980.

Yarnold, Edward. *The Awe Inspiring Rites of Initiation: Baptismal Homilies of the Fourth Century*. Middlegreen Slough, UK: St. Paul Publications, 1971.

Young, Robin Darling. "Martyrdom as Exaltation." In *Late Ancient Christianity*, edited by Virginia Burrus, 70–92. Minneapolis, MN: Fortress, 2005.

Index